INDIRA GANDHI

IN THE CRUCIBLE
OF LEADERSHIP

INDIRA GANDHI

IN THE CRUCIBLE
OF LEADERSHIP

A Political Biography

Mary C. Carras

BEACON PRESS · BOSTON

Beacon Press books are published under the auspices
of the Unitarian Universalist Association
Published simultaneously in Canada by
Fitzhenry & Whiteside Limited, Toronto

(hardcover) 9 8 7 6 5 4 3 2 1

Library of Congress Cataloging in Publication Data

Carras, Mary C
  Indira Gandhi: in the crucible of leadership.

  Includes bibliographical references and index.
  1. Gandhi, Indira Nehru, 1917- 2. India—Politics
and government—1947- 3. Prime ministers—India—
Biography. I. Title.
DS481.G23C37 1979   954.04'092'4 [B]   78-19598
ISBN 0-8070-0242-9

TO MY SISTER SASSA

Acknowledgments

Since I began working on this book four years ago, many people have helped me in innumerable ways to continue and complete this work. Without their support, the end of my labor might still be far off. Unfortunately, it is not possible to name each of them, but I am grateful for the opportunity to acknowledge publicly the assistance of a few of those to whom I owe a special debt of gratitude.

For facilitating my work in India, I wish to thank the following members of the Indian Government: B. R. Bowry, Press Information Bureau, Inam Rahman, Embassy of India, Washington, D.C., K. N. Sawhney, Parliament House Library, and H. Y. Sharada-Prasad, Prime Minister's Secretariat.

Others who helped in significant ways, through discussion, reading the manuscript and offering suggestions for improvement, or providing hospitality and facilities for work or other welcome assistance and encouragement, are: Peter Braunstein, Lee Cokorinos, Robert Hamilton, Charles Heimsath, Surjit Mansingh, Philip E. Jacob, Jagdish and Urmilla Kapur, Rita Mae Kelly, J. S. Lall, Leigh Minturn, Harry Shapiro, and Alison Sulloway. To all of them, I give heartfelt thanks.

Special acknowledgment is due to a special person, Marie Seton, whose humaneness and graciousness make heavy debts appear to fall lightly on the shoulders.

I also take this opportunity to acknowledge with thanks the generous support of the following institutions: the American Association of University Women, for providing the bulk of assistance for research in India during 1975; Rutgers Research Council, for bailing me out several times, with no questions asked; and the American Philosophical Society, for providing travel assistance.

As always, members of my family, through their steadfast love and moral support, provided the sustenance needed to see me through many agonizing moments. More than anyone, however, I am eternally beholden to my sister Sassa (Anastasia Cokorinos)—to whom I have dedicated this book—for her unfailing support, sympathetic understanding, insightful advice, and devoted assistance throughout these four years and especially during the darkest and most difficult days.

M. C. C.
November 1978

CONTENTS

PREFACE

When I first thought about writing a book on Indira Gandhi—in 1972—
I believed it better to begin with her participation than without it. In
1974, with this in mind, I approached the then Indian Ambassador,
T. N. Kaul, seeking his assistance in presenting the idea to her. After
several months of silence, I finally got word that the Prime Minister
had agreed to see me.

I met Indira Gandhi in February 1975, about three weeks after land-
ing in New Delhi. This first interview would, I hoped, create an atmosphere of confidence in which I could establish some rapport with her.
I must confess that I was a bit leery, having heard and read such sharply
contradictory views of her personality. At that point, the negative
stood out most vividly in my mind: she is reticent and shy, I was told;
she can be curt and icy if she does not like you; she has a tendency to
answer questions with a laconic yes or no at times; you should anticipate that your conversations with her will be punctuated by long,
embarrassing silences. With all these warnings whirling in my mind, I
entered her residence with great trepidation. But perhaps she was in a
good mood that day; or perhaps she sensed my nervousness. In any
case, she was cordial and gracious, and she put me at my ease at once.
Contrary to my expectations, she did most of the talking and, at my
request, the discussion remained general, touching on many issues of
the day. From her comments, it was clear to me that she saw herself
as a new and modern breed of politician, more flexible, pragmatic, and
rational than most old-style politicians.

One of my first impressions was that she was a quick study. She
glanced at an abstractly worded project statement I had brought along
and immediately saw the thread linking it with the questions submitted
months before to Ambassador Kaul. She struck me as a very confident

leader—an impression strengthened by later observation in Parliament, at rallies, or in interviews. I saw no signs of that reticence and shyness so many had warned me about. She gave the impression she was talking with candor, though her comments were cautious, as befitting her role. But she was not excessively guarded. Surprisingly, she brought up several controversial issues—without any probing from me. (I had decided to avoid sensitive topics during that first meeting in order to create an atmosphere of confidence.)

Perhaps because I am myself somewhat small in stature, she did not strike me as being so diminutive as many had described her to me. Nor did she seem particularly frail. She has lovely slender hands and a haunting face—the most striking feature being her large, black, sad eyes. Her manner was unaffected; she used her hands in natural gestures, to rub her eyes or cheeks or nose. She would lean forward, her elbows and arms resting on her knees. Sometimes she would run her fingers through her hair; suddenly, the white streak against her black wavy hair appeared as symbolic of the marked contrasts in her personality.

After observing her in Parliament, I saw her again at close range at the end of May and beginning of June when—in response to a request that I have an opportunity to observe her "in action" during political trips—I was invited to accompany her entourage when she campaigned in the western state of Gujarat (the present Prime Minister's home state). I went along on two such campaign tours, and what most impressed me during the endless whistle-stops at numerous villages, was her stamina—all the more remarkable in the extreme heat of the drought-stricken state. Up and down platform stairs she would walk briskly to address the crowds waiting for her in the sun for hours; after a fifteen-minute talk to fifty, a hundred, even two hundred thousand people, we would hurry back to the helicopter or car. Then on to the next stop. Her doctor, who accompanied her during these trips, thought that her partymen made far too many demands on her time and had unreasonable expectations of her energies during these election campaigns.

As she sat on the platform during the introduction by long-winded local potentates, she was anything but awesome. I noticed that she would twiddle her thumbs or take off one of her gracefully pointed oriental slippers and curl her big toe around the lower railing, unseen by the vast crowds below. I searched for signs of the charismatic personality, not knowing what exactly I was looking for. An aura about her? An irresistible charm? A captivating style of speaking? A compelling intellect? A lovable personality? I could find none of these and decided that charisma was in the eye of the beholder.

During these trips, she often asked me to join her and others for a casual cup of tea, so that I did not feel I was a burdensome foreigner with whom "correct" behavior had to be maintained at all times. At the same time, I never felt I got to know her on a personal level. That was intentional on my part (as much as it may have been on hers, I imagine). Wanting to maintain an objective distance and being shy myself, I never made an effort to cultive a personal friendship with her and doubt that I could have, even if I had tried. But I eventually came to feel that I had gained her confidence as a writer who was committed to principles of honesty, fairness, and balance.

Only once did she reach out to me. It was during a lunch break taken after a series of morning rallies. She asked to see me privately. "I've been invited," she said, "to attend the International Women's Conference in Mexico." In a charming and disarming way, she confessed that she had "drawn a blank" as to what she should say. At that moment I could see her shyness, as she sat with her feet up on a chair, observing me out of the corner of her eye. But before we could chat any longer, we were interrupted by someone who said it was time to move on to the next stop.

Another personal gesture was made later, when I was with her party on a visit to a local village temple. The huge inner courtyard was jam-packed. I was alone, barefoot, and clutching a camera in a vain attempt to capture on film the excitement, chaos, and peculiar grandeur of the scene. I found myself jostled in a sea of people who were following her to the inner sanctum. An inexperienced crowd traveler, I thought I would surely be trampled—when I felt someone pulling me out of the crowd. She had deftly reached out to bring me into the safety of the circle cordoned off by her security personnel.

The next time I saw her was in August 1975, nearly two months after she had declared a state of emergency. We spoke for two hours. She appeared weary. More so than I had ever noticed before, the burdens of leadership seemed to weigh heavily upon her. She was straining to defend her actions, and her comments did not stray from the official account and justifications of the emergency declaration. I was disappointed. She was in her most formal prime ministerial stance, surrounded by all the trappings of her high office. A few days later I flew home.

When I saw her again on a sultry July afternoon after three years, she appeared drawn, pensive, and seemed to have lost weight. She assured me she had not, though she thought she had probably aged. But at subsequent meetings, the freshness in her face had returned and she was her old buoyant self. It seemed, on reflection, that some temporary preoccupation on that first day had momentarily obscured her basic optimism. She was now serenely confident, convinced of the rightness of her decision to call an emergency, and insisting that the reports of emergency excesses had been exaggerated by her opponents within and outside the country.

It wasn't long before I understood the source of her confidence. Whether it was a taxi driver, servant, or successful businessman with whom I spoke, the feeling expressed was one of support, admiration, and sometimes even of affection for her. Simultaneously, the harshest judgments were made against her son Sanjay and the principal mood—whether in New Delhi or Madras—was one of disillusionment with the ruling Janata party. At a rally held in a resettlement colony of Untouchables in New Delhi, she was greeted by a jubilant crowd of about 50,000 people whose huts had been demolished and new quarters built for them during the period of Emergency Rule.

About two thousand miles to the south, Mrs. Gandhi addressed a public rally in Madurai, a city of about one and a half million people near Madras. There she was received with adulation by vastly larger crowds. Because of the great turnout on the streets, it took us about an hour to cover the seven miles from the airport to the government rest house. The distance from there to a famous temple (Meenakshi), and thence to the rally grounds, was also small, but the huge crowds along the way made travel by a convoy of cars, buses, and motorcycles a slow affair testing everyone's stamina and endurance of the heat.

Usually, I made sure I was close by wherever she went, and I noticed on several occasions that many who came to greet her would prostrate themselves at her feet. At one point I asked her, "How do you feel when people do that?" "Very embarrassed," she said. Yet why did she do nothing to stop them, I wondered.

But then I had a most peculiar experience. We were on our way to the Meenakshi Temple. I was trailing behind in one of the cars and thoroughly enjoying myself as I waved to the crowds in friendship. Suddenly I realized I was being mistaken for her. People clutched at my hands and nearly yanked them from their sockets. Rose petals were thrown into the car, and once, two tiny lemons were pressed in my hand—a gift of love. From then on I was told not to wave to the crowds and to stay within the car, which by now was like an oven. Finally, we reached the temple.

I was quickly whisked inside by my escort, a local woman leader. But more crowds were awaiting us there. I was again mistaken for her and the cavernous halls echoed with great shouts of welcome. On the way out, when I preceded her, the enthusiasm of the crowd could hardly be contained. A number of people broke out from the lines, throwing flowers before me and garlanding me. Twice, a few men prostrated themselves before me, touching my feet. I was acutely embarrassed and tried valiantly to lift them up from the damp granite floor, but it was quite impossible. They were determined to show their affection to this hapless "Mother." Then the local party workers were able to shield me, shouting, as we forged ahead, that I was not "the Mother." I finally escaped to the safety of the waiting car, and we drove away. For the rest of the trip, I never left the car and even hid my face.

It was an experience I shall never forget, and it occurred to me that, given the nature of the culture, such adulation dies hard. Any individual gesture to discourage it would likely be misunderstood and interpreted as ungracious and unbecoming a beloved leader and maternal figure.

Back at her house in New Delhi, no matter what the time of my visits—morning, noon or late afternoon—the stream of people going to her seemed constant and interminable; it included students or other youth, workers, politicians, and others. In short, I gathered that Mrs. Gandhi's confident outlook was based in good part on the visibly growing sentiments of nationwide popular support.

This new mood was manifest in electoral victories of her party in several state and parliamentary constituencies. At first, these successes astounded observers and caused many an anxious moment among her opponents. As time went on, however, her political comeback became more and more certain. Thus, people were not unprepared for her latest victory at the polls in early November 1978, when, after an absence of a year and a half, she was returned to Parliament from a constituency in the southern part of India which has become, for the time being, her strongest base of political support. As president of her party, which commands the second largest number of seats after the governing Janata party, she will now become the leader of the opposition. If the Janata continues to be divided internally, as it has been since its inception, she could well wean away some of its members (who are former colleagues and allies) and, together with other opposition parties, lead a successful motion of no-confidence against the present government, bringing it down. Her return to power at the head of the government would not be automatically assured after that, but she would certainly have an equal chance—if not a better one than most politicians—to lead the government.

The Indian people have paused at another crucial crossroads in their historical journey. They must decide whether they are to send their former Prime Minister to permanent political exile or once again place Indira Gandhi in the crucible of leadership.

CHAPTER I

The Leader and the Setting for Action

Indira Nehru Gandhi. Her name inevitably evokes images of two historic phases in the development of twentieth-century India. The nationalist stage of the drama was dominated by Mahatma Gandhi until his assassination in 1948.[1] He bequeathed to the Indian people ideals that have frequently been a source of inspiration to them; but, as few were able to attain his Himalayan virtues, they have more often been a source of frustration and even despair. Worst of all perhaps, in their earnest desire to live up to these ideals Indians have been prone to unwittingly mislead others and, more often, themselves. Jawaharlal Nehru, who ushered India into the stage of independence, was less demanding in this respect.[2] Yet he too towered over other men, and he projected an image of leadership—familiar, loving, confident, and reassuring—that the Indian nation needed during its years of infancy. But though he exacted high standards of performance from himself, Nehru failed to provide the firmness and direction his people sorely needed to tackle in earnest the staggering problems of development and national integration.

As for Indira Gandhi, she is the spiritual daughter of neither Nehru, her father, nor Gandhi, in whose aura she grew up, although she was influenced by both of them—most deeply by her father. Nor can we discount the legacy of her mother, Kamala. She drew upon the strengths—and weaknesses—of each of them, and of others too. Yet she is not a mere reflection of any of them; she developed a distinctive personality that marks her as a spiritual daughter of India, with many of the flaws and virtues that implies. She is, as Gandhi and Nehru were, in their own way, heir to the Indian cultural and historical traditions. She mirrors India in many ways: in the contradictions of her personality, the eclecticism of her thinking, her penchant for synthesis, and her singular

1

ability to evoke both hate and love—to alienate and to charm, to frustrate and simultaneously to delight. Perhaps it is only in this sense that "Indira is India," as the placards of her more ardent supporters proclaimed during the 1975 crisis. Yet at the same time she is a personality whose own motivations have blended and contended in unique ways with the imperatives and opportunities offered by her culture and the situation in which she found herself at any given moment. Only in the light of her environment and her personality—and especially of the interaction between the two—can we understand her political behavior and outlook.

This study looks at the antecedents of the decision to declare a state of emergency on June 25, 1975—which, along with later steps, resulted in the establishment of an authoritarian regime—in terms of that interaction. But, although the decision provides the focal point of concern, it serves primarily as a point of analytical departure from which to examine various features of her rule during the years that preceded it. To understand this brief but critical period we must consider the basic problems that have confounded India's leaders since independence—namely, the maintenance of national unity and stability on the one hand, and the effective pursuit of developmental goals within an evolving social and political framework, on the other. These issues, which have for long tested Indian leadership, do not lend themselves to easy resolution and will undoubtedly remain vitally important to Indian society for years to come.

Of all the actions taken since Indira Gandhi first assumed the office of prime minister, the emergency declaration provoked by far the greatest debate and acrimony—although in India its public expression was muffled by the censorship of the press. She had often been involved in controversy during the preceding decade and had taken actions that, though of questionable wisdom, beneficially jolted the Indian political community out of a prolonged state of animated aimlessness. Soon after Gandhi began to consolidate her political power in 1969, she displayed perceptible impatience with the pace of events. Over a relatively short period of time a body of legislation, significant in content no less than in volume, was enacted. Over half of the thirty-five amendments to the constitution added since 1950 (when the Indian Republic was established) were passed within a nine-year period beginning in 1966. Of course, only four or five of these could be considered major in their effect on fundamental questions of citizens' rights and "separation of powers," and almost all of the latter were engineered in a two-year period between 1971 and 1972.[3] Under her father's stewardship, by contrast, a similar number of amendments dealing with comparable issues were spaced out over fourteen years.

The landmark amendments passed under Gandhi were preceded by a political event of resonating significance. The Indian National Congress, the impressive but lumbering organization that had waged the nationalist struggle and that became, after independence, India's ruling party, was split in two in 1969, after a bitter struggle for control. Some saw the division not as a mere power struggle but as an ideological schism. In any case, the event shook Indian politics to its roots. Partisans on both sides still argue over who initiated the split, who was ultimately responsible for bringing about the "great divide," and whether it was in fact a power struggle or an ideological parting of the ways. It is certain, however, that Gandhi's role in the events leading up to the split was a central one; and her conduct in this political battle brought her public recognition as an astute politician and strategist. But it also changed potential rivals into implacable political enemies, and the seeds of deep mutual mistrust and animosity sown at this time still bear bitter fruit.

Another crucial event, which shortly preceded the split, was the nationalization of fourteen major commercial banks. In this case there is no doubt that the action was carried out on Gandhi's initiative. Moreover, the question has been raised as to whether political, rather than economic considerations were determining, as though the two are always independent of each other. In any case, bank nationalization, the dramatic act preceding the unceremonious fall of Congress party unity, caused many to stand up and take notice. Some worried about how far the prime minister's "radical socialism" would go, while for others, the action evoked admiration and hopes for a new beginning. It brought her national recognition and popular acclaim. The subsequent abolition of the "privy purses" and other privileges enjoyed by descendants of imperial rulers, kings, and princes of centuries past only added to these.[4]

The national elections of 1971 returned Indira Gandhi's party to power in a landslide victory that surprised many, though perhaps not the prime minister herself. She was developing a reputation for political timing and for her uncanny ability to appraise the popular mood. As she was herself approaching the peak of her popularity, it surprised no one that she won an overwhelming majority from her constituency of Rae Bareli in 1971; she polled over 66 percent of the vote, compared to less than 26 percent for her major opponent. But the 1971 election campaign in Rae Bareli gave rise later that year to the court proceedings that culminated, four years later, in the decision of the Allahabad High Court to remove her from her parliamentary seat.[5] The decision was stayed pending final adjudication by the Indian Supreme Court; the provisional judgment permitted her to remain a member of Parliament and attend its proceedings but deprived her of the right to vote.

Later this same high court ruling would precipitate the crisis leading up to the June 1975 declaration, but in 1971 little attention was paid to the gauntlet thrown down by Raj Narain, a long-time political enemy of Gandhi and her father. (Since Nehru's early days in office, Narain had been arrested almost every other year for agitating against the government.) His petition to unseat a victorious opponent must have seemed at the time like just another of the many petitions submitted to the high court. It could be safely ignored (or so it was thought).

What could not be ignored was the challenge shaping up across India's northeastern borders in what was then East Pakistan (soon to become Bangladesh). The adroit diplomatic and military handling of this crisis by Gandhi was applauded by most observers inside and outside India (a notable exception being U.S. President Richard M. Nixon). The event brought her to the very pinnacle of her political career in terms of popularity (even adulation) at home and respect abroad.

In some ways, however, this was a Pyrrhic victory, politically and economically. The cost in foreign exchange and, most seriously, in food reserves—which were depleted to feed the ten million refugees from East Pakistan who had streamed into India as West Pakistani armies wreaked havoc on their land—crippled India's ability to meet the economic crises that followed, with savage speed, one upon the other. Successive severe droughts and the international oil crisis were sharply reflected in critical food shortages and a staggering rate of inflation. As the developed nations of the world reeled under the impact of sharply rising oil prices, India entered the ranks of the so-called fourth world. Her limited exportable resources precluded any speedy economic recovery based on foreign exchange trade-offs between imports and exports.

Although the Congress party was returned to power in most state elections in 1972, from this time forward, the political fortunes of the prime minister and the Congress took a downward turn, reflecting the worsening economic situation and the accompanying popular discontent and disillusionment. Among the disgruntled were many in the administrative ranks who interpreted Gandhi's call for civil servants to demonstrate greater "commitment" to policies as a command to prove their political loyalty to the Congress party and to her personally.

By 1975, however, inflation, a source of much disaffection and political discord, seemed to have been brought under control, and the country appeared to be moving toward economic recovery. Before this could be consolidated, however, a new series of events, climaxed by the high court judgment unseating Gandhi and opposition efforts to bring about her resignation, overtook the prime minister; she reacted (some say overreacted) by declaring, through the president of India, a state of emergency in June 1975. It is interesting that a state of emergency, declared during the 1971 war with Pakistan, was already in force at the time. Even more than an earlier declaration—which had remained in effect for six years after the commencement of hostilities with China in 1962—this three-and-a-half-year-old emergency had become a hotly debated political issue by 1975.[6] The new declaration, however, was the first to be justified on the basis of the threat to Indian security posed by an "internal disturbance," which was said to be undermining "internal stability" and adversely affecting "production and prospects of economic improvement."[7] Earlier declarations (Article 352 in the Indian constitution makes provision for both types of emergency contingencies) had been precipitated by states of war.

The Political Personality

All the important actions taken by Gandhi, starting with those associated with the 1969 Congress party split, quickly became topics of serious and bitter debate between her supporters and critics in India and among outside observers of the Indian political scene. Certain constitutional amendments and other decisions passed during her administration had raised questions touching on the integrity of the Indian political process and the style of leadership as these had evolved up to that time. But none were more fundamental than those evoked by the emergency declaration and the constitutional amendments enacted thereafter, which served to consolidate authority at the center and, particularly, in the hands of the executive.

How can these actions by explained? What considerations entered into her deliberations? What happened to cause such a turnabout by a political leader who had long been apparently committed to democratic practices and values? Or was it really a turnabout and not a conclusive demonstration of her true colors, as her political enemies, who now hold the reins of government, assert? Our answers to these questions will assume that behavior is motivated not only by internal—that is personality—factors but also by a response to external—that is, situational—factors with which one interacts. We should, therefore, explore both Indira Gandhi's personality and the setting within which she operated as prime minister until her party's debacle and her own devastating defeat in the elections of 1977.

Though we are primarily interested in her as a political leader, we recognize that her political life is only the most observable aspect of a many-faceted personality that began to evolve when she was born on November 19, 1917—the first and only child of a politically and socially prominent Kashmiri Brahmin family in northern India. Before she assumed the prime ministership on January 24, 1966, nearly half a century of living, growing, and coping had molded her character. How did her life experiences influence her perceptions and her political philosophy in general? How might they have shaped her actions and predisposed her to certain types of behavior?

As the only child of Jawaharlal and Kamala Nehru, Indira saw from close up the struggles of her family and of Mohandas Gandhi to gain independence for India. Although the family was financially comfortable (indeed wealthy) and she suffered no physical deprivation, the fact of their opposition to continued British rule (in the twenties and thirties) meant that family and friends could be snatched away from her at any moment to serve long prison terms. Indeed, her father first went to jail when she was about four years old.

One of her reactions to the bruising insecurity she experienced after the age of three—when she was first separated from both parents—was an emotional aloofness. She also developed—on her own though at her parents' urging—a very early self-reliance that made it possible for her to survive these early separations. Also, as virtually no more than an infant, she became a fierce adherent of the nationalist cause and developed a strong predisposition to favor the oppressed and helpless in any situation.

Indira's mother was a shy, poorly educated young woman (by Western standards) of lower social standing than her in-laws; she had, unlike the Nehru women, received a traditional Indian upbringing and was looked down on by her mother-in-law and sisters-in-law. Her husband apparently never thought it worthwhile to protect her from their criticism and hostility, which sometimes extended to his daughter. During her short life Kamala Nehru too was an avid and active nationalist. She died after long years of illness when Indira was eighteen.

The young Indira, who was emotionally close to her mother, suffered from the same curse of shyness throughout childhood and adolescence. Even at forty-two, as a married woman and president of the Congress party, she is described as retiring and ill at ease in social settings. Nonetheless, she served for fourteen years as her father's official hostess—a task she performed efficiently and unspectacularly.

After her mother's death she studied history at Oxford for a time but returned to India in 1941 to work in the nationalist cause and to marry, at twenty-four and against her father's wishes, Feroze Gandhi. In 1960, after one term as president of the Congress party, she resigned to devote herself to bringing up her two young sons and to assisting her father. Upon Nehru's death in 1964 she accepted a post in the Shastri government as minister of information and broadcasting. Two years later, in 1966, she became prime minister.

In Chapters 2 and 3 we shall look in greater detail at her personal history and the development of distinctive character traits—independence, aloofness, achievement motive, nurturance, her response to authority, and her characteristic ways of dealing with conflict. These can tell us something about the sources of her motivation and how her personality interacted with the political setting, domestic and international. If, as psychologists tell us, each of us is the product of our individual experiences and develops a personality pattern that remains more or less stable throughout life, such an investigation into Indira Gandhi's past should yield rich ores of insight.

The Setting for Leadership

Inseparable from personality traits and attitudes is the environment in which these evolved over the years. For our purpose—the understanding of why the 1975 decision and subsequent actions were taken—it is particularly important to examine carefully the historical setting within which Indira Gandhi functioned as prime minister and de facto leader of her party as well as the immediate situation in which she made particular decisions.

Like most developing countries, India has been at a critical political and economic stage since independence was attained in 1947, and the Indian system has not yet decisively evolved to the point of assuring relatively permanent stability and continuous progress. Though remarkable advances have been made, further development depends to a great extent on the vagaries of nature and the goodwill and cooperation of important segments of the national and international community—all of which can be unpredictable and unreliable.

India's crisis has gone unnoticed in the past because, unlike many other newly emergent states, its political institutions function smoothly enough to produce leadership at regular intervals through orderly elections; leadership successions have occurred peacefully rather than through bloody (or even bloodless) coups. In a system in which one party overwhelmingly dominates all others, however, such successions can be effected mainly through informal personal arrangements that although guided by evolving conventions, are subject to modification by the particular leaders.[8] Changes in leadership were thus determined behind Congress party scenes rather than by the party as a whole, and the elections usually served merely to formalize these choices. Orderly succession thus masked a sustained, though low-intensity crisis in the political system.

In one sense, the emergency declaration of 1975 was the culmination of particular political events in the preceding three to four years; but beyond that, it was a manifestation of underlying, mostly unrecognized conditions and trends that had been converging for a long time—even before Nehru's death—toward a critical crossroads. Only the time and ultimate direction of the crisis could not be foreseen with any precision. The 1975 action, marking a critical juncture in Indian political history, may be interpreted as an attempt—grossly mismanaged, it now appears—to avert a tragic denouement of an unfolding crisis that is not over yet.

While potential anarchy may indeed have been lurking round the corner at the time, it is a mistake to assign responsibility for the state of affairs exclusively to the actions of opposition leaders, as Gandhi did in justifying her action. It would be correct to claim, however, that the political opposition substantially aggravated existing instability and, moreover, that the condition had its roots in political ailments Congress leaders had long neglected. As long as the task of creating a more equitable society remains unfinished to the present extent, we can expect to witness profound upheaval in India. Mahatma Gandhi himself foresaw this and warned: "A violent and bloody revolution is a certainty one day unless there is a voluntary abdication of riches and the power that riches give and sharing them for the common good."[9]

Appropriate remedies for its condition must be sought in both India's society and its leadership—the hero or villain theory of leadership is in itself inadequate to explain the course of events. Yet, there is a marked tendency in Indian society to personalize any struggle and to attribute to some person an almost unlimited capacity to affect the outcome, for either good or evil. Perhaps the charismatic personality emerges in India because people are predisposed to exalt the accomplishments of the individual and to disregard the impersonal forces that also govern events. By the same token, the declining charisma of a particular leader is often replaced by a kind of demon theory—which might account for both the wildly enthusiastic appraisals of Indira Gandhi as a *devi* or goddess in 1971—when such perceptions inspired the Indira wave—and for the later tendency to view her as solely responsible for the serious political, economic, and social ills of the country.

I am not suggesting, of course, that Indira Gandhi—nor any other Indian leader—should not be held responsible for failures, both before and during Emergency Rule. Grave errors of judgment, with both practical and ethical implications, were made by her. Prior to the crisis, Gandhi can be faulted for many other lapses: her reluctance to purge the Congress party of deadwood, opportunists, and corrupt elements; her failure to clean up the part of the bureaucracy under her command; her inability to persuade, coax, or coerce state Congress leaders to enact or implement agricultural reforms to effect a more equitable distribution of rural wealth, whether of land or revenue—her failure, in short, to carry out some of the political promises made to the Indian people over the years, particularly the promise to reduce economic disparities. The Congress party and opposition leaders at the highest ranks are equally to be faulted for consistently failing to set aside or subordinate personal political ambitions or private economic gain to the larger public interest.

The catalog of failings on all sides could be expanded indefinitely, but to go beyond apportioning blame requires that we identify the multiple sources of the problems and search for feasible solutions. Many of these are to be found in the setting itself.

Setting Problems

Three problem areas affect the ability of politicians to act effectively within the Indian political scene and deserve our close attention. First are the long-established—in some cases, ancient—social structures, attitudes, and values that coexist—albeit uneasily—with newly evolving democratic institutions and outlooks. Given these structures, and the inadequate supply of basic economic resources, it has not proven feasible to achieve, through existing political institutions, the goals defined by society (or rather by the Indian elite) and reflected in Prime Minister Gandhi's political outlook. A major problem, which sired many others, inheres in the well-intentioned but confused thinking of past leaders—including Gandhi—on the ends and means of government and social organization. Specifically, the official Congress philosophy of democratic socialism contains concepts and implies practices that have proven incompatible and contradictory in the Indian setting. Such incompatibilities, muted for various reasons under Nehru, became pronounced under Gandhi. Secondly, considering the radically reformist and even revolutionary nature of some of the socioeconomic goals the Congress government committed itself to over the years, one is struck by the remarkable lack of a carefully thought out strategy for change. Finally, there are obstacles that arise from conflicts inherent in the nature of all political systems. In India these are compounded by the nature of the political party system, the larger political framework, and the social setting; and they become increasingly apparent in the top leadership roles. Let us first look at the dimensions of the third conflict.

Cross-cutting conflicts of roles and functions: party *versus* government, integration *versus* adaptation The phenomenon of role conflict among Indian politicians reflects the contradictory needs and impulses that exist in any dynamic and complex unit of organization. Tension between established groups and new aspiring classes is normal in any social system attempting to respond to changing conditions. Moreover, there is in every social or political system an impulse to maintain a degree of integration and continuity of character, form, or identity. Ideally, governments aim for a balance between the need for order and the need for change. Revolutionary leaders and societies respond almost exclusively to the need for change, discounting, for a time, the need for order, whereas conservative governments sacrifice change to order. (The caste system of India is a prime example of what can happen when the latter policy is followed.)

Political, social, and economic change has been sorely needed in India for many, many years. Nevertheless, the changes wrought under Emergency Rule appeared to many Indians to be as drastic as they were unanticipated and unwelcome, and we are compelled to ask about their rationale. The "thirst-for-power" explanation sometimes advanced by Indira Gandhi's critics is not persuasive unless we view the pursuit of power through office as in itself psychopathological. (We will discuss this argument in more detail in Chapter 2.) Normally, however, it is conceded that leaders seek power in order to further goals perceived, rightly or wrongly, as beneficial to society. As a rule, these goals are well-served if the society remains orderly and responsive to the changing physical and social environment. The need to secure harmony on the definition of specific goals is reflected in the leader's drive to acquire and sustain the authority and resources necessary to formulate and implement appropriate policies. When there is agreement on the basic "rules of the game" and the broad purposes of government, the pursuit of political power and authority becomes essentially a task of integration—that is, of accommodating and reconciling the goals and activities of groups and individuals toward common public aims. Where such agreement is lacking, the task of integration becomes far more complex and intractable than the benign terms of "accommodation" and "reconciliation" imply.[10]

As prime minister, Indira Gandhi's principal instrument of integration was the Congress party. Public support had been cultivated and mobilized by Congress members directly and through special interests to which they were linked in urban and rural areas. Yet, although she needed the backing of such interests, we ought not to assume that she was wholly in their thrall. In a system in which support is expressed ultimately, through the electoral process, it is numbers that assure success, and the politicians' task is to manipulate such numbers to the party's advantage. In conditions of great poverty, social divisions, and their accompanying prejudices, opportunities for manipulation were legion. Often, however, Gandhi herself was the party's greatest asset, and, as its biggest vote-getter in populous rural areas, she was judged the best insurance for election to office at the state and national levels. Thus relations between Indira Gandhi, on the one hand, and the politicians and special interests, on the other, was symbiotic, and perforce collaborative, even though at times one or the other enjoyed the upper hand.

As noted above, the public welfare is served not only by national integration—an essential task of the political leader—but also by a nation's capacity to adapt to internal or external pressures for change—either in institutions, social structures, outlooks, or existing goals and priorities. Such change is implicit in developmental plans which set forth the changes in political institutions and socioeconomic structures necessary to promote more efficient control of resources. But such control, essential to the attainment of societal goals, will be resisted by the forces of the status quo. In India vested interests have successfully resisted governmental efforts to bring about meaningful land reforms aimed at more equitable distribution of land. There has been a similar subversion of local efforts to distribute political power more equitably at the grass roots.

Adaptation is thus the second imperative need every leader must acknowledge and deal with, both for the sake of maintaining political order and, by extension, of preserving or expanding his or her own bases of political power. In the pursuit of public goals, Prime Minister Gandhi's task was to adapt the political and social organization to the varying demands from within (and outside) India; her principal instrument for doing so was the government apparatus. She thus had to harness a different set of resources from those relied upon for the integrative task: she needed to mobilize capital and industrial and agricultural skills and products, as well as technological, managerial, and scientific know-how. These resources are found within sectors of the Indian and international environment that make demands on the political system for certain policies on a quid-pro-quo basis. Advancement of the public welfare thus depends to a great extent on the predisposition of a relatively small but powerful industrial, scientific, managerial, administrative, and agricultural elite both within the country and outside it.

When the demands of special interests collide with larger public needs (as they invariably do in India) a dilemma arises for the leader, as it did for Indira Gandhi: whether (and to what extent and at what pace) to concentrate on integrative tasks—whose successful completion could directly and immediately ensure her continuance in office—or on the adaptive tasks. In an underdeveloped country like India, it is by no means simple to make a categorical judgment about the relative priority these two crucial system needs should be given. Moreover, the attempt, on the one hand, to maintain some harmony or integration within the political and national community while simultaneously endeavoring, on the other, to mobilize resources toward attainment of change-oriented goals, merges these potentially conflicting tasks and assigns them to those interlocking organizations peculiar (until 1977) to India's one-party-dominant system: the Congress party and the government. Hence the inherent role conflict for the prime minister, who is head of both organizations. The conflict also extends to the personnel of both institutions. In India, even before Gandhi's tenure, this conflict was obvious in the well-known rivalries between the "organizational" and "parliamentary" wings of the Congress party.

The significant point to be noted here is that Indira Gandhi's situation was not unique—every leader is confronted with a particular system problem whose broad dimensions are not of the leader's making; and its successful resolution (either by compulsion or persuasion) distinguishes between effective and ineffective leadership. Analysis of this crucial intersection between the Indian leader and her environment (in what was then a one-party-dominant system) enables us to evaluate Indira Gandhi's relative success or failure to resolve the problem of orderly change.

Conflicting philosophies—democracy and socialism The abstract system needs of *integration* and *adaptation* may be clearer if we look at them in terms of specific, fundamental leadership functions. These functions (or roles) are defined formally by a constitution, laws, and so forth, and informally through conventions, traditions, habits, and established values. Adaptation signals the direction in which a society is traveling; as an intentional process, it is concerned ultimately with the ends of government. On the other hand, discussion of the integrative function directs our attention toward the means through which the decisionmaking machinery is activated and preserved—that is, the means through which ends are ultimately determined. In addition to role conflict then, there is another obstacle to achieving socioeconomic and political goals while preserving political stability: the incompatibility of political precepts defining the means with those setting forth the ends of government. This incompatibility, of course, intensified the problem of role conflict for the Indian leadership.

The political ideology of *democratic socialism* has officially guided the Indian polity in its actions and animated the institutions and workings of the system since independence. In essence, the values of democracy have impelled the integrative institutions and functions, while the goals of socialism have informed the adaptive institutions and processes. Democracy thus defined the organizing principles through which decisions were made, while socialism defined the goals of the society toward which specific decisions were directed. To what extent are the democratic principles inherited from the British rulers and adapted up to 1975 by Indian leaders incompatible with socialist principles as they have been defined since independence? The events of the last quarter of a century or so do not give us a complete answer, but they do suggest that some modification has become necessary in the democratic and/or socialist ideals. The present government of the Janata party, in fact, seems to be modifying the latter ideals and may eventually abandon them.

Democratic socialism attempts to answer, by implication, two fundamental questions about the role of Indian decisionmakers vis-à-vis society. The first—how will we make decisions of import, whether for purposes of maintaining order or for adapting our society's goals to changing conditions?—was clearly answered in the constitution: through democratic means, defined largely in terms of parliamentary institutions, universal suffrage, electoral competition between political parties whose formation would not be subject to any restraining conditions, and a free press. The second question—What will be our social and economic goals and values under given and changing conditions?—concerns the structuring of economic and social relations according to particular standards. The answer was stated ambiguously in terms of "a socialistic pattern of society," which implied at least a change from a rigidly hierarchical society to a more flexible, more egalitarian one—in terms of both social and economic rewards. It implied a more equitable distribution of social and economic goods and services as well as of other less tangible assets. Still there was little specific, extensive, or consistent elaboration of the term; and neither the government nor the party undertook to defend its rationale or speculate on its premises—particularly with reference to democratic values.

What are some of the major incongruities between these two philosophies? As already noted, socialism is primarily concerned with ends, while democracy (in its Western definition) dwells on the means of governance. As broadly interpreted in India, socialism posits a condition or goal of social and economic equality: that is, equality in distribution of goods and services, opportunities, living standards, and of such social values as the dignity of labor. (One can infer from official pronouncements that the equality envisaged by Prime Minister Gandhi's government was relative; the phrase commonly used was "a reduction of socioeconomic disparities.") Democracy, on the other hand, defined a means of achieving this desired social condition—the dimensions of which were to be specifically delineated through the democratic process itself.

Among other things, the social condition posited as desirable in socialism presupposes that, ultimately, the value of *cooperation* will govern relations among people (although struggle will still be the norm between "the people" and the vestiges of the bourgeoisie). The democratic method presupposes that the values of *competition* will govern human relations. (Incidentally, democratic competition should not be confused with the socialist class struggle, which takes place within an entirely different value framework.)

Whereas the freedom of the individual to pursue personal aspirations and ambitions is stressed in democracy—within broad societal limitations—in a socialist society, the welfare of the larger social unit is given priority (through it individuals will derive their rightful benefits). In other words, democracy is informed by an individualistic, competitive ethos, while collectivistic, cooperative principles inspire the socialist philosophy. Clearly, full and free competition in the political and economic arenas limits the areas of cooperation and blunts the cooperative spirit. Similarly, a philosophy that encourages the pursuit and gratification of individual goals must ultimately clash with a collective-oriented outlook; and one or the other must emerge as normative for a particular society.

Over the years, the acquisitive impulse in India, spurred by the democratic, competitive, individualistic values of the economic arena, has overshadowed traditional Indian ideas of self-restraint for the good of the community at large. Even in the social philosophy of Hinduism, where the group's welfare takes precedence over the individual's desires and aspirations, the group is usually very small and very narrowly defined—in terms of family and caste or, at the most, of language, region, and a particular sect of Hinduism. Increasingly in India, social divisions have crystallized along economic and political lines and have insulated a small but powerful elite from the masses of people whose meager economic resources have kept them outside the citadels of power. They have been effectively prevented from using their limited political power to effect social and economic changes favorable to them. Whatever else the poor people of India have gained through the vote in the past thirty years, one can plainly see—even from a brief visit to that country—that it has not brought about a more equitable redistribution of food, shelter, education, jobs, status, or other basic social and economic benefits. The separate identities of India's traditional groups have been strengthened by the competitive ethos and made even more fiercely separate.

It has been said that one cannot be both acquisitive and a socialist; giving free play to individual aspirations is no doubt more natural to believers in democratic philosophy. They seek to extend the competitive freedoms sanctioned in the political arena to economic pursuits. Hence democracy has generally been more at ease with capitalist than with socialist economic doctrines. In India, while socialism was acccepted only in modified form—embracing a concept of "mixed enterprise" that allows private enterprise to function alongside government-controlled activities—democracy was embraced as a whole. The common thread in the constitutional principles and conventional practices developed was the desire to protect individual choice and individual pursuit of wants and desires. The socialist philosophy, on the other hand, can be given substance only if attitudes of self-restraint, self-discipline, and concern for the community's welfare predominate over individual gratification. Up to 1975, such attitudes were not promoted in India.

Where democracy and socialism are combined against a background of sharp social and economic inequality; where inequalities are reinforced by a traditional hierarchical value system and conditions of appalling scarcity; and where a growing population further limits the per capita consumption potential—in all these conditions, it seems utter folly to encourage, concurrently with aspirations for greater equality, demands for more economic and social goods and services. Clearly these demands cannot be met; either the goal of equality or competitive ethos and practices must be modified or abandoned—one in favor of the other. At the very least, one or the other must be given primacy; or alternatively, both values must be substantially modified and redefined so as to work together rather than at cross purposes.

Strategy for change: emphasis on institutions versus values The third dilemma confronting India's change-oriented leadership concerns strategy and the style of conduct. Should one rely more heavily on instruments of persuasion (the competitive process, elections, political education diffusely administered, etc.), or on compulsion, coercion, and social engineering centrally guided and administered—whether to maintain order or to adapt to changing needs? In essence, the outlook of democratic socialism vis-à-vis socioeconomic change is, in the short run, reformist. In the long run, however, anticipated changes are revolutionary in the sense that socialist goals envisage a turnabout in certain attitudes (e.g., toward property relations) and the uprooting of certain ancient institutions (such as the rigidly hierarchical caste system). Democracy lends itself to gradual, reformist change, whereas socialist goals, given the condition of India over the past three decades, suggest that more radical and far-reaching actions are needed to achieve values like equality within the lifetime of the poor (or that of their children). Unless, of course, the choice is made to postpone that goal for a considerable time.

Once such changes are accepted as desirable, indeed necessary, strategies for change and style of conduct must be consciously thought through and instituted.

Two kinds of change then become important: (1) changes in socioeconomic institutions as a whole, in the way people habitually relate to each other—whether as dominant landlords and subordinates, dependent tenants, or agricultural laborers, as capitalists and workers, as political masters and passive subjects, and so on; (2) change, dynamically related to the first, involving popular attitudes and principles of action that guide behavior. The question then is, Can one bring about compatible changes in both simultaneously, or should priority be given to either institutions or values?

In some historical periods, no deliberation seemed necessary; changes were accidental or incidental (the Industrial Revolution, for example, was not centrally planned or engineered). In recent times, however, changes in the institutional structures and outlooks of societies have sometimes been conceived and implemented by a central political authority through five-year plans, intensive political training, and, often, coercion. Such devices have been favored as a means of both controlling the direction of change and accelerating it. Although centralized planning has been typical of Marxist socialist countries like the Soviet Union and China, many non-Marxist socialist or quasi-socialist countries have also adopted the principles and instruments of centralized planning, particularly in the economic field. Underdeveloped countries have usually instituted planning when it has been considered essential to accelerate the pace of change, and sometimes the strategy for change has been recognized as a crucial political issue. An outstanding instance of this occurred in China after 1949, as the leadership periodically shifted strategic emphasis from efforts to change values to policies aimed at changing sociopolitical institutions and structures—without, however, losing sight of the importance of both ideological and structural factors as catalysts for change.

India, however, has never boldly or consciously recognized the need for changing attitudes and values through political education by either formal educational institutions or a political cadre.[11] In the past, Congress leaders seemed to assume that institutional change would naturally bring about attitudinal and structural changes. Thus, while important institutional reforms were introduced, no parallel steps were taken to build up the requisite support for values on which to base a socialist society—which was, nonetheless, the goal repeatedly proclaimed by India's leaders. Indeed, the existing agents of political education, such as educational institutions and the press, fostered democratic competition and acquisitiveness rather than socialist cooperation and modest expectations.

In the area of institutional innovation, the Community Development Program, launched in 1952, attempted (unsuccessfully) to involve local populations in communally organized developmental activities within their villages and immediate environs. This was followed and supplemented by *panchayati-raj* legislation in various states during the late 1950s and 1960s, and by the expansion of cooperative institutions (mostly in the area of credit distribution). A number of large commercial banks were nationalized, as were many other economic activities. It was anticipated that many of these institutional innovations would act as vehicles of political and social education, particularly at the village level, and would generate needed attitudinal and structural transformations. But this did not happen—at least not to the extent nor in the direction desired. Time dashed the hope that such institutional innovations would extend the feeling of community beyond caste and kinship units, promote the spirit of cooperation, and spur motivation for the development of the community in social and economic areas that would spread benefits to the larger social unit at local or higher levels. Instead the introduction of popular local government and the establishment of cooperative institutions succeeded best in inspiring a fierce competitiveness. Such efforts mostly served the political and economic ambitions of the rural and urban elites and further reinforced the gap between political and economic haves and have-nots; and the socialistic goal of reducing disparities receded further and further into the background.

Moreover, as government expanded its sphere of social and economic activities, the values of political and economic competition encouraged the growth of expectations from government and intensified the assertion of individual and group demands. While the demands were growing, however, the economic resource base was not expanding sufficiently to meet the spiraling claims for economic and social goods and services. At the same time, to the extent that the democratic, competitive, self-oriented ethos was encouraged, the development of socialist values like egalitarianism and a collectivist, other-oriented ethos was impeded. This situation highlighted the incompatibility between the two political and economic creeds.

Furthermore—in terms of the strategy-for-change problem—the growth of the public sector tended to centralize (at both state and national levels) the function of economic reconstruction. In many instances this function was not carried out efficaciously. The function of social and political education, however, remained dispersed among various traditional and modern institutional agents: the family, schools, political parties, caste organizations, and the communications media—both public and private.

The three dilemmas I have discussed define the major critical issues generated by the environment within which the Indian leadership has functioned since independence. In setting them forth at this time, my purpose has been to outline a range of possible policy options and to highlight the fact that neither Indira Gandhi nor other Indian leaders have grappled in any systematic way with the thorny problems inherent in the country's social conditions. Rather, they have preferred to proceed on an ad-hoc basis, following the line of least resistance and avoiding hard decisions—the hardest being the provision, through their policies and programs, of a clear-cut direction for the nation. At the same time, one can well appreciate the predicament of leaders who must create, at one and the same time, a sense of national identity and commitment to common purposes *and* new forms of social organization to embrace the nascent national consciousness and cradle social aspirations.

The Leader's Personality in Interaction
with the Environment

Analysis of the setting indicates how environmental factors suggest, command, or compel one particular course of action to the exclusion of all others or, on the other hand, offer several feasible options. What must be established in the course of such an analysis then is whether the environment provides wide opportunities or dictates choices only within a very narrow range.

In addition, we should appreciate the nature of the interplay between a leader and the environment. Is the political player invariably moved by powerful personality compulsions that dictate almost preordained courses of action flowing out of these compulsions, with little regard to the "objective" environmental conditions (whether shifting or stable)? Do these compulsions distort the leader's perception of that environment and project his or her inner landscapes onto external "reality"? Three broad character types can be discerned. In the extreme case of the "power-mad" dictator, inner compulsions may be said to dictate almost all action, and environmental imperatives are either irrelevant or distorted by this "power" lens. At this same extreme are the saints or the heroes (symbolized in India by men like Gandhi and Nehru), who overcome obstacles that would daunt lesser people because they too are moved wholly by inner compulsions. Danger, for instance (whether physical or otherwise) may not be seen in the same light or—if seen—may be ignored or perceived within a different framework of value or importance. The saints and heroes, by the sheer force of their personalities, transcend circumstances and, possibly because their vision is clearer and more wide-ranging, it appears, by conventional standards, to be distorted. They truly "make history" by creating new circumstances to clear the path to their goals. Whether "villains" or "heroes," they share a strong will and the skills to satisfy it. At the other extreme of the "personality-environment" spectrum are leaders almost totally at the mercy of their environment, who are impelled to act because they have neither the skill nor the will to control events. They are mere playthings of history, of their circumstances and conditions, succumbing to pressures arising in their social environment or to the vagaries of nature. In a sense, they too "make history"—but by default, as it were. Between these extremes of very strong and very weak leaders is a whole range of others who respond to both inner motivation and outer situations with their own characteristic rhythm. They fall somewhere in between and do not lend themselves to clear categorizations.

Men like Gandhi and Mao truly "made history" because they had the skill and the will to control and shape circumstances that would have overwhelmed others. A Chamberlain, by contrast, could not transcend the limitations of the conditions.

Where might Indira Gandhi be placed in this typology? One thing is clear at this point: she has not been a helpless pawn of circumstances, nor, for the most part, of people; but neither did she prove to be a trail-blazer. She was neither a weak leader nor yet strong enough to over-come the undoubtedly formidable obstacles of the political environment she faced, as her predecessors had, and whose nature we shall explore.

To understand the dynamics of the interplay between environment and personality, we need first to focus on each of them in some depth. The next chapter begins with a personal and political sketch that high-lights some of the outstanding features of Gandhi's personality and their relevant political ramifications. Are there certain contingencies under which she might behave in certain ways? Under what circum-stances are given traits and attitudes engaged or activated, and why? We shall be searching for connections among various characteristics, events, or conditions central to her life. How did her past experience, the political and social climate of her early years, and other influences contribute to the development of her personality traits? How do these characteristics predispose her to perceive and act in a given situation or in the general course of events?

As noted, our analytical point of departure is Prime Minister Gandhi's decision to declare a state of emergency in June 1975 and to follow this up by a progressively authoritarian reorientation of Indian political institutions. Taking such a reorientation as a fact, we shall try to under-stand it as a product of certain situational factors prior to the emer-gency declaration in dynamic interaction with her personality. We shall not assess the failings of Emergency Rule, nor determine the proper allocation of blame, nor yet speculate on its impact on India's political future.

Most efforts to explain the introduction of emergency rule and re-lated actions have hinged upon several assumptions I wish to explore in the suceeding chapters. One is that Indira Gandhi was driven by an overweening ambition for power. Second, it is asserted that because she was dictatorial by nature the 1975 actions can only be interpreted as vehicles for imposing authoritarian rule. Third, it is assumed that the actions were irrational (or that the rationale offered was dishonest) because the situation could have been adequately dealt with within the existing political and governmental framework.

All of these assertions raise questions about Indira Gandhi's personality and her setting. In dealing with assumptions about her personality, we need to answer two questions. (1) To what extent was she oriented primarily toward the aggrandizement of personal political power rather than toward national goals (which may render the pursuit of power an instrumental value)? (2) Could she be characterized as predominantly an authoritarian or a democratic personality type?

Even if we assume that hers is an authoritarian personality, we still need to identify the situational factors that activated a behavior syndrome that had apparently lain dormant during the preceding ten years, when Gandhi headed a government universally recognized as democratic.[12] On the other hand, if we assert that prior to the emergency proclamation her conduct and outlook were not authoritarian, how then do we explain the discrepant phenomenon of a democratic personality acting in an authoritarian way?

Further, we need to make a judgment as to whether the prime minister's perception of events—that the situation preceding the emergency declaration was dangerous to Indian stability and to developmental goals—was rational. Here we need to ask whether the situation required extraordinary intervention to preserve or enhance order and development, as Gandhi and other officials asserted. (If not, we may conclude that personal compulsions were at work or that her judgment was inadequate.)

The latter questions are deemed of prior importance to the analysis, for socioeconomic and political conditions define the limits of a leader's behavior as well as providing opportunities for action. My basic assumption is that an explanation of Mrs. Gandhi's authoritarian policies lies primarily in the political and economic environment within which she operated as prime minister after 1966 (especially in the four years or so preceding the emergency declaration) and secondarily in her personality characteristics. I shall, therefore, emphasize the trend of political and economic events during the ten years prior to Emergency Rule and the nature of the opposition to her government (discussed in Chapters 4 to 6). Insights into Gandhi's political personality will be found in the historical/cultural background in which she was raised, as well as in her family relationships and other learning experiences (described in Chapters 2 and 3).

To guard against the pitfalls of such a comprehensive perspective, I have strictly limited the investigation to events, trends, actions, or ideas relevant to the three questions set forth above. In Chapter 7, I shall conclude with a final assessment of Gandhi's political behavior, drawing upon discussions of her personality and the setting for action. Shifting to the period following Gandhi's 1977 defeat, Chapter 8 analyzes the Janata government's case against the former Prime Minister, which alleges that the Emergency Declaration and subsequent actions were motivated by her obsessive desire to hold on to and extend her power.

CHAPTER II

The Motivation to Power *versus* the Motivation to Achievement

The Elusive Chameleon

Whether Indira Gandhi has been primarily power oriented or goal oriented is a question that can be answered in part by considering the development of her personality. No doubt some distortion will mar our image of her, seen as it is through the lens of time, space, and our own particular culture. Many Westerners' perceptions of her personality have been shaped—understandably—by the news of developments in India during the period of Emergency Rule. Thus even a brief look at her life may startle us with some unexpected facts and bids us exercise caution and not relegate her too quickly to the category of compulsive powerseeker.

We find, for example, that the pursuit of public office did not engage her energies in any sustained way until she assumed the office of prime minister at the age of 48. Even this event does not seem to have been the result of any determined and concerted effort—initiated and orchestrated by her—to capture political power.[1] She held only one major party position prior to her father's death in 1964—the presidency of the Congress party in 1959, at age 42. She occupied the post for less than a year and could have continued in it. After a period of indecision, however, she resigned, in order to prevent political duties from interfering with her maternal obligations.

Prior to that time (and thereafter), she regularly turned down requests to run for Parliament (requests, she says, were made before each national election). On one occasion, soon after independence, she offended a top party leader by refusing his virtual command (transmitted through Mahatma Gandhi himself) to run for a seat in Parliament. She was concerned about her children, who were very small at the time, and told the Mahatma she would not be bullied.

Upon Nehru's death, she rejected suggestions by a small but growing number of supporters that she succeed her father. One of Nehru's biographers reported that, by her own account, "she would have preferred a long spell of privacy to attend to her father's papers and other memorial activities." He added Jagjivan Ram's testimony that she "was not very keen about the post" and remarked on "the utterly passive nature of her involvement in the process."[2] When Lal Bahadur Shastri became prime minister, it is thought that she was offered the external-affairs portfolio, among others. Instead she chose the Ministry of Information and Broadcasting, a less prestigious and politically weighty post.

If this behavior suggests a long-term strategy to realize ambitions of power, one can only assess it as a very peculiar one that repeatedly disregarded excellent opportunities to pursue power—independently of her father while he was living and on her own merit after his death. Of course, this does not necessarily mean that a power motive was not operative at all and never had been; but it does suggest that it cannot have been too dominant an impulse since it surfaced actively so late in life. A random survey of such political personalities of this century as Winston Churchill and Charles de Gaulle shows that the pursuit of power through public office—civil or military—consciously engaged their thoughts and energies from an early age.

Still, the fact that she did not actively pursue office does not in and of itself preclude the possibility that she consciously desired power. It may be argued that as Nehru's constant companion and confidante since 1950 she was perceived by others as powerful and had always at hand the opportunity to exercise power—albeit behind the scenes. And she did in fact undertake more political responsibilities than was generally known at the time. This role, however, was always played out in the shadow of her father and depended ultimately on his will; moreover, its exercise would not have yielded the volume or quality of prestige presumably needed by the avid powerseeker.

The public image she brought to office in 1966 was certainly far from that of an ambitious, aggressive powerseeker; instead she was perceived as a shy, retiring woman who for fourteen years had been the efficient, charming, but unspectacular official hostess and constant traveling companion of her father. It was a phantom image, but it was well earned, for her name appeared only as one among several others— in the newspapers of the countries they visited, indicating that she aroused little if any political curiosity, even though her duties and activities were not confined strictly to the social sphere. She is not known to have made any overt effort to promote herself in these years; on the contrary, she apparently assiduously avoided publicity. Only when Nehru's end seemed near did speculation about her as a possible successor begin; a book devoted to this subject placed her in the lower ranks of the potential candidates.[3]

Such a public perception, to which she herself contributed the main elements, is clearly not that of the hungry powerseeker (although her political opponents and critics have repeatedly characterized her as one). Nor does it seem credible that she would have purposefully culti- vated such a mild impression for all those years in order to cash in on it when conditions were ripe. For the time could not be foreknown with any precision, nor could "proper" conditions be defined ahead of time.

Nonetheless, if she cannot on the basis of this preliminary evidence be easily defined as a compulsive powerseeker in the years prior to 1966, we should at least consider the possibility that her personality was radically transformed the moment she stepped into office. While we cannot exclude (indeed we should anticipate) significant changes in her attitude toward power after she came into office, we should also not ignore earlier conduct that provides clues to the predispositions toward power she brought with her.

Nehru's role in his daughter's rise to power is by no means clear either, although the assertion was commonly made—not only by her political opponents (some of whom were Nehru's rivals) but also by analysts of Indian politics—that Nehru "groomed" his daughter as his successor. There is some evidence that Nehru asked his daughter to be hostess to the prime minister because of his earlier failure to permit his wife to share fully the responsibilities of public life. The fact that he felt compelled to encourage his daughter this way suggests that he felt her self-confidence needed bolstering. Indira Gandhi herself has spec- ulated that her principal foray into the political arena while he was alive may not have been wholly welcomed by her father. She said that he greeted her decision to accept the Congress party's nomination for the presidency in 1959 with a look of disapproval; and rather than en- couraging her to accept the nomination, he told her the decision was hers to make[4] (advice that was, as we shall see, typical of Nehru). Nevertheless, the conviction persists among many Indian analysts that Nehru orchestrated both her nomination to the Congress presidency, and her ascent, two years after his death, to the prime ministership. (A number of opposition leaders I interviewed in 1975 expressed the same conviction.)

It would be difficult to document the truth of either assertion, and in any case this is a barren argument. Our concern is not whether Nehru wanted his daughter to lead India after his death, but whether she was motivated to pursue political power and, if so, to what purpose. We have returned then to our opening question—Indira Gandhi's motivation for accepting or pursuing office. Is it a desire for power to gratify ego needs or a desire for achievement that transcends egotistical concerns—or perhaps combines them with larger social goals?

While it can be argued that Gandhi, as prime minister, was impelled by a strong sense of public duty and by a desire to achieve worthy national goals, it is also acknowledged that achievement for the public good may have served several psychological needs that were in the past inadequately filled. Achievement brought Gandhi recognition for hitherto unappreciated talents and an enhanced self-image; it also provided an outlet for aggressive impulses that would otherwise have been repressed. As the overt expression of such impulses would be considered unworthy by Indian social standards (particularly for a woman) and by her own value system, the role of disinterested national leader allowed her to channel aggressive energies toward many praiseworthy activities. It also offered her a degree of challenge that suited her personality and the opportunity to exercise skills and develop capabilities—thus satisfying need for self-fulfillment.[5]

We need to know, then, how Indira Gandhi's needs and aspirations were generated by her life experience and to what depths the roots reached. What sort of balance was attained between needs and satisfaction—a balance (or lack thereof) that shaped her character traits in an enduring fashion? Psychologists define "personality" as a characteristic pattern of styles of thinking and acting that tend to remain stable throughout life. Thus linkages between past and present are far from unusual.

Our first concern will be to determine whether Indira Gandhi's actions have been conditioned by her experiences to reflect a predisposition toward power as an expression of aggression and hostility to others coupled with a will to dominate in anticipation of deriving pleasure; or whether, on the other hand, they may represent an earnest desire (whether misguided or not) to serve the national good—an effort springing from the higher needs postulated by humanistic psychology. Some insight into this question can be gained if we venture into Indira Gandhi's early years, from infancy to adolescence; a sketch of her life may help us gain some understanding of her personality. More details will be filled in as we go along.[6] I make no claim to have penetrated the inner recesses of her mind or psyche; few have done so, perhaps least of all Gandhi herself. Rather, my interpretation combines impressions and some intuitions with the facts as they are known and the insights of personality psychology.

Childhood years: the 1920s Indira Gandhi's childhood spanned the 1920s, a decade marked, for her, by many lonely moments, anxiety about her mother's health, and a generally unstable setting. But the first two years of her life were relatively uneventful, happy, and secure. According to family accounts and Gandhi's own testimony, Kamala Nehru was an affectionate, attentive mother. She personally attended to her baby, rather than leaving tasks like bathing, clothing, or even feeding to servants, as is sometimes common in wealthy Indian households.

Her mother's unstinting gifts of love and tenderness were richly supplemented by her grandfather, Motilal Nehru, who cherished her as a "personification of innocence." Remembering him, Indira Gandhi has said: "I loved him and I admired him, and, of course, like many grandchildren, he spoilt me terribly and gave me everything I ever asked for which my parents didn't. But I was impressed by his personality because he always seemed to fill a room although now I realize he wasn't really that tall but at that time I thought he was very tall and broad. . . . when he laughed the whole house shook and laughed with him."[7]

Around the age of three, however, life became increasingly insecure, as political tension began to mount throughout the land, animating the Nehru household more than most others. First she was separated from both parents by being sent to her maternal grandparents in Delhi, over 350 miles from her home in Allahabad. The intention was to provide her with a more stable environment than was available at home, for the family residence had been virtually transformed overnight into a bustling Congress headquarters. Indira attended a local kindergarten in

Delhi but was so homesick that within a few months she had to be sent home. Shortly after her return she saw her father and grandfather tried and imprisoned and British police raid their house of furnishings and other possessions. With her grandfather's arrest and imprisonment, his laughter, which she has said filled the house, was stilled for six months. Then, almost throughout the fourth year of her life, she was deprived of her father's presence as he began traveling within India; his leadership qualities were being increasingly recognized, and his appeal soon became nationwide. Nehru himself wrote of those years that he "lived in offices and committee meetings and crowds [and] . . . almost forgot my family, my wife, my daughter."[8]

Often during her childhood the traditional rivalries between her mother and the other women in the joint household threatened the child's sense of personal dignity. Kamala, and increasingly her daughter (who identified strongly with her mother) were treated with condescension and even hostility by the more sophisticated Nehrus. During these impressionable years, until she left home in 1931 to attend school, she must have witnessed countless incidents in which her mother was hurt, embarrassed, and humiliated by Nehru's mother and sisters, especially the oldest one, "Nan" (familiar to Westerners as Mrs. Vijayalakshmi Pandit, former ambassador to Washington, Moscow, and the United Nations).

The Nehru household was, of course, among the more socially advanced and, therefore, "liberated" from many of the more cumbersome and pointless traditions. When it came to in-law rivalry, however, enlightenment seems to have been sadly lacking. The rivalry in this instance, though originating in jealousy, fixed on status questions as its concrete manifestation. Kamala, who had been personally selected for Nehru by his father (at Nehru's request) was from a less well-to-do family than the Nehrus. Her lack of sophistication, on which Nehru himself remarked, was at first perhaps more noticeable to the Nehru clan than to her. "Modernity" and "sophistication" were defined by the degree of westernization: whether you had a Western education, used a knife and fork, and, presumably, could carry on "sophisticated" chitchat with English aristocrats or other westernized Indians. Kamala failed to meet these and other tests, and such disparities provided an easy handle for her sisters-in-law to demonstrate their superiority.

In 1926 and 1927, there was a two-year interlude in Europe, where her mother was taken for medical examination and treatment. Indira was placed in a Swiss school and remained there while Kamala was confined to a sanatorium. She was on her own a good deal, and it was a time of adjustment and, no doubt, much anxiety. Plucked from an intensely political atmosphere and deposited in this European playground, she felt out of place; she was too sober and mature for the usual children's games and not compatible with others of her age. Still, she worked at her studies and is remembered as a bright child by one of her teachers. Whenever Kamala's condition improved, she and her daughter accompanied Nehru and his younger sister, Krishna, on their travels throughout Europe. Indira was eight years old when the family went to Switzerland; when they returned in December 1927, she had just turned ten.

In terms of psychic gains and losses, we find that the balance sheet is not wholly negative. She must have felt alone and deserted at times, especially when her father and aunt traveled around Europe without her and her mother. Once she was left behind when both parents and her aunt accepted an official invitation to visit Russia. Her tendency to withdraw from people, which became marked later on, was noted in the Swiss school; and her sense of being different, of being unique, began at this time. The fact is that she was different from the Western children in this European school and from most other Indian children of her age.

Nonetheless, her accounts of this period show that she had a sense of being loved. She saw a good deal of her mother, who had always been demonstrative. And when her father was not traveling, he always picked her up from school; one teacher remarked on the warmth and devotion that clearly bound father and daughter at the time. Having learned to ski, she probably shared many moments on the Swiss mountain slopes with her father, who was fond of the sport. Referring to that time of her life, as prime minister she recalled: "I learned very soon to stand on my feet all alone. I was eight years old when I first went to Europe. I moved all alone between France and Switzerland because my parents were in different places and I had to join them."[9]

On their return to India, Nehru resumed his political activities and travels, which were interrupted during the thirties by extensive periods of imprisonment. As long as her mother was alive, Indira saw more of her than of her father. But by early 1925, Kamala's ailment had been definitely diagnosed as tuberculosis, and Indira was discouraged from excessive physical contact with her mother, even when she was not hospitalized. Her grandfather once cautioned Nehru about this, noting that Indira's tendency to kiss her mother frequently ought to be stopped. No doubt this precautionary advice was followed, with painful results for both mother and daughter. Even so, there had been concern about Kamala's health as early as 1919-1920, so that her mother's well-being must have been a constant source of anxiety for Indira from the age of three. The premature birth and loss of a child in November 1924 may have heightened the child's awareness of her mother's fragility; the infant, a boy, lived for two days. Within four years another pregnancy ended in a miscarriage. In the meantime, Kamala's health was constantly deteriorating.

Indira was now in the eleventh year of an already-intense childhood. Her transition to adolescence was hardly less eventful: in October 1930, as her twelfth year drew to a close, her father was arrested, less than a week after his release from a six-month term; her grandfather, who was ailing, had been arrested two months earlier; and her mother had thrown herself into the nationalist movement when Mahatma Gandhi launched his civil disobedience campaign with the famous Salt March at the end of April.[10] By this time, everyone in the family—aunts, uncles and both parents—were active in the movement and were subject to arrest. Friends, other relatives, and even servants followed her family into British jails.

Adolescent odyssey: the 1930s The most traumatic year of Indira's life was yet to come. During 1931, shortly after she turned 13, her mother was imprisoned for the first time—to the great joy of both parents.[11] A month later, while she was revelling in her mother's release, her grandfather died, piercing her with grief. Before the end of the year, after a happy family holiday in Ceylon, her mother's condition again took a turn for the worse, and her father began his fifth sentence and first extended stay in prison. Between the end of 1931 and September 1935, he remained in jail continuously, with only a six-month reprieve in 1933. Indira too experienced a traumatic "first" when, in May of 1931 (after the return from Ceylon), she was enrolled in an experimental school founded by the great Indian poet Rabindranath Tagore; it was located in Pune, about a thousand miles from home. Apart from some younger cousins who also attended the school, there were no familiar faces to ward off anxiety and loneliness. Indira was now a decidedly shy, retiring adolescent, and this was the first time that she had been away from both parents for so long. She felt totally alone. However, her sense of autonomy and responsibility were further strengthened during this period; for not only did she have to take care of herself, but as the eldest representative of the Nehru clan in Pune, she also had to keep an eye out for her young cousins' welfare. She remained in Pune for the next three years (except for brief holiday homecomings), deprived of comforting family presences. Her closest link with home was Mahatma Gandhi, who was incarcerated in a nearby prison; she was able to visit him once.

Her rearing was different from that of most Indian children in so many ways, and at school this set her apart from others of her age and, later on, from her colleagues as well. It probably accounts for her sense of uniqueness and for the resentment she produced in many of her rivals and foes, who interpreted this sense of being "different" as hostility. In actuality, her self-image of uniqueness seems to stem from the fact that she was not reared in typical Indian fashion and from the frequent separations from her family. Hers is an uncommon experience in India. Even less typical was the sustained permissiveness practiced by her family well past her third year. Normally, Indian parents are indulgent with their children until the age of two or three; after that restrictions escalate as social, moral, and (especially among Brahmins) intellectual training begins. In addition, the average school child gets used to daily absences from home at an early age, whereas for Indira, the pattern was too inconsistent even to accustom her to the separations caused by political and other partings. Sometimes her schooling took place at home, and sometimes in schools; in the ten years after her third birthday she attended at least six different schools. Moreover, while other children could look forward to seeing their parents and other loved ones at the end of each day, young Indira did not have this advantage. Especially after the age of thirteen there was a rather sharp drop in the amount of time spent with her family. Even before then, contact with her father had been sporadic and that with her mother restricted because of health taboos.

The three years she spent in Pune were not very happy ones, though she did develop an enduring bond with the couple who managed the school. In spite of this warm relationship, the young girl apparently welcomed the move, in 1934, to Santiniketan, another experimental school, this one in the state of Bengal, founded by the Tagore. She nostalgically recalls the brief time spent there as "perhaps the only relatively calm period in my life."[12] She was just seventeen.

By the time she returned home to Allahabad in April 1935–after a four-year absence–she had traced a huge three-thousand-mile triangle across the length and breadth of India. Within a month, she would embark from Bombay with her ailing mother and their family doctor. She was not yet eighteen. Within three months after crossing that threshold into young adulthood, she lost her mother. By the time her father joined them in Europe–on leave from a jail term–it was clear that Kamala did not have long to live. But even during this most private and anguishing time, her father was constantly badgered by political friends. Nehru captured the mood of stress and urgency during that last month of Kamala's life, as friends pressed him to return to India. He recalled later that the month before her death:

> I went to Paris for a few days and paid another brief visit to London. Life was pulling at me again and news reached me in London, that I had been elected for a second time president of the Indian National Congress, which was to meet in April. It was a dilemma for me: to leave her as she was or to resign from the presidentship.
> Meanwhile the call of India was insistent and friends there were pressing me to return. My mind grew restless and ever more occupied with the problems of my country. . . . I was straining at the leash.[13]

His election in absentia and the news from home seemed to wrench Nehru from his dying wife's bedside; he finally agreed to return briefly to India when Kamala's condition seemed to show some improvement. About a week before her death, however, the doctors apparently warned him that the end was approaching, and he postponed his departure. Kamala Nehru died the day her husband was to have returned to India.

Her father left for India after a few days of quiet mourning at a nearby retreat, and Indira Nehru was herself soon on the move. She headed for England to continue her schooling at Oxford, but her education was frequently interrupted: by a return trip home the next year and the year after that, by trips to Southeast Asia and various European countries, and by an eleven-month stay in a Swiss clinic following an attack of pleurisy. After a long period of uncertainty about her academic future, she decided to abandon her studies and return to India to participate in the history-making activities of her family and country. She left Switzerland for London in November 1940–taking a rather circuitous route because of the war–and in February 1941 sailed for home with her husband-to-be, Feroze Gandhi. They landed on Indian soil a month later.

This flitting about during the five to six years that followed her mother's death reflects the mood of restlessness and indecision with which she greeted adulthood. Frequently such indecision betokens inner conflict, and it is likely that her anxiety stemmed from a desire, on the one hand, to honor her mother's memory by completing her education, and, on the other, to return home and join the movement for independence alongside her father. It is also possible, as Nehru himself believed, that she really did not wish to return home but felt that her duty to her father dictated that she do so. Certainly the matter of her education must have been linked in her mind with her mother, for Kamala Nehru had promoted women's education throughout much of her adult life. As a young woman of 28 she wrote to a friend: "Daily I grow more determined that on my return, taking your wife along with me, I shall urge Indian women to have faith in God and fight for their own freedom—*and educate their daughters so that they may not be in trouble like us.*"[14]

The young Indira was no doubt well aware that Kamala would unquestionably have urged her to complete her studies. On the other hand, the young woman had been involved in practical activities for much of her life. As a child, she had not been content merely to play at leadership roles or the role of the freedom fighter. She had wanted to be one and even organized her own "army"—the Monkey Army—when she was denied the opportunity to join the Congress. At Oxford, she pursued an interest in history sparked by her father; but rather than learning about history (and other peoples' history at that), she may have decided that it would be more exciting to help shape it. And so, finally, she was drawn back to India. Her decision to abandon her studies would not have pleased her mother, and she seems to have carried a burden of guilt about it ever since. She tends to be rather defensive on any question touching on education, particularly her own. When discussing the subject of education in 1975, she said: "The 'old' Indian approach (to education) brought out certain qualities in the individual which is far more important than merely going to school. Many of the world's top people never finished school. Why even the first aeroplane was sent up by two bicycle repair people, after top scientists had said such a thing was impossible. Look, I am not against education—but going through the routine is not education." Is education "for mere decoration," she asks, echoing her father, or is it something to be used for a larger purpose? "Education is not just knowing something more, but becoming something better."[15]

On another occasion she pointed out that school examinations do not always accurately gauge ability, and she cites Churchill, who "did extremely badly in school, and yet he was one of the great men of the world and also a great leader of his country."[16] The fact that she herself was a poor student and twice failed her examinations at Oxford makes such references meaningful. Even when she was a small child, her father had expressed concern about her schoolwork.

Her ambivalence toward education, then, can be traced back to this period when she was trying to decide whether to stay on at Oxford or return home. Her indecision was resolved in a pattern that has since become typical of her; circumstances guided her in the direction she was to take ultimately. First her illness (an attack of pleurisy) incapacitated her for eleven months; then the Second World War broke out, which made it advisable to return home before the lines of communication and travel were closed.

The wanderer returns Her return to India in March 1941 seemed to signal the end of a ten-year odyssey and a twenty-year period of instability. After constant separations from loved ones and all kinds of uncertainties, at age 24 the wanderer had returned home at last. The Indian artist Satish Gujral, who later painted her as a refugee, captured in that image the essence of much of her early life.

As if to assure herself and those around her that she was now determined to set anchor, she resolutely announced her decision to marry Feroze Gandhi—despite her father's reservations. (Their marriage was considered "mixed," as Feroze Gandhi's family followed the Parsi religion.) The Quit India movement intervened in August 1942 by channeling all their energies into political activities, and the newlyweds were soon forced apart. They were both arrested, and Indira spent eight months in prison under trying physical conditions. Following this test of her physical and emotional fortitude, she tried to settle down to domestic life. Although housekeeping had never enchanted her, she did relish being a mother and has described the feeling of holding her first child in her arms as the most wonderful moment of her life. What she "loved mostly" about being a housewife was bringing up her two sons.

After independence, her domesticity in Lucknow was interrupted by periodic visits to New Delhi (270 miles away) when her father's social duties as prime minister required her presence. For a while, she shuttled back and forth between the two cities, returning to her husband whenever he asked her to; "but if my father called and said, 'I need you, please come,' then I would leave Lucknow and run to my father."[17] By 1950, she had moved into the prime minister's residence with her two boys (then aged 6 and 4); for a time her husband also lived at Teen Murti (as the residence was officially named). There Indira Gandhi remained for the longest period of her life yet. In a very real sense, however, the return to her father was a decision to postpone a decision, for during the next decade and a half, she lived in Nehru's shadow, at peace and contented—so far as anyone knew or cared.

In fact, her early adult years were not a period of personal achievement or real contentment. In all likelihood, however, they were a necessary preparation for self-fulfillment. Of course she must have gained some satisfaction from her behind-the-scenes participation in some important decisions and she showed considerable promise of her abilities on such occasions. But few people knew of this, judging by the condescending attitudes most politicians took toward her in 1966 when she was being considered for the highest office. Even during her first three years as prime minister her talents and abilities were not widely recognized or appreciated. She alluded to this fact by stating once that she had had experience in making political decisions before she became prime minister, "though nobody ever made a fuss about it." Although referring to India's hurt national pride on another occasion, she might also have been thinking of herself when she said: "Always undervalued, underestimated, not believed."[18]

Leadership Style in Embryo

It should not surprise us that Indira Gandhi's life, which began on the crest of the wave of nationalism, was not only exhilarating but filled with anxiety and tension, menacing deeply rooted needs. But those experiences also required her to develop, early on, a variety of techniques for coping with life. Directly and by their example her parents taught her independence and self-reliance, and these allowed her to adapt to a difficult environment while maintaining some degree of inner harmony. This reinforced a self-image of self-reliance that was positive in most ways and enabled her to deal adequately with life's problems on a conscious level and to respond effectively to the urgent, more or less unconscious, drives for safety, love, and respect.

At all stages of her life, what is significant about her way of dealing with various problems is that she tended to develop, both instinctively and deliberately, a varied repertoire of coping techniques and to alternate among them. It is this variety, more than anything else perhaps that helped her develop in a more or less healthy way, without becoming rigidly or compulsively fixed in any one response pattern.

At various times in her life she appears to have gone through and overcome periods of severe depression; and the emotional deprivation and insecurity she endured in childhood and adolescence are present in traits of chronic indecisiveness and ambivalence—which psychologists tell us are sure signs of conflict between wishes (or instincts) and conscience. Frequently her periods of indecisiveness are followed by spells of resoluteness—particularly when she has been challenged and her dignity or beliefs have been threatened. On such occasions, she responds with aggressive decisiveness, clear thinking, and attempts to reach out to people—for friendship, advice, or support. Such tendencies were clearly reflected in her leadership style as prime minister, which was characterized by extended periods of drift interspersed with periods of decisive action. Perhaps fearing rejection, rebuff, or defeat, she has usually been disinclined to seek help, has aspired to self-sufficiency, and has tended to shun unpleasantness and conflict. Her aloofness, which has been manifest since early childhood, is one of her most distinguishing and persistent character traits. Yet, as prime minister when she sensed a challenge to her leadership or dignity or to goals she perceived as important, she was often able to transcend her reserve. This pattern of alternation between aggressiveness and aloofness was evident from her earliest years; at times both have been expressed simultaneously.

While we do find early signs of reticence, self-control, and determination alternating with hesitancy, there is no evidence that she ever tried in youth to relieve her insecurity and self-doubt by aggressive means. Rather than attacking pre-emptively to ward off anticipated threats, she more often withdrew into herself, for both the cultural environment and her own psychological and physical needs precluded a spontaneous expression of aggressive feelings. However, she has confessed to a stubborn streak as a child, and stubbornness is a passive way of expressing aggression. As they were in personalities like Woodrow

Wilson and Winston Churchill, repressed defiance and hostility to adults were reflected in persistent weakness in her schoolwork.[19] For the most part, however, she must have turned any hostile feelings back on herself by restricting her impulses and her conscious desires. And she reached out, in her way, toward people.

Looking at her childhood, however, one might not suspect that she was reaching out to anyone. She apparently made little effort to evoke affection if it was not spontaneously forthcoming. Her aloofness, a means of overcoming the anxieties of her unstable and insecure childhood, was necessitated by the absence (and hence unreliability) of those who might have eased those anxieties.

It is instructive to compare this aloofness with the passivity she exhibited later on in regard to the pursuit of power. An enduring and pervasive attitude seems to be—"Let the mountain come to Muhammad." Such an image is implied in an introspective assessment of herself given to an interviewer when she said, referring to the loneliness of office: "As your capacities draw you, you may leave some people behind. It's one section of you they can understand but they can't understand the whole of you. So the loneliness comes because there are so few people who have been through all the experiences which you have been through."[20]

We ought not to infer from all this that either the child or the adult Indira Gandhi wholly abandoned her need for affection. However, she tended to emphasize the giving more than the receiving of love over the years, which is in accord with expectations of women in most cultures and especially in Indian society. Indira Gandhi's personal circumstances moreover reinforced a nurturing attitude because the people toward whom she would normally have turned for affection during her childhood and adolescence were frequently absent or not responsive in ways that were wholly satisfying. Hence, she was inclined from childhood to expend her need for human affection on abstract symbols like the "nation," which were readily available in the historic times of her growth. And over time, either by choice, by chance, or by necessity, the circle of personal friends and loved ones has narrowed more and more.

However, what may have started out as a means of defending herself against unhappiness came eventually to be a positive source of rewards. Gradually a need to nurture developed, a desire to look after, to care for someone or some group that needed a champion or simple sustenance. Her concern with and for children is well known in this respect. One former cabinet minister I talked to pointed to this as one of her distinctive characteristics; and she herself once told an interviewer that if she ever had more time she "would like to do something with children. Anything worthwhile, with children."[21] While her father was alive, she was extensively occupied with a variety of projects relating to children and with social-welfare programs generally. Nor should we forget that even her decision to return to her father when he became prime minister was in large part a response to his expressed need for her.

Repeatedly during her public career, Indira Gandhi has espoused causes for helpless groups or individuals—rescuing Muslims during the communal riots of 1947-1948 and supporting the rights of minorities in the abstract. Such groups have in the past provided her with the largest and most consistent source of political support. Indeed, her commitment to socialism, which—in its articulation if not always its implementation—is above all a championing of the weaker members of society, is a natural extension of this impulse. Emile Durkheim once poetically described socialism as a "cry of grief and anger."[22] Her socialism expressed just such a sentiment, rather than a detailed, internally consistent statement of planks, programs, and goals.

Finally, one of her most basic needs, which has been perhaps the most stable aspect of her personality as child and adolescent, is the need to achieve, to grow, to expand, and to realize her potential. This need expresses her highest impulse, but it is at the same time the most vulnerable of all to external frustration. A friend spoke of this vulnerability in describing Gandhi's "inner core . . . which is religious in nature—which arises out of a deep feeling of love and respect for human life—for life in general. She has a sense of sacredness . . . which is not projected to many people." Speaking just three months before the emergency declaration, however, the friend stressed her concern that this core might be destroyed by the political environment.[23]

This outline of Indira Gandhi's dispositions, inner needs, and efforts to overcome problems does not fully illuminate her character. Her chameleon quality of constantly, and perhaps deliberately, eluding us is partly an instinctive effort at defensive evasion. Nonetheless, one key to her personality does emerge from this brief sketch—the contradictory nature of her character and conduct. Though impelled by her early experiences to maintain distance between herself and others, she has entered a profession that constantly thrusts her among people. A very private person, she has nonetheless assumed a very public role. Although she prefers to shun conflict, she can not only meet it head on but positively enjoy it once she enters the fray. She is indecisive, yet capable of firm decisions. Though she can be aggressive, Indira Gandhi is also shy by nature; she has a reputation for ruthlessness, yet can be gentle. She can be sociable and charming, yet confesses to being utterly miserable at social functions. A good judge of character at times, on other occasions she is seemingly blind to others' shortcomings.

Given these inconsistencies, it is not surprising that she projects sharply contrasting images to various people. Such contradictions also leave her open to charges of deception, opportunism, and manipulativeness, and she has given indications from time to time that she is somewhat aware of her inconsistencies. She seems to have marshalled her inner energies toward integration within and adaptation to her environment without through her varied defenses and through her system of beliefs, style of thinking and conduct, and by appropriate molding of her temperament. The keynote in all these areas of her personality is balance, equilibrium, reconciliation, and synthesis. These personality tendencies were reflected in her political outlook and style during most of her tenure of office.

Challenge and Response: Mastery, Achievement, Aggression, and Seclusion

Let us look now in greater detail at some of the patterns in experience, outlook, and conduct that sound familiar themes at various critical points of her life and are reflected as dominant traits of her personality.

Turbulence, challenge, and conflict—both within and without—have been the normal conditions of Indira Gandhi's life, and from her many trials she has emerged a scarred but toughened fighter. Without seeking out battles, she has relished the challenge when confronted with them, perhaps finding a legitimate outlet for feelings she would have otherwise repressed as improper to her cultural setting and upbringing. An old gentleman of transparent integrity (and a seasoned politician) talked to me about this aspect of her character. Uma Shankar Dikshit was a member of her cabinet who had also served in her father's government, and he has known the family since her early childhood. He described her behavior during the power struggle preceding the split of the Congress party in 1969 in the following way: "Her first reaction is to avoid confrontation . . . even to yield to a demand which is reasonable and expedient. But if the other side is obstinate or moved by malice according to her, or something vicious which is averse both to her ideals or public ideology or objectives, but also to her personality as a leader, then at that point, she gives up all idea of compromise or settlement and resolves to fight it out. And in that situation, she is at her best."[24]

Several other people mentioned this characteristic of being "at her best" when confronted. I myself saw a glimmer of it during her election tour in the state of Gujarat in May and June of 1975. The fifteen-minute stops at various points had been mostly uneventful; crowds ranging in size from ten thousand to a hundred thousand people often waited in the sun for as long as two or three hours to see her. Although the gatherings were large, they were also quite orderly, and her speeches after a while sounded like echoes reverberating in the vast, thirsty plains of Gujarat. But on two or three (out of about seventy-five) meetings during the six days I accompanied her, there were some rather ugly incidents, including rock-throwing. The trouble always seemed to start in the rear of the crowd. There would be a shout or some sort of disturbance, which slowly but perceptibly rippled to the front as people stirred, wondering anxiously what was happening. Suddenly, her voice and her mien would be suffused with defiance; anger and, mostly, a determination to stand her ground were unmistakable. Someone has said of the Kashmiris that they are fire and ice. During these moments of challenge (and again just a few days before she declared the emergency), I saw that Indira Gandhi was indeed "fire and ice."

Courage is a virtue she prizes greatly and possesses in the highest degree (and it is one of the three attributes that define the able leader in classical Indian political thought). Many stories attest to her physical and personal fortitude and to her political fearlessness; and, as they span decades, it does not appear to be a new trait. A doctor I consulted, quite by accident, in New Delhi during 1975 turned out to have attended Jawaharlal Nehru during his final illness. He recalled that when she was told that her father was gone, "there was a momentary look—of grief perhaps. Her eyes may have filled up." He was not sure. But it was over as quickly as it came, and after that, he said, she was in full control of herself and the situation. Another time he told her that her first grandchild, who was born prematurely, had died. Again, she seemed for a mere moment to be enveloped in grief; but then she turned around and said calmly, "These things happen sometimes."[25]

Such equanimity in the midst of crisis is an essential condition facilitating (though not always ensuring) wise decisions. It is equally crucial in reassuring colleagues and subordinates and preventing wholesale panic in the ranks. Many of her colleagues, in their remarks to me, stressed her ability to remain calm in the midst of crisis. Commenting on her political courage, the old family friend and colleague said to me: "She seems not to appreciate, not to realize the . . . invincible power on the other side, either internally or externally. She does not seem to accept this fact. And she creates . . . a . . . spiritual atmosphere around herself. She kind of works herself up, you might say, not consciously . . . and then she goes forward, reckless of the consequences."[26] Yet if she displays recklessness, it would seem to be born of calculation and thorough preparation, so that it is certainly not reckless in any literal sense. She is said to be unstinting in preparing herself for any sort of demanding task—whether a major speech or a high-level meeting with colleagues or a foreign dignitary. And when a battle is shaping up, she will "prepare herself and also her colleagues and organization, and the machinery available to her with a thoroughness of her own style. She will think of every conceivable factor or source of assistance or possibility—whether averse or favorable—and provides for all eventualities."[27] Clearly there is no impulsive, irrational "jumping into the fray" but well-thought-out action executed with a coolness that evokes admiration from her colleagues and consternation from her enemies.

Such thoroughness is perhaps related to the fact that she does not gamble. "I do not believe in luck," she says with conviction. "Luck comes only to those who have the character to attract it and who have the character to hold it. It is not something that by chance flutters in through the window. You have to work jolly hard"; moreover, "fate itself is moulded by character and action."[28] She has repeatedly denied assertions that she is superstitious, believes in astrology, and is influenced by "holy people." One of her bitterest enemies privately told me he was convinced—because of her dress and the fact that "she goes rushing around all the temples in India"—she was susceptible to such influences.

Such criticisms of her dress and supposed religious beliefs were made quite often and stressed rather heavily, I thought, considering the really serious Indian problems that might be raised. It seemed to me (though I may have missed some deeper political significance) that she simply has an aesthetic flair and dresses in good taste, with elegance and simplicity. Nevertheless, sinister motives were imputed to her because she dressed less conservatively abroad than she did when visiting a poor Indian village, a practice I would attribute to common sense and good taste rather than an intent to deceive.

Criticisms of her religious beliefs, which often seemed contradictory, are somewhat more serious in India; when she was not attacked for extreme religiosity, she was excoriated for being an atheist. I heard one important political leader addressing an election campaign crowd in Gujarat in 1975 and trembling with indignation as he reported that she was, by her own admission, an atheist. She goes abroad, he said, and tells people, "I do not believe in God," but when she returns home, "she goes to the temples and prays for help."[29] It is true that she made such a statement in an interview on BBC television; but read in its entirety, it strains the imagination to interpret it as a confession of atheism. Responding to a question about her religious faith or lack of it, Gandhi said: "I don't believe in God *in that particular way as a person.* I do believe or feel that each person has something within him which for want of a better word I suppose one would call 'divine' but I certainly don't believe in a bearded gentleman sitting up above."[30]

A reasonable explanation for her imputed religiosity came from a civil servant who in many respects was sharply critical of her. In his view, her behavior in these matters was in the nature of a concession to public expectations. In this respect, he said, she was "similar to Gandhi who also preferred to accept some of the superstitions and some of the traditional modes of behavior of the people in order to sway them to his point of view on something more important, without offending their sensibilities on matters of tradition."[31]

She was also influenced by her mother and learned to have greater tolerance for traditional religious beliefs and practices because Kamala Nehru was tolerant and also had a strong religious bent herself. Thus through both identification and precept, she absorbed a sympathetic outlook toward diverse religions. This breadth was reinforced by her secular-minded father who bequeathed to her a questioning and irreverent attitude toward organized religion. She recalls that when she and her parents sat together (which was not often), "we always read the Gita in the morning, the three of us, and Ramayana in the evening. I am sure this was her move rather than my father's."[32]

Indira Gandhi has very definite views on what she calls India's "third culture" of superstition, fatalism, and outdated habits and customs; and they are negative. She sees such attitudes as forces of inertia to be resisted and eradicated so that India can progress socially and economically. Self-reliance is one of her favorite themes—both personally and for the nation—and she rarely misses an opportunity to bring that message home to her audiences.

The impulse to control one's life, which is so strong in Gandhi, has been traced to a basic human need to gain control over one's "physical and psychological life-space." On the political plane, it is manifested in a "feeling that individual political action does have or can have an impact upon the political process."[33] There is no doubt that Indira Gandhi's childhood fostered feelings of self-reliance—the belief that she could exercise control over her environment—and, hence, self-esteem. Though her environment was full of insecurity, her parents and the exigencies of life helped her to develop a degree of autonomy that was very unusual for a child and ensured a rapid growth of personal control and, with it, a feeling of self-confidence. Her needs for security and self-esteem, therefore, were not entirely frustrated; and to the degree that they were satisfied, they paved the way to self-fulfillment, enhancing her natural impulse toward personal growth and maturity.

All the outlooks described earlier—her rejection of superstition, fatalism, and the notion of "luck,"—point to a basic view she holds of the world and life in general. "Life," she says typically, "is one series of problems and mankind has to face these problems with courage, with determination and with the will to succeed. . . . My experience of life has been that as soon as you solve one aspect of a problem, another problem arises in its place." Among the common themes in her speeches and interviews are those of challenge, achievement, hard work, and struggle. "You can never have achievement unless you have challenge and hard work," she said once, speaking at a press conference shortly after India's victory in the 1971 war with Pakistan. And she added (perhaps in response to the national mood of confidence at the moment): "In India we do not want a soft life. . . . *We want to have challenges so that we can prove that we can meet them and we can overcome them.*" She may well have been expressing her own personal inclination. Then, to emphasize this sentiment, she paraphrased the poet Robert Browning, saying, "life should be a stuff on which to try the strength of one's soul." And to a friend she remarked: "The whole of my life has been meeting tests and transcending them." Her utterances, public and private, are often dominated by this theme.[34]

It is clear, then, that she sees struggle as an impetus to growth and places a positive value on it. But more than that, she seems to find challenges irresistible and has in fact said so. She asserted once: "I have never said I can't do a thing." A friend described her state of mind when she decided in 1962, during the China war, to go to the state of Assam to reassure its people; at the time the military situation was so dangerous that the local authorities were considering evacuation. Yet, said her friend, "she was compelled by the challenge."[35]

Earlier, when (by her own account) she was hesitating about whether to accept the Congress presidency offered to her in 1959, she expressed her doubts to the then-president. What made her decide is once again indicative (whether as fact or as recollection of fact) of this temperament: "And then he said the one thing which he knew . . . would have effect was (sic) that 'All the newspapers are saying that you can't do it. Now are you going to allow them to get away with this.' I said, 'All right.'" Clearly she has a very strong conviction about her ability to control herself and her environment and to overcome obstacles, an image that no doubt enhances her self-esteem. She says with obvious satisfaction: "I am one of those who always choose the most difficult paths, and between a straight road and a mountain road, I invariably go for the mountain road."[36]

There is a stubborn tone to all these assertions, and stubbornness, as noted earlier, is a sign of aggression. Indira Gandhi herself might use a different word to describe this attitude; "I am a very determined person," she says. Shortly before she was married she was advised that she ought not to have children because she had been ill in her adolescence and might not survive a childbirth. "Had they not said this, I might not have married. But that diagnosis infuriated me." She told the doctors: "I don't want to hear that I cannot. I want to hear what I have to do so that I can have them." When her doctor's diet for putting on weight did not work, she says, "I ignored all the doctors' instructions and made out a regimen for myself. I succeeded."[37] The ring of triumph is unmistakable. So is the tone of self-satisfaction, stubbornness, and above all, the will to overcome obstacles.

Perhaps the most common symbol of struggle and achievement for her is the mountain. Its repeated use can hardly escape attention. She has often said that she loves to climb mountains; in this respect, as in many others, she resembles her father. Speaking to a group of academic women in New Delhi in 1967, she stressed this positive aspect of struggle, singling out the mountaineer as a model of the happy man.

"What does he not put up with to scale a mountain? Every step is agony, is hardship. It is difficult to breathe. There is danger of frost-bite. There is danger of pneumonia. And yet he does it for fun. He is not being paid to do it. Nobody is forcing him to do it. He enjoys doing it, because it calls into play the best of his mind and body, and that is enjoyment."[38] In the same way, she added, Indian freedom fighters were happiest when they were sacrificing themselves for a noble ideal. She clearly believes that devoting one's life to a greater cause gives the same sense of fulfillment that one might enjoy in mountain climbing. And though she denies that in this or other respects she resembles her father, the similarity between her expression and a sentiment voiced by Nehru is too striking to dismiss as a chance convergence of thought. In 1933, as she approached her sixteenth year, he wrote to her:

> The ordinary course of life becomes dull at times, and we take too many things for granted and have no joy in them. . . . Many people go up high mountains and risk life and limb for the joy of the climb and the exhilaration that comes from a difficulty surmounted, a danger overcome; and because of the danger that hovers all around them, their perceptions get keener, their joy of the life which hangs by a thread, the more intense.
>
> All of us have our choice of living in the valleys below, with their unhealthy mists and fogs, but giving a measure of bodily security; or of climbing the high mountains, with risk and danger for companions, to breathe the pure air above, and take joy in the distant views, and welcome the rising sun.[39]

One can discern in both these personalities a love for the excitement that accompanies great undertakings. Indira Gandhi says, "I actually enjoy . . . physically dangerous pursuits,"[40] a clear echo of her father's words. But there is a difference; for Indira Gandhi, the great undertaking is rarely separated from the notion of duty. One who knew both well and assessed them as decidedly distinct personalities thought that a dominating disposition in Nehru's character was a sense of dedication that emphasizes the *personal* nature of commitment to a goal or a cause. In the case of his daughter, according to her friend Marie Seton, it is a sense of duty, that stresses the *social* nature of the obligation to which one is committed. Others have remarked on Gandhi's sense of duty, and it is a common theme in her public and private statements, emerging as a dominant consideration at important decision crossroads—

whether to postpone marriage, abandon higher education, forego an active political career (when her children were small), or respond to her father's call.

For Indira Gandhi, then, the "mountain" symbolizes sacrifice and duty, as well as excitement; and, as the latter is not stressed, we can assume that it is a secondary source of satisfaction. When she was imprisoned by the British for eight months shortly after her marriage in 1942, she named the small corner of the prison barracks to which she, her aunt, and a cousin were confined "Chimborazo," after a mountain range in the Andes. It symbolized for her "all that was beautiful but far away."[41]

This notion of sacrifice for a greater cause also has very early roots. Every biographer has mentioned that, when she was a mere tot, she daydreamed of being Joan of Arc. An aunt has described seeing her "standing at the balustrade of the veranda with outstretched arms—one hand pressed resolutely against a stone column, the other hand raised high as if persuading an audience of her mission." She told her aunt then that she was preparing to lead her people to freedom when she grew up and had been practicing being Joan of Arc.[42] Her fantasy clearly reflects leadership aspirations, and her model, a manifestly military one, reflects her own militancy at the time; yet its aggressiveness is tempered, or perhaps legitimized, by the saintly character of the figure with whom she identifies. Some fifty years later, she said of her childhood and her life in general, "it's a privilege to have lived such a difficult life. . . . *Suffering builds so much.*"[43]

She recalls that as a child, all her games were political and that the symbolism of her doll play was not usually maternal but military: "I had many dolls. And I played with them, not necessarily seeing them as babies to feed. In fact, I used them as men and women to perform insurrections, battles, and so on."[44]

It is noteworthy that in her play she could assume "male" aggressive roles such as military commanders, without compromising her female identity and without conflict; in fact she was encouraged to do so by her parents. She recalls her mother's story of being brought up as a tomboy until suddenly, at an appointed age, she was told she could no longer play as she had before but had to accept her destiny as a woman: "staying home, learning to cook. . . . And she hated that destiny." So, later on, her mother fought for the rights of women and raised her daughter to be free of the traditional constrictions: "I was brought up

as a boy when I was small. I climbed trees, I ran, and I never had any
feeling of inferiority or envy toward men." Invariably, interviewers
asked her the "how does it feel to be a woman prime minister" type of
question. Her typical answer was: "As Prime Minister, I am not a
woman. I am a human being. I suppose I grew up taking equality for
granted." She sees no significant difference between man and woman:
"Every man has some female trait in his character, and every woman
has some male qualities. Thanks to my upbringing, I have been able to
develop a strong character."[45]

The attitudes of duty and equality were reflected in her earliest fantasies and in her games: by age twelve, the child's play had become the
adolescent's reality, as she organized the oft-mentioned Monkey Army
or Vanar Sena. This army was made up of children and young adoles-
cents pledged to volunteer their time and energies to the Indian National Congress in the struggle for independence. Among their tasks was
the transmitting of messages when adults would be too conspicuous,
"intelligence" work (such as eavesdropping on policemen to learn about
arrests, house searches, and so forth), and other more minor activities.
At a young age, Indira also occupied herself with nonmilitary, social
work tasks. Even before organization of the Monkey Army, she was
involved in the movement to spread Gandhi's message of economic
self-reliance through the spinning wheel.

Her commitment to duty seems to have developed from an excep-
tionally strong conscience and an equally strong political consciousness
at a precocious age. When she was only three, she burned a treasured
doll for the sake of the nationalist cause, principally to close the gap
between her beliefs and her conduct; this may have been the first conscious conflict between her desires and her conscience. The incident,
reported in all of her biographies, was no doubt a traumatic experience,
and much insight into Indira Gandhi's personality and the conditions
under which it developed can be gleaned from it. It occurred shortly
after the Nehru family had burned all their foreign clothes in a huge
bonfire—to signify their rejection of British ways and assert their Indian
identity and independence of foreign imports. The child was taunted by
a relative, recently returned from abroad, for refusing to accept the gift
of a foreign dress. Her mother had told her the choice was hers to make
but reminded her of the bonfire a few days earlier. (This incident is
also significant as an illustration of the early encouragement her parents
gave her to be autonomous.) Young Indira reached out her hand as if

to take the frock but then moved it back, whereupon the visitor mocked her, saying that the doll she was carrying was also foreign. The child pondered this, and, after a few days of what must have been agonizing conflict, she took her doll to the terraced roof and set a match to her, crying copiously as she watched her burn.

The poignancy of this act is more striking because she was an only child and had no playmates of her own age. It must have been a devastating experience to "kill" her companion, as she afterward put it. She recalls that the doll was not a mere inanimate toy but a "friend" and her "child."[46] Even so there must have been also some inner satisfaction, for the stronger impulse toward duty won out. This deeply painful experience of "killing" her playmate must also have infused her with a terrible sense of guilt, for she manifested a loss of appetite, sleeplessness, and a high temperature immediately preceding and after her decision. After so many years traces of the trauma remain, and she confesses that "to this day I hate to strike a match!"[47]

In a very real sense, this experience was her initiation into the nationalist struggle and its meaning. Her political awareness was reinforced when, a short time afterward, she sat on her grandfather's lap while he and her father were tried for defying British laws. A few days later, she shouted and tugged at British policemen who came to confiscate some of their household possessions in lieu of a fine her grandfather and father had refused to pay. But the burning of her doll was the first personal sacrifice she made of her own accord. It was also the first of many separations (or losses through "death") from someone dear to her.

Throughout her childhood and later on, as we have seen, sacrifices of one kind or the other were exacted from her—the most significant being separation from her parents. Nonetheless, there is no indication that she or her family considered these deprivations unusual; she was just doing what was expected of her. Speaking of her imprisonment in 1942, she says she had decided that she "had to go to prison. Without that . . . something would have been incomplete. So that I was glad to be arrested." It was a matter of family as well as national honor. Her secretary, Usha Bhagat, who had been with her for many years and probably knows her better than most people, stated that the sense of duty that prompted her to go to her father shortly after he had become prime minister was "not just duty to her father but her sense of what her father meant to the country."[48]

It bears repetition that an accounting of her early years does not give

us a picture of someone who is principally concerned with ego gratification. Indira Gandhi's impulse toward nurturance and growth expanded
the boundaries of her ego-consciousness, and her actions during these
years seem to have been directed toward satisfaction of these needs in a
creative and personally rewarding way. She learned during her youth
to reconcile duty and pleasure, either by subordinating the latter to the
former or by defining duty as pleasure.

Devi or Demon?—Problems of Trust and Image

Many of Indira Gandhi's "image" problems, according to a friend,
have arisen from the fact that she was unknown for so long. Few people
knew her intimately enough to understand her and to share their understanding with others; and those who did were not involved in politics,
so that their insights were not passed on to her colleagues and rivals.
In retrospect, however, it is clear that a fatal flaw in her character—her
reluctance or inability to make friends, particularly among politicians—
has been more damaging. A more affable person might have evoked less
rancor among opponents and associates. A more balanced view of her
might have emerged—of neither *devi* (goddess) nor demon—the two
images I encountered so often in my interviews and reading.

Besides personal inhibition, important external constraints dictated a
reserved style of conduct. As one cabinet colleague said, "Don't forget
that . . . she is a woman in a male-dominated society and one which re-
tains its traditional outlook towards women. Because of this, she cannot simply drop in on people, the way her father did, or the way any
other man might for example, go into another man's office, put his
arms around him and say, 'Look here, I wonder if you could drop me a
memo giving me your views on this, that, or the other thing.' She cannot be too intimate with people. That explains a great deal about this
question of trust."[49]

There is much truth in this. Often, while observing parliamentary proceedings or other political occasions, I noticed that the men embraced
one another in friendship or used gestures of spontaneous intimacy that
are common in many Oriental, Middle Eastern, and Mediterranean
societies. And I recall that when Gandhi was in Parliament, it was rare to
see anyone sitting right next to her, except to give her some specific
information. A colleague might lean over her from the aisle or from the
row of seats behind her; at times, she might go over to a colleague and

lean over, usually standing, to say whatever she had to say before returning to her seat. Otherwise, she spoke to her colleagues from a distance; and although her manner of speaking was not cold, there was always a tinge of restraint in her look.

While I was in New Delhi I also tried to establish the identity of her close personal friends. Their number, which is very small, is in inverse proportion to their loyalty, and they are remarkable for integrity, strength, and fine character. I was more than ever perplexed by the contrast between the images she projected in public and in private. In this respect, she seems to resemble her mother. Nehru said of Kamala that: "She was reserved to those she did not know or did not like . . . If she disliked a person, it was obvious, and she made no attempt to hide the fact." Indira Gandhi has described her own attitude in much the same terms: "I never put on an act; I am always what I am. If I'm cross, then I show myself cross; If I am happy, then I show myself happy."[50] Though she has alienated many of her political colleagues and acquaintances by appearing cold, aloof, or ruthless, her private image, as projected to close friends, remains consistently one of warmth, depth, and richness.

This difference points to a problem rooted in her personality, which mars her ability to function well as a political leader under certain conditions: she is severely limited in her ability to reach people at an intermediate level, though she functions extremely well in large crowds and at intimate gatherings. This inability might not create very serious problems under ordinary circumstances, but for a leader, it is a serious handicap; and in Indian politics, where personal relationships count for so much, this flaw can be disastrous. It is a defect traceable in good part to her aloofness and is part of the broader tendency noted earlier—a general inclination to put as much distance as possible between herself and others. The tendency to "pull down the shutters," as someone described it, is apparently activated whenever she feels threatened and vulnerable. It is a form of detachment, which in Indira Gandhi vies with the opposite propensity to aggression and sociability. Although none of these dispositions are mutually exclusive, the impulse toward restraint dominates and even modifies the others. The need to seclude herself did, however, become increasingly dominant during her later years as prime minister, and it more and more compromised her ability to function effectively as a leader. The good commander must rely heavily on the ability to inspire confidence among subordinates, and here she was found wanting. A prominent newspaper editor, otherwise well-disposed toward her, emphasized this flaw, saying that Gandhi had tried to keep the party together through fear rather than trust. One of her major shortcomings as a leader, he thought, was her inability to evoke trust and loyalty, along with her reluctance to formulate decisions jointly with others. (Ironically, she once cited with approval her father's penchant for consulting others before making decisions, which she saw as the defining characteristic of the democrat.)[51]

This element of reserve in Indira Gandhi's personality is not one single trait but rather a blend of mutually supportive characteristics that, taken together, describe the syndrome of detachment.[52] It is not, for example, merely a desire for occasional privacy, which is quite natural; if it were, it could coexist comfortably with her general impulse for social intercourse, which apparently it did not. She has said that she hated functions where she had to smile and talk when she did not really feel like it.

Although she shed much of her shyness after becoming prime minister (as she once told an interviewer, "if one has to do a thing one might as well do it well so I grew into it"[53]), she did not lose her inner reticence, which was most noticeable when she addressed her peers—including rivals and political enemies—in Parliament. Throughout her childhood she identified more with adults than with her peers, and she was only rarely forced to compete with other children. Having modeled herself after adults, she tended to relate to her age-mates more as an adult than as a peer and to feel uncomfortable with them. The uneasiness that characterized her then apparently stayed with her into adulthood and has bedeviled her political relationships.

Commenting on some people's unfavorable reactions to her, Indira Gandhi herself attributed these to her inclination to be "direct," without taking time for the social preliminaries to which Indians are so deeply accustomed. That may explain the reactions of some—but only in part. The fact that there is so much variability in others' perceptions of her rather suggests that she interacts with and reacts to different people in very different ways. The important variable seems to be her intuition of them as either well-disposed or neutral toward her or ill-disposed in some degree. She is particularly on her guard with politicians or anyone involved in the political process; no doubt such people have been the greatest threat to her self-esteem. In a highly competitive system (which the Indian system has been and in many respects remained even under emergency rule), this was perhaps a normal reaction. In her case, moreover, a cautious attitude was accentuated by her earlier experience. She developed a mistrustful attitude toward the many who approached her father for favors and tried to influence him or otherwise pursue political ambitions and interests. She was privy to all the "secrets, the games" of politics and became acutely conscious of people's opportunistic motives in approaching the seat of power. Like many others, she felt Nehru was too lenient with people who were unworthy of his trust.

Referring to politicians and others she disapproved of, she said, as far back as 1957: "It does not matter who they are, if people do not function, they must go. No one is indispensable."[54] This was a significant remark and presaged the style of leadership that characterized her as prime minister, for her tough and ruthless image has been earned precisely because she usually showed no compunction about dismissing ministers and other appointees—even if they were old friends or former political supporters—when she felt they had failed her or their responsibilities. At the same time, the yardsticks she applied in making such decisions were often far from clear. I was told by several individuals whose information was highly reliable that prior to June 1975 she had been advised many times by friends and loyal supporters to put some physical and political distance between herself and her son, Sanjay, and certain other unsavory characters. She consistently resisted these sound suggestions.

In general, however, her tendency to maintain distance from others enabled her to deal with people dispassionately. Even some of her opponents saw this as an asset, compared to her father's inclination to "lend an ear" to too many who tried to influence him for their own gain. To maintain that distance, however, a leader must have or strive for certain other qualities: self-reliance, autonomy and independence, self-sufficiency. All these traits have in common the urge to master oneself—one's emotions, thoughts, and will to action—and one's environment. It is such mastery that, in a very real sense, assures physical, social, or spiritual survival for those who are isolated. In Indira Gandhi's case, however, physical survival has not concerned her so much as social, political, and "spiritual" survival—the survival of her personal integrity and sociopolitical identity as an Indian, a nationalist, a Nehru, and a "progressive" political and social leader.

There is little doubt that the need to master herself and her environment has always been powerful and dynamic. Self-reliance is one of the basic threads through almost everything she has said—statements on public policy as well as assertions of personal belief. It takes fortitude for a child of eight years old to travel alone through foreign countries, as she did. She grew up "with the idea that courage was the most important thing. My mother and father both drummed it into me."[55] Autonomy, therefore, became natural to her and reflects an attitude that was reinforced frequently over the years. Deprived of steady parental guidance and urged on by her mother and father, she made her own decisions on a variety of matters, such as education and her political career.

Then too, Indira Gandhi has learned through bitter experience that dependence on others can be disappointing, and she asserts her independence and self-sufficiency by remaining unattached to either things or people. Like her father, she shuns ostentation, which betrays a dependence on material goods. Though her father was raised in luxury, by the time she became conscious of her surroundings, the Nehru household had shed its trappings of opulence for a life-style more suited to the austere political and social ethic fostered by Gandhi. Evidence of this influence still lingers, although she does not pretend to live an ascetic's life. Nonetheless, she rarely wears jewelry, other than a string of beads (and certainly not the gold that most Indian women of the upper classes display), and she dresses in simple good taste. The prime minister's residence she used was hardly impressive compared to the stately mansion she and her father occupied when he was prime minister. During her tenure in office, she lived in a bungalow that was modest for an official residence by almost any standards, especially when compared to residences of other heads of government. It was certainly much less pretentious than some of her ministers' residences I visited.

Her desire to be free of strong attachment to material things is surpassed by a desire not to be overly attached to people outside her family. She invariably shuns relationships that may somehow restrict her freedom of action. Years ago, when she was in prison, she says she "made a rule" that nobody should speak to her before a certain hour of the day because she did not want to be interrupted from the routine she had set up for herself. This stern tendency to separate herself from others—which we see here in its most explicit expression—was also evident in her reluctance to form intimate bonds with others during her school years and later in adult life. Her courtship with her husband-to-be is revealing in this respect, for she took eight years to accept Feroze Gandhi's proposal of marriage, which was first made to her when she was about sixteen years old.

Although she and her mother agreed it was too early for her to marry then, she concedes that she began to change her mind about marriage by the time she was eighteen or nineteen. Even then she did not wish to marry yet because she thought marriage might limit her participation in the nationalist movement. She finally married Feroze Gandhi at twenty-four but never seriously considered marrying again after his death, although she was then only forty-two. She said once that she had never met anyone with whom she wanted to live; and in any case, "even if I had, I do not believe that I would have married again." As prime minister of India, she said quite firmly: "Think well: Why should I? Why, now that my life is so full? No, no. It is out of the question."[56]

This cautious attitude toward long-term commitments is typical of the personality that tends toward detachment, and is accompanied by fear or anxiety about any dependency needs. Though Indira Gandhi has not articulated such a concern for herself, she has expressed it within a broader framework—perhaps it is her way of avoiding admission of a trait she considers defective. Referring to the importance of developing self-reliance among the Indian people, she said (prophetically) that the danger of India reverting to a paternalistic system of rule, such as had existed under the traditional maharajas or kings of India, was in "our own need for dependence. I suppose it comes from being insecure, from having been poor and deprived, and dependent, ruled by others so long."[57] If we substitute psychic deprivation for economic poverty and paternal rule for British rule, she might have been referring to herself. One suspects that the inclination to lean on someone is anathema to her, though at times it must be irresistible. Her reliance on her children and their families for moral support, especially on Sanjay, can be partially explained by the need for dependence, which in detached personalities surfaces when their "ivory tower" has been violated.

Indira Gandhi does indeed tend to see herself as an "ivory tower" person—as someone whose life experiences and background are unique or at least unusual, which in many ways, of course, they are. Speaking of the many quarrels between herself and her husband, for example, she ascribes them to the fact that they were both strong-willed and sees them as positive influences on their characters; without them, "we would have had the usual banal sort of life, and we did not deserve the usual banal sort of life." She also sees her ability to relate to people outside of the traditional mold of sex-defined roles as unique: "But you have to remember that I received a very special education, that I am the daughter of a man like my father and of a woman like my mother."[58]

She also believes that she has a special talent for handling people— that is, "crowds." Even as a small girl, she notes, "I always felt at home in crowds, even if they were hostile." She adds, with the conviction appropriate to a leader, "I think that I can calm them more than almost anybody that I know."[59] She is probably correct in this assessment, but since this talent does not extend to the important intermediate level of human or political relationships, we must question her claim to be an "expert at dealing with people."

This sense of uniqueness, of being separate and apart from others, enhances her self-esteem; but carried too far it can damage her "sense of wholeness." As one political psychologist has pointed out: "Solitude destroys, among other things, the sense of being someone in the eyes of others," just as "complete submission to others destroys the sense of being someone in one's own eyes."[60] In other words, a balance must be sought, and this balance has perhaps eluded Indira Gandhi.

She insists on preserving her independence and, in this, she yields to nothing—except her conscience, which usually responds to duty (a blend of traditional, social, and political standards with her own personal values). It is here perhaps that her personality has achieved the highest degree of harmony between conscious desires and conscience. Even so, it is an exaggeration to say, as she does, that she has "never felt a conflict between intellect and emotion."[61] At least her father was certain—around 1940—that she was experiencing a very difficult period. He wrote to a friend: "I was convinced in my mind that she (Indira) had really no desire to come to India, but her affection for me and a wish to be of some help to me were forcing her to want to return to India."[62] There was, he felt, a conflict between her duty and "her own clear wishes." Later, when her father had become prime minister, there must have been some conflict between her desire to be with her husband and her sense of duty. She herself has alluded to this conflict, saying that she shuttled back and forth between Lucknow and New Delhi when either her husband or her father called.

Her decision to give up the Congress presidency in 1959 was also preceded (according to a friend) by considerable conflict between her

maternal obligations and her desire to continue in that office. In retrospect, she is on the whole satisfied that she did not neglect her children
when they needed her. As a rule, she took them with her when she
went to Teen Murti: "I didn't believe in leaving children to others."
When she did have to leave them behind, she wrote to them daily
letters that were always warm and intimate. She adds: "I only started
doing things after the children went to school. Even then, I'd organize
my day to be home with them after school." With the assurance of one
whose household is maintained with the help of servants and, at times,
obliging family members and friends—typical arrangements in non-
atomized, organic societies—she disagrees with the premise that a
woman can give more time to her home if she does not have a career.
"It is the quality of time that the mother spends at home that is
important."[63]

Still, there has not always been such a happy resolution between her
emotions and instincts, on the one hand, and her conscience, on the
other. Invariably, her sense of duty (however much it may seem at
variance with conventional interpretations) wins out over her own
personal desires. This is perhaps why one gets the impression that her
independence sometimes has rather negative connotations, expressing a
desire *not* to be influenced, *not* to be coerced, rather than a desire to be
free to do or to be. Explaining the origins of the Monkey Brigade, for
example, she recalls that she formed it in response to the refusal of the
Congress to make her a member so that she might become a "freedom
fighter." Her rejection, which was due, of course, to her age (only
twelve), so "infuriated" her that, "in a fit of temper,"—as she put it—
she decided to form an organization of her own.

Thus any efforts that hint of coercion or an attempt to thwart her
will are almost instantaneously interpreted as assaults on her self-esteem.
Her reaction is immediate—and it is aggressive, particularly when she
sees her sense of duty or right compromised. We see it when she was advised not to have children or, conversely, to do something—such as run
for office—when she felt her first duty was to her children. One cannot
help but notice the similarity between her reaction to being refused
membership in the Congress and her response, forty years later, to
efforts to expel her from the party. Nor can one escape the implication that the emergency actions represented a similar response to
challenge.

What is fascinating, and significant, about her efforts to preserve her independence is that she appears to have recognized the importance of finding a compromise between the impulse toward attachment to others, which can give pleasure, and her instinctive aloofness, which protects her from possible and actual assaults on her self-esteem. On the one hand, we find her yielding to the need to relate to others through her tendency to nurture children and others weaker than herself. At the same time, she shields herself from any possible hurt issuing from such relationships by depersonalizing or neutralizing the objects of her affection as crowds or as abstract groups: minorities, the poor, the untouchables, the Muslims, and so on. Similarly, she depersonalizes hostility by directing her aggressive impulses toward "things"—rather than people—within her environment, symbolizing them as mountains or identifying them as "social problems" or environmental obstacles such as poverty or illiteracy.

In the past, she has felt more comfortable "attacking" problems than people—at least when she was under public scrutiny. There is a strong tendency to deny hostile feelings about people; only rarely are hostile or negative expressions directed toward individuals, although she no doubt experiences such feelings at times. Every society, of course, has a few groups that are acceptable targets of criticism; Indians, like Americans, among others, take great pleasure in venting their aggressions on "politicians." In turn, politicians like Gandhi can "legitimately" express hostility against certain political groups—communal parties like the erstwhile Jana Sangh, for example. But even though she seizes every opportunity to criticize such groups, she makes a point of saying that she is not criticizing people but the principles and ideas and policies they espouse. Speaking to Winston Churchill she denied harboring hatred for the British; and to another Englishman she said: "We never were against Britain as a country or the British people as a people." Rather, it was the "colonial system" they fought.[64]

She also tends to almost entirely avoid expressing hostile feelings toward family and close friends. Particularly when her emotions are tinged with ambivalence (which is the case with her father, as we shall see in Chapter 3), she is quite circumspect. She ventures to express negative sentiments only about those whose affections she felt most sure of: her mother and her husband (both of them deceased). She acknowledges, for example, that there were frequent quarrels between her and Feroze Gandhi and goes on, in a roundabout sort of way, to minimize her love for him. She has said, for example, that although theirs was a love marriage, when they were engaged *he* loved her, rather than she him (though she concedes that her affection did grow after marriage). In fact, she adds, she probably would not have married at all if she had not wanted children.

Even when discussing influences on her character and personality development, she minimizes or denies influences by people as such. What shaped her character, she says, was her life, with its difficulties and sorrows. "So, you see, when people ask me, 'Who influenced you mostly? Your father? Mahatma Gandhi?,' I really don't know what to answer. Basically, what influenced me was a certain attitude toward life: a feeling of equality that was taught to me in childhood." Finally, she concedes: "This feeling came mostly from my father, yes, but my father got it from Mahatma Gandhi."[65]

One of the most common characteristics shared by detached personalities is a certain objectivity, as though they were onlookers observing themselves and life in general. The clearest expression of this attitude is found in a statement in which she confided that: "I do have the feeling sometimes, if I am addressing a meeting, that I am watching the whole procedure from the outside. And I sort of say: 'Now I wonder what she is going to say or what she is going to do!'"[66] Her father had the same ability to look at himself from the outside, as we shall see.

This capacity for detachment vis-à-vis herself and life in general is related to her ability to suppress (and repress) her thoughts and emotions. She has described on various occasions how she managed to retain mental balance and equanimity while in prison: "I think I sealed myself up and said, 'I am not going to allow anything to happen to me, I mustn't fall ill and so on.' So I was just living on the surface." She has retained to some extent this ability to seal off her mind: "I do remove myself from a place if I need to, or if I am tired." "I can retire into myself, not only when I am alone but sometimes even when in the midst of a crowd."[67] When the artist who painted her portrait (and her father's) asked her why she wore a mask, she replied: "I don't wear my heart on my sleeve."[68] Confirming this, several political colleagues and personal friends told me that they could never be sure what she was thinking when they spoke with her. "She keeps her counsel" or "gives the impression that she doesn't know what she wants to do." She confided to a friend, however, that she had developed a certain apathy to unpleasant events, though she was not sure if this "is a good or a bad thing."[69]

Because of these tendencies (but also because of her role imperatives and her cultural setting), she has had all too often to suppress any natural spontaneity. Close friends insist that she *can* be spontaneous and "let her hair down," that she can shed completely that reserve, that mask she normally wears, and reveal her innermost self.

The portrait that emerges here, insofar as it is relevant to the power motive, is that her most persistent impulse has been towards self-control rather than domination over others. The detached nature of her personality suggests that she was inclined to avoid entanglements that could compromise her self-respect and independence of action. She has not overtly pursued domination over others. Only when her self-esteem was actively threatened were her aggressive impulses diverted from things to people. Otherwise, they have either been repressed or channeled into the manipulation of abstract forces. Thus, it seems to me, it is achievement—whether as mastery over herself or her environment—that is her primary motivation and that the basic drive behind it is her need for self-esteem that, along with an urge to realize her potential, are dominant forces directing action. I believe she uses power primarily as an instrument in the service of some self-defined national goal—the attainment of which would satisfy, ultimately, her need for esteem and self-fulfillment.

Fulfillment of these basic needs is, however, frustrated by inadequacies in her own character, including an inability to relate effectively to people. She can be very perceptive in gauging people's motives and moods in a private atmosphere of mutual candor; in the public, competitive political world, her vision about people or events is clouded at times by an almost compulsive need to preserve and publicly assert her autonomy and privacy. In satisfying such a need, she often inadvertently or purposely discourages or inhibits friendly and impartial—but healthy—intrusions into her autonomous, private world—intrusions that could enrich and clarify her perceptions of the outer, public world.

Self-esteem, according to the humanist psychologists, is derived from a conviction that what one does is right and that one is basically "good."[70] On the other hand, the esteem in which one is held by others is based on *their* conviction that one's actions and character are essentially "good." In an "open" situation such as existed prior to the emergency declaration, the rightness or wrongness of actions could be directly communicated to Gandhi, and she could reflect upon the merits of opposing views that were genuine—not inspired primarily by self-serving motives or opposition for opposition's sake. For nineteen months, during Emergency Rule, this valuable communication was blocked. The prime minister was effectively isolated from others so that information about their regard for her was either not forthcoming or, worse, distorted. There were few checks to guard against such distortion.

Under these circumstances, she might easily have succumbed to a desire to accept at face value all "good tidings" and even unchecked, unfiltered flattery. Without accurate information about the actual state of affairs, her decisions would certainly have been flawed. Her need for the esteem of others, which was kept in perspective in "normal" times, became tainted by a susceptibility for flattery, which opponents, and even some friendly critics, have agreed is part of her make-up. She recognized this herself, according to one friend, and her recognition was the best guard against such susceptibility. For many different reasons, however, her defense was demolished and its positive effects were neutralized during the months of Emergency Rule.

At the same time, the actions taken on and since June 25, 1975, were an effort at reconciliation between promises and actions; between her dream of what India could be and the reality of 1975. They represented further an attempt to resolve patently contradictory aspects of the main political philosophies to which she subscribed—namely, democracy and socialism. No doubt, the resolution of conflict by such means created other, equally serious inner conflicts and threatened the personal integrity she had sought so hard to maintain. The "return to democracy" may be interpreted, in part at least, as a desire—indeed a compelling need—to preserve intact that part of her self-image and self-esteem that, in her mind, had always been closely linked with a perception of herself as a champion of democracy.

In June 1975, therefore, and in the months that followed, her actions were in part a defensive reaction to a self-esteem endangered by those who were openly intent on removing her from office by any means possible and in part a challenge to her will, her personal integrity, and her vision of India. The dominant impulse was not fear of losing power as such, but the resolve to thwart her enemies' plans. It was a stubborn determination not to "let them get away with it." And, once taken, the emergency measures released the floodgates of long-suppressed feelings of aggression against foes who had for long (since the split of the Congress party in 1969) tried to weaken, ridicule, belittle, and denigrate her. In 1975, the challenge was total, and her actions were undertaken in the firm conviction that the duties and obligations of her office demanded them, as did her personal commitment to the vision of a united, strong, and prosperous India.

CHAPTER III

Authoritarian *versus* Democratic Aspects of Indira Gandhi's Political Personality

Authoritarian or Democrat?

When a state of emergency was declared in June 1975, Prime Minister Gandhi was thought by many to be acting "out of character." She imprisoned many of her political opponents, effectively neutralized opposition in the press, and launched a program of constitutional reforms that, together with earlier amendments, promised to bring about truly fundamental changes in the form and spirit of the Indian constitution. The result of these actions was to point the Indian political process in a decidedly authoritarian direction. Our judgment of the merits of this political style and underlying philosophy will be offered in later chapters. For the moment, the question is whether the actions taken by Indira Gandhi in 1975 and thereafter were those of a confirmed authoritarian personality and reflected internal compulsions that nullified the democratic image her earlier actions and public statements had projected. Was the earlier democratic image itself valid and genuine? On what basis can we say it was or was not? If Gandhi can be described as a democrat prior to June 1975—or if we can establish that her lifelong conduct and outlook do not fit the authoritarian mold in terms of the characteristic traits, motivations, and upbringing usually associated with that personality—then we should seek an explanation for the discrepancy between a posited democratic personality, on the one hand, and authoritarian actions, on the other, in the situational context. In other words, to what extent were her actions called for by the situation and trend of events at the time? First, however, let us try to establish whether or not she can be described as an authoritarian or a democratic personality type—or some mixture of the two.

While she was prime minister, Indira Gandhi's political opponents

often complained—especially after the Congress party split in 1969—
that her conduct was authoritarian. For them, her actions in 1975 were
confirmation of their earlier assessment; she had acted very much
"in character." If they are correct we should find evidence of an
authoritarian pattern of thought and behavior in some form or another
throughout her adult life. Such a pattern should be visible not only
since 1966 or 1969 but also before, and not only in politics but in
other spheres of life. An authoritarian in politics is not likely to be
democratic in family relations or with friends, and *vice versa.* Moreover, he or she ought to display authoritarian trademarks in the broad
social and intellectual sphere.

Thus we shall first turn once more to Indira Gandhi's early years to
see if we can identify some of the forces that might have favored the
development of either an authoritarian or a democratic personality. The
actions of June 1975 and thereafter, if seen as clues to her personality,
might arouse certain expectations of her childhood and later development. Specifically, we would look for signs of a restrictive, paternalistic,
stifling, or repressive home environment. We would expect to find cold
and unresponsive parents or other elders.[1] And we would not be surprised to find that the world around her was perceived as very threatening, as an unmanageable "jungle" in which the basic rule for survival
was—in its extreme form—"kill or be killed." The strategy for coping
with threats from others induced by these circumstances would rest on
the principle that the best defense is offense; we would thus expect that
the "pre-emptive attack" would be her usual tactic in interpersonal relations. In addition, living in such a world would generate much anxiety
about her safety, and—feeling weak and helpless—she would seek
security in an alliance with the strong and suffer from low self-esteem.
The weak would be scorned, and power over others would be seen as
the best insurance against physical or social annihilation.[2] But do we, in
fact, find that her early environment deprived the young Indira of
safety, love, and a sense of worth?

The childhood world of Indira Nehru does not fit this picture very
well. There was insecurity to be sure, but her world was in no sense a
"jungle," even though she had real cause to be anxious because of her
father's frequent absences from home, her mother's deteriorating health,
and the constant moving about from place to place. And there was, of
course, a real "enemy." Yet the British empire and its representatives in
India were for the most part an impersonal enemy. The "sound of

boots" that remains a part of Indira Gandhi's childhood recollections was not scary enough to keep her and other children from milling about in front of police stations to pick up bits and pieces of information that might be helpful to their elders. Although the British did not always conduct themselves in a civilized manner in India, there were among them many men of character who could respond to the civility and integrity of men like Gandhi and Nehru. Somehow one cannot quite picture a Nazi-type "viceroy" permitting a prize prisoner to leave the country to be at his dying wife's bedside. (On the other hand, few such prisoners could have been expected to return to complete their sentences.) Nor can one imagine—today or then—a national leader who would permit his offspring to attend a university in the enemy's homeland.

The influence of the Mahatma undoubtedly served to neutralize much of the personal threat and hostility Indians might have harbored against the British soldier. I once asked an old-time "freedom fighter" whether he felt any hostility against the British in whose jails he had spent twelve or thirteen years of his life and who had, on one occasion, placed him in solitary confinement and chained him to the ground because of an unfounded and untrue charge of conspiracy. No, he said, he held no grudge against the British, now or then, for "we were after all much influenced by Gandhi, who told us that the British were there simply to do their job; and of course, the Indians had to do what they had to do, and so no one should hold a grudge against anybody else."[3] This sentiment was echoed by many others like him—hardnosed and hardheaded politicians. Strangely, the words did not sound incredible on their lips, for while the British could be harsh rulers, they could also show nobility of character and compassion. On the Indian side, although there were numerous instances of terrorism, this never became the dominant style of the nationalist struggle. Indira Nehru was thus reared not in the midst of terrorists but at the feet of Gandhi, the apostle of nonviolence, and of his main disciple and lieutenant, her father.

We do not mean, of course, to dismiss altogether the notion that imperial rule could be and was a source of some anxiety but only to urge that it be viewed in perspective. Apart from the fact of British colonial rule and some intrafamily rivalries (which were certainly not physically threatening), neither the larger sociopolitical environment nor the immediate family setting can be described as pervasively threatening. To the extent she felt menaced at times, she was equipped to handle herself with some resourcefulness and without fear. In many respects, then, her surroundings lacked the basic ingredients of the authoritarian's world. On the contrary, wherever one looks, there are signs that her training by both parents, her life experiences, and the ideas and personal style suggested by models with whom she identified represent the antithesis of authoritarian influences and would have worked toward the development of a democratic personality. It must also be acknowledged, however, that, although the dominant direction was toward openness and democratic standards, there were certain mitigating factors, so that latent strands of authoritarianism—subject to release under certain circumstances—can also be discerned.

Let us look first at the dominant pattern, many elements of which have been identified in a different context in the preceding chapter. We have seen that the most compelling motivation for Gandhi's conduct has been achievement, in terms of self-mastery and of larger social goals, rather than domination over others. When she was a child, self-control was often called for in her efforts to cope with a difficult environment: when she was alone in school away from home; when she was at home while one parent or other close relatives were in prison or traveling; or when she had to travel alone. Somehow, she always managed to cope, and these successful efforts generated a positive image of herself—as did the organization of the Monkey Army and other social and political work she undertook as a child or adolescent. Nor was she deterred by others' disapproval from pursuing a desired goal—for example, from marrying Feroze Gandhi.

Yet, paradoxically, the motivation to be self-reliant was reinforced in her early years not only by her ability to overcome challenges but also by her desire to ensure her parents' approval. Both her father and mother demanded self-reliance, for political or other reasons—such as her mother's health. The latter often meant that the girl had to control the impulse to take her problems and anxieties to her mother. Of course, her father's political travels, imprisonments, and the knowledge that he carried a heavy leadership burden precluded any thought of relying on him for help or comfort or guidance in concrete moments of need. Even if there had been an inclination to lean on her parents (which undoubtedly there was at times), this must have been supressed in response to their constant urging that she be strong and self-reliant. In a revealing turn of phrase, she says, "Courage was *drummed* into me."[4] Indeed, it must sometimes have appeared that their continued affection and regard depended on her ability to be self-reliant. Not only did she find that she *could* cope successfully with a variety of problems, but also that such competence was rewarded by the affection and, even more, by the respect of her parents. So she was motivated to be resourceful, independent, and brave in coping with problems; the situation called for it, and her own needs dictated it.

Rather than seeing herself as a helpless pawn in an overwhelming environment, she grew up believing that she was and must be master of her own fate, and that there was a solution to any problem confronting her. She came to believe also that this solution rested with her ultimately, not with any superior authority or supernatural force. Nor was defeat some other person's fault. The world was not a battleground for her; it was an obstacle course. Her future was not in the hands of fate; it was her own handiwork.

In this and other respects, her upbringing must be described as "democratic." Her mother trained her from an early age to resolve by her own lights any conflicts between conscience and impulse, and she was encouraged to think and act independently. Moreover, as long as she was alive, Kamala Nehru saw to it that, as much as possible, her daughter would not have to abide by sex-biased restrictions. She was at times permitted to wear the male attire of the Congress worker, as her mother had done. Such an environment also explains the ease with which she adopted the leadership role when forming the Monkey Army.

Throughout much of her short life, Kamala Nehru fought doggedly against a debilitating illness and stifling social prejudices. She resisted her in-laws' efforts to dominate her and tried, timidly and without much success, to enlist her husband's support. She defied both her physical limitations and social restraints by vigorously participating in the nationalist movement and in the cause of the emancipation of women from the dead weight of tradition. Her daughter identified strongly with her and learned from her, above all else, a determination against powerful odds. Whatever her mother's flaws—or indeed those of the Nehru women in general—they were all strong and proud women. Indira Nehru Gandhi could be no less.

At the same time her mother provided a rather ambivalent model of resistance, combining as she did passive with active impulses. When working for a cause, whether the nationalist movement or women's rights, Kamala could be quite aggressive. According to her husband, a favorite topic was "women's struggle for freedom against manmade laws and customs"; she often urged women "not to be too submissive to their menfolk." Even on the topic of servants, she held a most unorthodox, egalitarian view: "Before we are free, let our homes be free. Look how we treat our domestic servants—as low and despicable creatures. We have much to do to put our homes in order."[5] I dare say even today few high-caste Indian women share this outlook. One of her most cherished projects was the organization of a hospital founded by her father-in-law, Motilal Nehru, to treat both freedom fighters and the general public. She expended her waning energies on this undertaking, which, according to Mahatma Gandhi, was on her mind right until the last moment before she left India for the last time in 1935.

Yet, for all this determination and fearlessness, when it came to asserting her rights as a wife vis-à-vis her in-laws, she was shy and shrank from open attacks. Suppressing an impulse to assert herself more forcefully, she modeled herself after the ideal Hindu wife, the self-effacing, self-sacrificing Sita of legendary fame. Even her husband remarked on this—after her death.

Neither in her actions nor in her words do we find any intimation that Kamala Nehru passed on to her daughter a view of a world as a "jungle" or of people as either "superior" or "inferior," according to a scale of power and prestige. Her religious bent alone, which led her to see Mahatma Gandhi as a kindred spirit, precluded such a view. Indira's closeness to her mother and her propensity, even as a child, to speak up in her defense have been mentioned before. Perhaps partly out of this sense of identity, she has seemed to welcome deprivation and sacrifice, as Kamala Nehru did (and, of course, as her father and others close to her did).

To the extent that Indira's mother encouraged her to think for herself, to treat others as equals, to shun power, money, and prestige as criteria of a person's worth, and to aim towards competence (particularly through education), Kamala Nehru's impact on her daughter's character must be adjudged positive and deep-rooted. Indira's admiration for her mother was perhaps exceeded only by her love. At the same time, a qualification is in order. According to her own statements, she reacted early against her mother's passivity, even though she may have blamed her father for not defending her mother within the family. This is a significant element that contributes—in a negative way—to her personality development and the evolution of democratic outlooks.

As far as her father is concerned, there is little doubt that Nehru's influence on Indira was for the most part positively related to the development of a democratic temperament. The tendency to treat her as an individual aspiring toward ever higher levels of maturity and deserving of respect is apparent very early. Along with his wife, he bequeathed to her that crucial legacy in democratic training—namely, independent thought and action—that encouraged her through word, deed, and example. Her father and other adults entrusted her with responsibilities that reinforced not only her self-reliance but also her self-esteem. As a young adolescent she was expected to take care of her younger cousins at the Pune school. Then, at seventeen, her father asked her to accompany her mother on the long sea voyage to Europe while he remained in jail. Although she was not completely alone—the family doctor accompanied them—she was the only member of the family at her critically ill mother's side for several months. During these months before her father was released to be with them, the mental burden must have been a heavy one for a young girl plucked from the tranquil atmosphere of Tagore's school at Santiniketan.

Nehru's efforts to instill in his daughter a sense of independence are evident in several areas. Among other things, he believed firmly that she should make her own decisions on matters of education, whether on subjects to be taken, leaving the Pune school in 1934 to go to Santiniketan, or remaining at Oxford. Even when, at twenty-four, she decided to marry Feroze Gandhi, he did not forbid it outright, although he tried to discourage her. Having prided himself on being a "modern" father who felt strongly that "decisions must not be imposed on the modern girl," he could not now reverse himself.[6] And in political matters too, Nehru encouraged his daughter to make her own decisions.

Although he was somewhat less demonstrative than either her mother or grandfather, he showed his affection and, above all, his respect for her as a person. When she was a child and adolescent, he invariably included her in trips he and his wife took, whether it was to Europe in 1926-1927 for her mother's health or to Ceylon (now Sri Lanka) in 1931 for a holiday after the death of his father. Above all we see this tendency in his many letters to her, which are full of interesting references to their many discussions on various significant topics. We gather from the letters that these talks were often initiated by his daughter, and her many questions attest to a growing curiosity and an open mind.

Reading the letters, one becomes increasingly aware that he never talked down to Indira, even though they were written when she was quite young. He wrote them over a period of several years. She received the first batch in 1928 while vacationing with her mother in the Himalayan foothills. These thirty letters could be described as a summer course on "An Introduction to the Evolution of Man and the Universe." They touch on astronomy, biology, botany, archaeology, and anthropology. The second set, written between 1931 and 1933, were a sort of delightful three-year program on world history and politics—with considerable emphasis on political and economic thought and social mores. From the letters one can extract (or absorb) some of Nehru's notions about human psychology.

He was clearly a born teacher, invariably managing to make his topic interesting, alive, and relevant to the human condition—whether writing about the evolution of the universe or the French Revolution. He could simplify without excessive or deliberate distortion; yet he was not reluctant to take his daughter into deeper intellectual waters. Midway in his "summer course," he acknowledged that the letters were "getting a little complicated"; but, he added, "the life we see around us is itself very complicated." Unless they tried to unravel some of these complications, he said, "we shall never be able to understand all that is happening around us."[7] No fairy tales, hobgoblins, or good and evil witches for the ten-year-old Indira! At the same time he never passed himself off as an authority and indeed cautioned her to check out facts for herself and to form her own conclusions. It is one piece of advice, among many, she took well to heart. (Her disregard of it in 1975–1976 proved nearly fatal to her political career.) Her colleagues in government and the party with whom I spoke in 1975, and some others outside of government, invariably mentioned that she checked out information given to her, got as much relevant data as possible from as many sources as possible, and reached her own conclusions.

The letters also contain frequent references (particularly in the 1928 letters) to museums, gardens, and places of historic interest they had visited together in Europe between 1926 and 1927. Father and daughter ventured on educational sightseeing jaunts around London, Paris, Geneva, and in Germany. They also met and talked with various famous people, which suggests that Indira was seldom excluded from adult company or conversation. Her sense of dignity was thus preserved and enhanced; and she must also have seen this as a clear sign of her father's affection and solicitude, about which others have also remarked.

It is important to stress these positive aspects because all too often, only the insecurities, loneliness, and negative qualities of her childhood are emphasized. It *was* no doubt a difficult childhood, but it was not without its happy interludes and rewarding experiences. Had it been one of unrelieved pain and distress, we could perhaps convincingly argue that her behavior in 1975–1976 was the product of irrational fears, anxieties, and insecurities traceable to such a childhood. But, to the extent such an argument ignores the positive aspects of her early years, it would be a distortion.

What other aspects are there to her upbringing that might be considered supportive of a democratic or an authoritarian ethos? Her self-image and her views of the world and its people neither support nor reject either ethos in an absolute way. How were these images shaped by her father? Specifically, how did Nehru influence his daughter's political perceptions, feelings, and values?

We have discerned some democratic influences in the basic character training given her by both her parents, most noticeably in Nehru's attempts to provide her with an integrated view of life and politics. That he succeeded in placing the stamp of his thought on her philosophy of life and political value system in many areas is evident from her speeches, interviews, articles, and press conferences.

During her tenure as prime minister and in the years prior to 1966, one is struck by the vivid parallels in her opinions and those of Nehru on any number of subjects. I have already referred to one sentiment that echoes her father's outlook on life—comparing it to the challenges and sacrifices of mountain climbing—and there are other striking similarities. Let us try, then, to glean the major attitudes and values reflected in Nehru's letters, the common themes, moods, styles of thought, and feelings that permeated them—particularly those which shaped her views of humanity in relation to political authority.

The Shaping of Political Thinking: Nehru's Influence

Several themes in the letters are relevant to our special concerns. The principal one is humanism. Nehru's writing (and his whole life) attests to an abiding and sympathetic interest in man's achievements, ideals, and aspirations. Through a cluster of related ideas, he conveys a distinctly personal and simultaneously Indian perspective on human history. Indeed, it was the desire to cultivate in his daughter a broad vision of human evolution, to pass on to her an attitude that looks upon men of different times and places with sensitivity and understanding, that inspired the letters. Throughout them, he expresses an outlook best summed up in the Latin playwright's dictum: "I am a man; nothing human is alien to me." To be sure, Nehru would have been more at home with this formulation than its restatement by his contemporary, the Spanish philosopher, Miguel de Unamuno, who viewed the terms "human" and "humanity" as abstract, cloaking the awareness of "the man of flesh and bone." The Spaniard preferred to say, "I am a man; no other *man* do I deem a stranger."[8] The distinction is not trivial; its significance dawns upon us as we read through Nehru's writings. Although the genuineness of his concern for human suffering cannot be doubted, still his conception of man is somehow remote; the letters speak of "great men" and "the people" with insight and sympathy but invariably in an impersonal tone.

The image of humanity Nehru projects is, for the most part, hopeful and optimistic; there is little to make his daughter distrustful of her fellow man. Shunning ethnocentric prejudices, he speaks of peoples in times past and in the present as brothers and sisters, or cousins whose family bonds are evident in the major language families. Only in the last eight months of his imprisonment in 1933 did his optimism waver, as his literary journey through time brought him closer to the grim realities of the twentieth century.

We tend to think of Nehru as a highly westernized Indian leader, and in many respects he was. Yet, though it may be comforting and flattering to Westerners to think of Asian and other non-Western leaders in this way, it is wrong to do so. The "Western image" projected by Indians is, it seems, most often an instinctive act of courtesy to put Westerners at ease. Or it may be a vestige of the obsequious colonial mentality. The tendency to project such an image has perhaps contributed to much personal and international misunderstanding, friction and disappointment in the relations between India and the West. For Westerners have come to expect Indians not only to act like themselves but also to think like Westerners. And why should they, after all?

In many of his ideas and outlooks, Nehru was very much a Hindu of the monistic tradition of Indian philosophy, which yearns for oneness, absorption, and synthesis. It is as if the confounding diversity, dissonance, and disparities of Indian society propelled thinking people toward its polar opposite—harmony. Nehru too, perhaps because he yearned for it so much, believed deeply in the underlying unity of mankind. Some seek to understand man, he said, by examining the world he lives in; others probe his inner world, guided by the advice of ancient Greek and Indian philosophers who urged man to: "Know thyself." But as Man is *of* Nature, said Nehru, echoing Indian philosophers of past ages, both approaches ultimately lead to the same knowledge.[9]

This impulse toward integration, passed on to his daughter undiminished in fervor, inclined both of them toward a lifelong commitment to the promotion of communal harmony. Perhaps because Nehru valued such harmony he could forgive Akbar his autocratic ways; for this great sixteenth-century Moghul emperor, inspired by a "universal toleration in religion," had tried to forge a synthesis among different Indian religious and social groups, Himself an adherent of Islam, Akbar nevertheless brought Hindus, Parsees, and Christians into his government. He urged mixed marriages and followed his own precept in this respect. Such a spirit made Akbar a heroic figure in Nehru's eyes, although he never imagined that, in his nodding approval of Akbar's views, he was sanctioning his own daughter's mixed marriage ten years in advance of its consummation. Speaking of Ashoka, another great Indian emperor of the third century B.C., Nehru praises, again, the spirit of tolerance and persuasion by precept and example.

Incidentally, such references to Akbar and Ashoka are in themselves meaningful. Although, as noted, Nehru ranges far and wide over the surface of the globe and through vast expanses of time, he frequently returns to Indian history. These historical homecomings no doubt gave form to some of his daughter's dispositions and self-perceptions, among them her sense of Indianness and its political expression in strong nationalist feelings. While Nehru never shrank from pointing out the drawbacks of Indian civilization, he also communicated his sense of pride in the achievements and high aspirations of Indians in many different fields—philosophy, the arts, and, of course, government. As he approached the nineteenth and twentieth century events, we see building in his correspondence a crescendo of that nationalist feeling with which his daughter was already so strongly imbued. Throughout her younger years, as we saw, the struggle for independence was the centerpiece of her life, and most of her personal decisions were subordinate to this national goal. So too, her fierce pride in being Indian, expressed frequently during her tenure as prime minister, must be attributed in no small measure to these letters, which dwelt so often on the glories of India's past.

Nehru also saw to it that her pride in things Indian would not be
narrow in perspective. He also extolled the greatness of other peoples
and pronounced as the ultimate criterion of a great civilization its
ability to produce a "fine man." In speaking of Indian "heroes" and
achievements, he managed to convey to her his notion of social and
religious tolerance—his secular outlook—not only in explicit terms but
also in more subtle ways. For example, included among the great
Indians he discussed were women as well as men to provide models of
conduct for the young Indira. Similarly, his Indian heroes were Muslim
as well as Hindu.

Nehru's religious and social tolerance was but one expression of a
broader attitude manifested in his respect for the diversity of life. It
bordered on awe before the vastness of space and time and man's place
within such boundless dimensions. He sought to impress upon his
daughter the impermanence of things—whether cities, civilizations, or
human life. If somehow she could be made to grasp the concept of
eternity, he thought, she could more easily maintain equanimity in the
face of hardships, petty annoyances, and failures. Within that immense
framework, cultural values were seen as relative; human qualities of all
kinds and shades were perceived as broadly and rather evenly distributed across cultural spaces as well as within each individual. Such views
led him not only to accept and indeed rejoice in social and cultural
differences, but also to appreciate the worth of cultures and civilizations, past and present, and to be indulgent of their imperfections.

Patiently, with sensitivity and in an almost poetic style, he mused on
the follies and virtues of man; he cajoled her to greater flexibility and
receptivity of ideas; and he instructed her in his accumulated wisdom.
Almost like a Brahmin priest—except in his diffidence (the analogy
would have made him shudder)—he passed on to her his own "vedas."
He cautioned her against ethnic as well as personal vanity, reminding
her of the humble simian origins of the human species. He urged her
not to judge indiscriminately the past by the present, nor the present
by past values; he commended to her, instead, the wisdom of an eclectic synthesis of the old and new—sensitive to the good and bad in both.
The letters themselves, of course, exemplified just such a synthesis.

By 1933—after a year in which Indian nationalism was harshly repressed, and divisions had appeared within the ranks of the movement—Nehru's moods, as reflected in the letters, begin to vacillate
between optimism and deep disillusionment regarding the selfishness,

cruelty, and narrowness of outlook of man. But he fights against such "dismal" views and invariably balances his despair with expressions of hope. Rejecting Oswald Spengler's negative view and his philosophy of hate and violence, Nehru urges Indira to adopt a realistic outlook on life—expecting both good and bad in all things and people—and to adopt ideals without allowing them to distort reality or provide an escape from it.

Yet even at his most pessimistic, he does not invite his daughter to indict all men. His disenchantment is mostly with "the great," the kings and princes and priests—leaders who are not only authoritarian but who combine this behavior with cruelty to the common man, injustice, neglect, and lack of compassion. Among such elite classes, the "priests" are the most heavily criticized; their sin is greatest because it offends the mind and the spirit. More than their dogmatism, Nehru deplores their sustained and often successful efforts to establish a monopoly over knowledge, which is then used to frighten people into submission.

Here we see most vividly Nehru's commitment to the open mind and his clear recognition that knowledge is power, which, like material goods, can and should benefit people by wider and more equitable distribution. As a rationalist, he considers the human intellect the special ornament of man. And when, again, he speaks of the Moghul emperor Akbar, he dwells on his intellectual traits—his curiosity and his consuming search for truth—because from these sprang his tolerant temperament. It is plain that Nehru sensed in Akbar a kindred spirit, seeing as a virtue what Jesuits scorned as the flaw of the atheist—namely, supreme reliance on reason over faith. In this spirit, Nehru extols the virtues of the scientific outlook, primarily its regard for the open mind and the experimental method as a tool in the search for truth.

Time and again, he urges his daughter to think independently, to question authority—even his own—to make decisions slowly and with deliberation, and to train herself in the refinement of this faculty. At the same time, although he plainly admires the life of the intellect, he sees greater virtue in a life combining thought with action; the pleasure of reading history, he says, is only exceeded by the joy one feels when actually helping to shape it. When his daughter was at the impressionable age of fourteen, he even proposed that she herself might one day help form the course of events. Recognizing that impersonal and mighty forces are at work shaping man's future, he believes never-theless that the individual can and often does count "in every crisis of destiny." Scorning fear and submission to such forces, Nehru lauds the heroic response: "to ride the tempest and control it a little and direct it, willingly facing the perils that this involves for the joy of helping actively in a mighty process." In one of his last letters, he reminds his daughter that human progress was attained not "by helpless submission to the ways of Nature, but often by a defiance of them and a desire to dominate them for human advantage." The future of the world "lies with you and your generation, the millions of girls and boys all over the world who are growing up and training themselves to take part in this Tomorrow."[10] These are heady words for an adolescent girl living in her historic times and in the Nehru family; many times thereafter she responded to their call. She also took to heart his warning that fear must be put aside in the face of the challenges, for it "blinds and makes men desperate."[11]

The greatest danger of fear, said Nehru, is its offspring, irrationality. Fear causes governments to rely on senseless repression, clouding men's vision and making it "difficult to distinguish between the guilty and the innocent." The prime example of this process, according to Nehru, is the fascist philosophy, which elevates violence and terror to a principle of governance, demanding unquestioning and blind obedience. This principle may be "suited to an army perhaps, but certainly not to a democracy." Fascism is dangerous because it has "no fixed principles, no ideology," except, possibly, the people's well-being, which he points out, is no policy; anyone can say, as Mussolini did, that the fascists' program was very simply designed "to rule Italy." The origin of such misguided ideas and evil deeds, Nehru stressed, was "the simple desire for power." Earlier he warned his daughter that the "quest for over-much power is a dangerous one" that brings "downfall and ruin" to those who seek it. This is why ruination came to Napoleon, a leader in whom Nehru recognized many virtues; his major flaw and his un-doing was his quest for personal power rather than "the pursuit of an ideal."[12]

It was not only, however, its reliance on violence that Nehru found so repugnant in fascism. As he ruefully told his daughter, violence has been practiced throughout man's history. In the past it has been "con-sidered a painful necessity and it is excused and explained. Fascism, however, did not believe in any such apologetic attitude towards violence." It ennobled violence, especially in war, and deified the state on whose altar individual freedom and rights were sacrificed.[13]

Comparing his views on fascism with those on religious authority, we find that he rejects the legitimacy of both on similar grounds—namely, that in one way or the other they violate the human spirit, depriving it of freedom. Citing John Stuart Mill on the question of individual liberty, Nehru tells his daughter that such an outlook "could not be reconciled with that of dogmatic religion or despotism." In a glance backwards at his own country's ancient history, he remarks that it was just such a love of freedom which marked the early Aryans. This spirit was conquered, he says, only because "people were not vigilant enough" about preserving freedom. They fell victim to "superstition . . . the authority of the 'sacred books' and customs and conventions. . . . Authority and authoritarianism reigned over us and controlled our minds." Today, he says sadly, the Aryans' "descendants in India . . . have little courage and hardly feel the loss of their freedom."[14]

In all these discourses we can discern an effort to implant in his daughter the basic elements of a free and democratic spirit, if not the precise components of a democratic philosophy: the open, fearless mind, and the questing intellect; the maintenance of a flexible outlook; the wisdom of respecting social and intellectual pluralism and of preserving the individual's dignity and autonomy; sympathy for fellow human beings and equality of opportunity; freedom of conscience (whether religious or political); and freedom of speech. Consistent with such ideas is Nehru's rejection of authoritarianism, especially when it inhibits the questing mind and, in so doing, serves only the vanity and well-being of the ruling elite. He deprecates the most extreme manifestation of this mentality, fascism, which exalts violence and the state at the expense of individual freedom. He conveys, in short, an unshakeable intellectual commitment to the conception of freedom postulated in classical Western liberal philosophy.

Viewing Nehru from this perspective alone, we can understand the claim made by many of Gandhi's opponents, who have maintained that, if her father had been living under her regime in 1975, he would surely have been imprisoned for his outspoken views. And indeed, there is no doubt that Nehru was marked by a democratic temperament, as I have tried to point out. But this cameo portrait is incomplete unless we look at his larger political and economic philosophy, which incorporated elements of socialism and his views on Western democratic theory and practice.

The topic of democracy engaged Nehru's exclusive attention in three long letters, as well as being touched on in numerous others.[15] In them, he embraced the ideals of liberty and equality as the most praiseworthy in democratic theory. Some interpreters, however, have vigorously questioned some of his views on democracy.

Nehru's letters draw a sharp distinction between political and economic democracy, noting that the artificial separation between them, in practice, had nullified political forms of democracy first introduced in modern Europe during the eighteenth century. The ideal of democracy came to be symbolized, at this time and in the following centuries, in the vote. But although the right to vote was expected to guarantee to the people a share in political power, it in fact assured no such thing; for by the nineteenth century, it had become clear that the political franchise unlinked to economic power would never enhance the political power or well-being of the average individual. The problem, Nehru suggests, lay in such eighteenth-century documents as the French Declaration of the Rights of Man, which, though liberal for the time, continued to defer to the status quo by viewing as inviolate the right to private property. Because of this outlook, other noble ideals, such as free speech, effectively remained the privilege of the wealthy elite.

Nehru's account, then, ushers his daughter into the nineteenth century and all its intellectual, social, and political turmoil. He seeks to sharpen her consciousness of social injustice and the economic and political exploitation of the many by the few; he instructs her in the virtues of socialism and begins to share with her his doubts about democratic theory and institutions. The Industrial Revolution, he says, had spread all over Europe by the nineteenth century, bringing with it far-reaching social and economic changes. The most important change was a sharpening awareness of the economic injustices of the existing political and economic systems (i.e., democracy and capitalism) and a growing desire to share more equitably in the wealth produced through labor. The elites, however, clung to outdated eighteenth-century democratic ideas; the conservatism of feudal society had simply been replaced by that of capitalism—with its veneration of private property. Having dwelt earlier, in his 1928 letters to the ten-year-old Indira, on the inequities of private property, he now reaffirmed his point more authoritatively.

As socialistic ideas began to animate people in the latter half of the nineteenth century, says Nehru, political democracy weakened. The very idea of "majoritarian democracy" may have paved the way for this trend. The latter introduced the idea that the happiness of the greater number may require sacrifices by the smaller number. Socialist philosophers began to promote the idea that government regulation of private enterprise might be the best way to ensure the "happiness of the greater number." After this time, Parliament, the representative of the people and as such the chief democratic institution, progressively lost its position of strength vis-à-vis the executive branch of government. Young Indira further learned that the twentieth century saw a diminution in the number of those who revered even the idea of "formal democracy."

Nehru's reference to democracy as "formal" was explained in terms of the Marxist assertion that democratic forms were not real but only a "shell to hide the fact that one class ruled over the others." The vote, Nehru said, only gave people a choice among exploiters; thus, democracy was really the dictatorship of a capitalist plutocracy.[16] Such sentiments reflect an early stage in the evolution of Nehru's political thought. As others have pointed out, Nehru had been deeply and favorably impressed by Marxist thought when he visited Europe in 1926-1927 and made a short visit to the Soviet Union. He retained this favorable attitude toward the Soviet Union, communist ideology, and Marxist philosophy in general throughout most of the 1930s. Thus, in the letters he wrote his daughter in the summer of 1928, he propounds a wholly Marxian view of history, social organization, and the dynamics of revolution through class struggle. The view permeates all his letters, up through 1938, as well as his autobiography. Paralleling this attitude is his consistently negative view of "Western imperialist powers," whose principles of conduct he equates with Machiavelli's *Prince;* his attitude contrasts starkly to his less well-known respect and admiration for Western thought and civilization in general. Both of these conflicting attitudes he passed on to his daughter.

Nehru acknowledged that Marx's expectation that the working class would be a revolutionary force was confounded by its twentieth-century Western European conservatism. He attributes the worker's complacence to subversion of labor's socialist ideals through the sharing of capitalist profits. Nonetheless, he believed that the future of political democracy remained dim as long as it continued to serve the propertied classes. The major weakness of democratic forms was thus the inherent contradiction between democracy and capitalism. The former implied equality—social and economic as well as political—whereas the latter was predicated on economic inequality. The prime struggle within democracies was for control of economic power, and at its peak, this conflict could be resolved only by abandoning democratic forms. Equating democracy with socioeconomic equality, Nehru noted that many people had "become dissatisfied with the old idea of giving a vote and calling it a democracy."[17] The equal society that was of the essence of democracy could not be attained solely through the vote and parliamentary institutions. In short, Nehru persistently impressed upon Indira a single commanding idea: political equality was not enough; economic equality had to be included within the "boundaries of democracy."

We shall see later that the entire argument distinguishing political from economic democracy was repeated practically verbatim by Indira Gandhi many, many times after she came into office and more frequently and insistently during the later years of her tenure. After June 1975, it became one of the central official and unofficial attempts to explain, justify, or defend the emergency declaration.

Nehru tempered his ideas about democracy and socialism after the 1940s (and his belief in Soviet policies—domestic and foreign—was considerably dampened by the Soviet-German Non-Aggression Pact of 1939). With India's attainment of independence, his faith in Western democratic institutions increased; he acknowledged their value for governing a highly fragmented society that was sorely in need of the safety valves of democratic practices. One might say that his reliance on democratic institutions and ideas increased in inverse proportion to his implementation of socialist ideals; and the two ideologies became the twin cornerstones of official Indian political and economic philosophy. He left to his daughter the problem of resolving the contradiction between them in the Indian context.

We should note one other facet of Nehru's temperament which, for want of a better word, we shall call "populist." The essence of its political plank was expressed in simple affirmations of regard for "the people." Nehru often expressed sympathy for otherwise offensive individuals and events if they were somehow beneficial to the people. Both Akbar and Napoleon are admired in great part because, though dictatorial, their autocratic ways ultimately benefited the people. Nehru approvingly cites the Portuguese model of the good leader (drawn from their observations of Akbar) as one "who can command, simultaneously, the obedience, the respect, the love and the fear of his subjects." Nehru looked up to this complete autocrat because, among other things, he treated all men justly, regardless of their rank or origin, and "did not think manual labour beneath his dignity."[18]

Similarly, the French and Russian revolutions, bloody though they were, fascinated Nehru; and he passed on to his daughter the excitement he felt about these elemental upheavals. He believed that both revolutions held valuable historical lessons for India because they were revolutions of the people. He could readily excuse revolutionary repression because it "acts on behalf of the masses," while reactionary repression invariably serves only the privileged. The French Reign of Terror, he assured his daughter, was emphasized in the history books because the privileged were often its victims: "we are so used to honouring the privileged classes that our sympathies go out to them when they are in trouble." Not that he wished them ill, but "those who really matter are the masses, and we cannot sacrifice the many to a few." The Reign of Terror, although terrible, said Nehru, was but a "flea-bite" compared to the long-term evils of poverty and unemployment that had injured or shortened the lives of many more people than the revolution.[19]

In every way possible his loyalties and sympathy were with the masses, and Nehru tried to convey this sentiment to his daughter. He was thoroughly committed to an ideal of social progress that brought within its compass more and more people. But, he added, improvement could only be brought about through changes that went against vested interests. Injustice could not be corrected merely by a rational appeal to wrongdoers, but by changing the unjust system. Like the Marxists Nehru thought it unlikely that any privileged group would voluntarily acknowledge the injustice of the status quo and give up its privileges. Hence, a clash was inevitable. The sanctioning of compulsory change was thus implanted in his daughter—although he subsequently abjured this path for himself.

We know that many of the views Nehru expressed in the 1930s were considerably modified after he became prime minister; but since he did not write any more personal documents of this sort after 1944, we cannot trace the origins or patterns of change nor the manner in which his evolving thought was transmitted to his daughter. We can only surmise that, during the extended period when she lived with him in the prime minister's residence, she must have absorbed his philosophy as it was actually being modified, incorporating some of his ideas into her own thought pattern and, perhaps, rejecting others. That pattern awaits our examination. Yet, even at this point, we cannot discount the impact of the political views Nehru imparted to his daughter during her impressionable childhood and adolescent years—in recent years many of them have surfaced almost intact in her own political expressions and policies. Moreover, although Nehru did change some of the attitudes and values of his early and middle years, there were certain strains he never quite abandoned. The notion of an egalitarian society made concrete in social and economic benefits (as well as in political rights) remained one of the pillars of his socialist philosophy (as it has of hers). He always kept before him the goal of a more equitable distribution of political and economic power sustained by a cooperative ethic. Individual motivation would have to be transformed, eradicating attachment to private property, human greed, and the profit motive in favor of a nonacquisitive, cooperative ethos.

Thus Nehru's "democratic" temperament, while extolling and embodying the virtues of the open mind, the free spirit, individual liberty, and tolerance of diversity in social and intellectual expression, could also justify repression in the name of the "good of the people." For the same reason he praised authoritarian rulers and, when necessary, bloody revolution. Perhaps it was these contradictory impulses and views that caused him to wonder whether he might not himself have "the makings of a dictator." In a now-renowned article (first published anonymously in a Calcutta journal), he warned his followers (and himself no doubt) to beware of his ambitions. Had he not traveled throughout the length of India "like some triumphant Caesar, leaving a trail of glory and a legend behind him? . . . Is all this just a passing fancy which amuses him . . . or is it his will to power that is driving him from crowd to crowd. . . . His overwhelming desire to get things done, to sweep away what he dislikes and build anew, will hardly brook for long the slow processes of democracy." But then, as if to admonish himself, Nehru wrote: "We want no caesars. . . . It is not through Caesarism that India will attain freedom, and though she might prosper a little under a benevolent and efficient despotism, she will remain stunted and the day of the emancipation of her people will be delayed."[20]

The intensity of Nehru's inner struggle comes through distinctly and forcefully in his letters. His efforts to supplement his daughter's education by sharing with her his own "glimpses of world history" conveyed some rather mixed signals about the proper conduct of the individual and the leader in society and about the priority of values in personal, social, economic, and political realms. His philosophy combined eternal Indian themes and nationalist ideas and ideals with classical Western philosophy and Marxian thought; but he never attempted to reconcile the conflicting strands among them. Nehru was able to live with these conflicting impulses and ideas, not only because the Indian mentality is congenial to contradictions but also because his people's political and economic awareness had not yet developed to a level sufficient to erode his charismatic appeal and to force him to reconsider the practical consequences of such contradictions. The process of erosion was set into motion during his lifetime, however, following (and accelerated by) India's military defeat at the hands of China in 1962. His daughter was to bear the brunt of its effects.

Before we go on to consider the changed political, social, and economic environment with which Indira Gandhi has had to grapple, we shall explore one final aspect of her relationship with her father, in the hope of garnering some further insights into her political style.

The Turbulent Years—Childhood to Young Adulthood

Indira Gandhi's relationship with her father is generally seen as that of a dutiful and loving daughter, and she was both—in full measure. As we have seen, her father influenced her deeply, politically and in other respects. From him she inherited and developed her socialist beliefs and views about democracy. What is rarely recognized, however, is the possibility that Indira Gandhi may also have harbored mixed feelings toward him—because of his relationships with her mother, grandfather, and aunts, on the one hand, and her relations with them, on the other. If so, it is possible that her ambivalence toward him attenuated— under very special circumstances—the democratic conception passed on to her by Nehru throughout her life, particularly during the years spent as his companion and confidante, when he was the principal mentor of the new democratic Indian state.

Of course, her actions of 1975, which introduced an authoritarian overlay on existing democratic institutions, can in no way be traced solely—nor even mainly—to this ambivalence. As we have seen, the formative experiences of her childhood and adolescence were more likely to foster a democratic than an authoritarian temperament, in spite of Nehru's sometimes conflicting signals about democratic and authoritarian ideas and ideals. In succeeding chapters I will argue that the circumstances preceding the emergency declaration are a more adequate explanation for the decisions of 1975 and thereafter than any character analysis. The present discussion of her relationship to her father serves merely to explain how and why Gandhi might have been predisposed to question, under certain circumstances, the validity of her commitment to democracy and to react with the intensity that characterized her actions following the emergency declaration.

Turning once more to her childhood years, we find that the anguish of frequent separations was compounded by a home life that generated much inner conflict in the young Indira. When parents argue, for example, a child is beset with anxiety because the situation seems to require it to shift loyalties to one parent, when in fact it has already committed affections and loyalties to both parents simultaneously. Among the signs of such emotional conflict in children and adults are fatigue, anxiety, depression, and indecision.[21]

Throughout young adulthood, Indira Gandhi seems to have exhibited precisely these symptoms, which may have been brought on—in part at least—by an ambivalence toward her father that began in childhood. Though there are many indications of such a conflict, I found that Indira Gandhi had never squarely faced her negative feelings or acknowledged them as perfectly natural, whereas she has spoken quite freely about friction with her mother, whom she loved deeply. That the emotions toward her father have remained unacknowledged (deliberately suppressed or unconsciously repressed) may be a measure of how painful they are. There are, of course, cultural as well as psychological compulsions to hide such feelings from consciousness; the powerful Indian family ethic demands absolute respect for parents and elders. In addition, Gandhi's principle of nonviolence—talk of which permeated the atmosphere when she was growing up—was drawn from the mainstream of Hindu religious philosophy, which also required the suppression of hostile feelings, even toward enemies. It is therefore not surprising that Indira Gandhi has tended to avoid expressing hostility toward her father, other members of his family, or even outsiders.

The inner discord she felt was generated, for the most part, by divided loyalties between her father and grandfather and between her mother and father. It may be recalled that after the first political trial of her father and grandfather in December 1921, four-year-old Indira was separated from both of them for three or four months. Another prison sentence for her father followed almost immediately; this time he spent about nine months in jail until the end of January 1923. There ensued an interlude of seven to eight years before the next jail term for either Nehru or his father, Motilal; but these years were by no means peaceful for Indira, nor for India's nationalist leaders. Her father, now actively involved in Congress politics, held office at the local level of the nationalist organization, sometimes working alongside the Mahatma and at other times clashing with him.

There was also strain and conflict at home; Indira experienced it first at age six when she began her formal education. She was shifted by her grandfather from a school under nationalist auspices to a local one run by English nuns. As a result there was a falling-out between Nehru and his father. Motilal dearly loved his granddaughter, who amply reciprocated the emotion. Especially during the very early years, before the family was so actively involved in the nationalist movement, he indulged her whenever he could. His insistence that she be enrolled in this particular school was motivated by his "desire to give Indira companionship of children of her age regardless of instruction."[22] It was a sensible concern, for it must have been obvious to him that she was a lonely child. Although Nehru at first agreed to the change, he ultimately had his way; Indira remained isolated from other children for several more years while she was tutored at home. By the end of 1927, however, after the family's return from Europe, the young girl was enrolled in a convent school in Allahabad; at the same time she was tutored at home in Hindi.

The discord between Nehru and his father no doubt had many expressions and multiple roots—cultural, historical, and psychological. But little Indira understood only that there were repeated arguments between the two men she most loved and admired. One of her aunts has confirmed that the atmosphere in the household was tense at such times. Referring to the time when Gandhi's views on *satyagraha*[23] began to gain wide appeal among Indian youths (including her brother), Nehru's youngest sister reports that: "The arguments between him [Motilal] and Jawahar put our peaceful home in a turmoil."[24] Such a home environment must have created powerful anxieties in the little girl whose affection for her father was equalled and possibly surpassed by her love for her grandfather. The anxiety was compounded during the 1920s when the friction extended to her mother and father.

While her mother and grandfather showed their affection spontaneously, with a gesture, a word or a deed, her father was rather inhibited, particularly during these early years. That Nehru loved his only child can hardly be doubted. Nevertheless, as two of his biographers have suggested, he was undemonstrative: "His sense of the essential pushed private life to the background, and led him to a conscious withholding of emotion." Nehru himself once told a friend that he never discussed personal matters with others. "I would not do so even with Kamala or Indu [a diminutive of Indira meaning "little moon"]. Such has been my training."[25] This reticence inhibited expression of his feelings during Indira's childhood and probably accounts, in part, for his unsatisfactory relationship with his wife. He once told an interviewer: "I may be very popular. It is true. But I cannot function as an individual."[26]

Jawaharlal and Kamala were married when he was twenty-six and she only seventeen. In his autobiography Nehru confesses that they often quarrelled over petty matters because they were both young, sensitive, and quick-tempered, and "we both had childish notions of keeping our dignity." At bottom, however, the problem may have been a certain ambivalence toward women that Nehru seems to have shared with Indian men in general. He once wrote to a friend: "India is so like a woman—she attracts and repels."[27] The expression is akin to the Indian attitude toward power—at least its public pursuit and display. Whatever their origins, Nehru had very mixed feelings about his wife (and possibly about Indira, who, as a pitifully thin and awkward girl, lacked the urbane appearance and confident bearing of most of the other Nehru women). His own words, written after Kamala's death, reveal the complexity of his feelings for her:

> I often wondered if I really knew her or understood her. There was something elusive about her, something fay-like, real but unsubstantial, difficult to grasp. Sometimes, looking into her eyes, I would

find a stranger peeping out at me. . . . Except for a little schooling, she had had no formal education; her mind had not gone through the educational process. She came to us as an unsophisticated girl. . . . With all my tremendous liking for Kamala, I almost forgot her and denied her, in so many ways, that comradeship which was her due.

What was Kamala? Did I know her? understand her real self? Did she know or understand me? For I too was an abnormal person with mystery and unplumbed depths within me, which I could not myself fathom. Sometimes I had thought that she was a little frightened of me because of this. I had been, and was, a most unsatisfactory person to marry. Kamala and I were unlike each other in some ways, and yet in some other ways very alike; we did not complement each other. Our very strength became a weakness in our relations to each other. There could either be complete understanding, a perfect union of minds, or difficulties.[28]

One of the things he disapproved of was his wife's religious interests, to which she turned more and more in the last years of her life. In a disarming confession, Nehru reveals in his autobiography that even as he watched his wife "lying ill, struggling for life," he felt "a little irritated at her for her carelessness about her health." This incident took place in August 1934, while he was temporarily out of prison to visit her; at that time her condition was deteriorating rapidly. Yet a few months earlier, he wrote in his diary: "felt greatly cheered at seeing her. I am *much too fond* of her." About a year later, he wrote: "What a child Kamala is! That irritates me often enough and yet I think that is partly her charm. How my moods change when I think of her. How much she means to me and yet how little she fits in or tries to fit in with my ideas. That is really the irritating part, that *she* does not try, and so she drifts apart."[29]

Nor was Nehru inclined to come to the defense of his young wife in the rivalry played out, no doubt daily, in the joint household, where there was friction between Kamala and her mother-in-law, who "was quite a queen in her own domain and Kamala . . . a spirited girl."[30] Nehru's mother apparently resented Kamala during the early years of her son's marriage, for the young bride encouraged her husband's nationalist views, which were bound to get him into trouble with the British authorities. But the most serious and enduring conflict was between Kamala and her sister-in-law "Nan." Nehru's youngest sister,

Krishna, has said that her sister Nan had the "usual complicated sister-in-law's feelings"[31] toward Kamala (who was about two years her senior). Such "complicated" feelings are in fact a common feature of in-law relationships in India. According to a well-known Indian anthropologist, there are certain members of a household who are "natural enemies"—a woman and her husband's sister and a woman and her husband's mother.[32]

Thus, the usual in-law rivalry in India has been developed into a fine art, if not a science. Even in the socially advanced Nehru family the atmosphere apparently generated much anxiety for the young bride, who was used to a simpler living style than that of the wealthy, anglicized Nehrus. And, of course, as Gandhi herself has pointed out, it was simply a clash of personalities. All of them were very strong-willed women.

The situation was troublesome enough to cause Kamala to write to her husband about it while he was serving a prison term. She was concerned that "irresponsible" tales were being carried to him. She wished she could tell him her side of the picture and even wanted to be arrested in order to avoid such unpleasantness. Nehru, however, seems to have dismissed these incidents with a casualness he later regretted. One suspects that in those early years, he shared (unconsciously perhaps) his sisters' condescending attitude toward the unsophisticated girl his father had selected for him. Nehru's latest biographer reveals that there are few references to his wife in his diaries of the 1920s; there are more in the 1930s, especially shortly before her death, when Nehru seems to have grown more deeply attached to her. During the earlier decade Kamala could not have failed to sense her husband's indifference, and she must have been terribly hurt by it. She hinted at this in a letter to a friend in 1926: "Today in this world only the educated are honoured. People do not want to talk to those who are uneducated; indeed *close relatives and even husbands do not wish to talk to them.* Under such conditions the lives of the girls become unbearable; and then will it be a life or a curse?"[33]

Nehru's ability to look at himself from the outside, exemplified by the article he wrote about the possibility of becoming a "Caesar," was paralleled by the detachment with which he could view his wife and their relationship. During one of the visits the British allowed him to make to the sanatorium where she was being treated while he was serving a sentence in a nearby jail, he sat by her bedside and wrote a note for her doctors in the form of a "case history." In it he referred to himself in the third person as "the husband" and to his wife as "the patient." Referring to her mental state, he said: "She is definitely neurotic, probably due to some repressions and maladjustment *during her early years.* . . . When she has herself taken an active part in public affairs she has been mentally far happier and the neurotic element has faded into the background."[34] Although in his autobiography and later writings, he seemed haunted by his neglect of her, at that point, shortly before she and Indira sailed for Europe in 1935, he did not seem to connect her "neurotic shortness of breath and feeling of suffocation" to her anxiety about their relationship and his attitude toward her. Instead he attributes them to "maladjustment" during childhood. Yet right after her death he wrote:

> She wanted to play her own part in the national struggle and not be merely a hanger-on and a shadow of her husband. She wanted to justify herself to her own self as well as to the world. . . . Like Chitra in Tagore's play, she seemed to say to me: "I am Chitra. No goddess to be worshipped, nor yet the object of common pity to be brushed aside like a moth with indifference. If you deign to keep me by your side in the path of danger and daring, if you allow me to share the great duties of your life, then you will know my true self." But she did not say this to me in words and it was only gradually that I read the message of her eyes.[35]

Feeling the regret implicit in this passage, it is difficult to avoid the speculation that Nehru tried to make amends for neglecting Kamala by asking Indira to share his "path of danger and daring" and the "great duties" of his life.

This "neglect" and the undercurrents of emotional tension between her parents and other family members could hardly escape the sensitive mind of the child. She apparently spent many hours comforting her mother when Kamala sought escape from the oppressive atmosphere of the household in her bedroom. As an adolescent Indira frequently felt called upon to defend her mother: "I loved her deeply and when I thought that she was being wronged, I fought for her."[36] Her own selfhood was so tied up in her mother in those days that defense of Kamala was also a form of self-defense. Although when she spoke about that period of her life later she made a noticeable effort to temper her comments about her father's side of the family, one got the distinct impression that the memories of those times are still fresh and still rankle. Asserting that she is better able to face life than her mother was, she says that her determination grew as she watched her mother's distress: "I saw her being hurt and I was determined not to be hurt"[37]—one of many indications that a defensive personality style was taking shape in these early years.

As we reconstruct the picture of this relationship, it seems likely that she shared her mother's disappointment in her father, that sense of being abandoned in a sometimes hostile household. Perhaps this is what prompted Indira to vow, while still in her teens, that she would never marry. Later, when as a young adult Indira Gandhi personally felt the sting of rejection and condescension from the same family member, she must have recalled her mother's disappointment in her father; the whole sad drama was being re-enacted. A friend who came to know Gandhi when she was living with her father at the official residence, observed that even then the aunts "looked down on her as socially inept since they couldn't induce her to imitate their own sophistication." Indira Gandhi confided to this friend that "all would have been well if she had been willing to be made into a carbon copy of them." Buried in some of her "half-sentences," according to the friend, was the plaint that her father "should have protected her from the aunts." Publicly, however, Gandhi limited herself to a very temperate comment: "People find it difficult to understand somebody who is entirely different."[38]

There is, then, adequate reason to believe that Indira Gandhi's feelings toward her father were deeply divided. It is clear that she loved him very deeply and that certain aspects of his life and character as a statesman and political thinker represent models to which she is powerfully drawn and which she wants to emulate. At the same time, she fiercely resists the idea that she is a mere reflection of her father. The fact that she has not, even to intimate friends, laid bare her feelings of anger and disappointment toward him is itself a sign that they have been a source of severe anxiety. They slip out, nevertheless, in unintended ways and are evident in some of her earlier conduct.

In spite of the clear two-sidedness of the term ambivalence, people are often tempted to stress the reality of only the negative valence. One cousin of Gandhi's I interviewed, for example, was sincerely convinced that Indira Gandhi did not love her father, which is hardly likely. As she grew into adulthood, Indira Gandhi saw many signs of his concern and affection, particularly after her mother died. And long before then one finds touching expressions of his solicitude in his letters and references to her. Although always concerned about her health and her education, he was also particularly careful not to stifle her initiative. From his letters we learn that he always encouraged her to make her own decisions; and when he saw her evolve into a reticent, diffident young woman, he tried to bolster her self-confidence. She confided to a friend that only her father's belief in her "had brought her out of her shell of shyness enough to cope with strangers. He made her believe in her potentialities and she tried to overcome her limitations in order to live up to his belief."[39]

Indira Gandhi's decision to return to her father to manage his household and attend to his personal and social needs when he became prime minister has been interpreted in ways that are not always charitable. From the start, say her enemies, the limelight and being near power attracted her. The reality of the situation, however, suggests otherwise. Before she went to live permanently with her father in 1950, she and her aunt Mrs. Pandit ("Nan") took turns serving as the prime minister's hostess. However, as Nehru assigned more and more diplomatic responsibilities to his sister, the task of attending to his official and personal needs at home fell increasingly on his daughter's shoulders. This job, which required periodic trips to the capital from her own home outside of New Delhi, and absences from her husband and (when they did not accompany her) her small children, disrupted the Gandhis' home life. Far from taking the first opportunity to avail herself of a more permanent share of the "limelight" and the proximity to power, she had to be persuaded to accept; she did not in fact move in with him until three years after he became prime minister. Her decision to do so, therefore, seems to have been motivated by a sense of duty as well as of love. She herself has said: "I just saw my father as somebody who needed help . . . in certain areas where there was nobody else to give it. And that's why I came to Delhi and looked after his house and so on."[40]

Nonetheless, however self-effacing she may have appeared during her years as official hostess—perhaps she was unconsciously reflecting and replacing her mother's "Sita" image—she was also, like Kamala, very proud and, like her, possibly silently resentful that her abilities were not always recognized. During these years, her aunt, who had so often slighted her mother and condescended to Indira as socially awkward and otherwise incompetent, was gaining international recognition as

India's representative to the most powerful nations of the world and, at the United Nations, to the entire world. It would have been surprising if, given the background of the family, Indira Gandhi had not felt some animosity toward her aunt. And might not some of this resentment have been directed unconsciously against the father who, until his dying day, kept by his bedside pictures of his sister and his wife—the two "natural enemies" side by side in spite of themselves, sharing equally a place of honor and affection in Nehru's heart?

When discussing her childhood, Indira Gandhi's most spontaneous and unqualified expressions of love are for her mother. Since she identified more strongly with her mother and saw much more of her than she did of Nehru, this seems perfectly natural. Her expressions of affection for her father, on the other hand, are more subdued, more tentative, and less tender. Contrasting her father with her mother or her grandfather, the less vivid, less positive image is that of her father. Once, when asked if she had been close to her father when he came out of prison, she replied: "Yes, *I think so because I had nobody else with whom I could talk.*"[41] This lukewarm endorsement contrasts sharply with her unsolicited and unqualified expressions of love for Kamala. Of her grandfather, Motilal, she invariably speaks with a warmth and tenderness that are almost totally lacking in references to her father.

Others have noticed this implicit contrast in her comments. C. L. Sulzberger, the American journalist, noted: "I got the impression . . . that she wasn't quite as influenced by her father as many people make out. She wanted to stand on her own feet, to be accepted by and as herself." He thought that "she clearly paid more regard (to her grandfather) in our talk than to her far more famous father." A friend who was close to both Nehru and his daughter has the same impression. She recalls telling Nehru at a family luncheon one day that she had read all the way through his *Glimpses* (a volume of about a thousand pages). Immediately after lunch, recalls the friend, "within seconds of our leaving the dining room, Indira gave me a book to a great extent concentrated upon Grandfather's letters to Papa. And I got the vivid impression, not in words, but in feeling, that Grandfather was her ideal rather than Papa."[42]

Nehru, we must recall, was not a person to show his feelings directly or effusively. Unlike her mother's letters, which contain expressions of tenderness and convey a sense of intimacy, her fathers' letters (some of them written while he was in prison) were usually impersonal and didactic in tone. He seemed to have been conscious of this failing and tried to avoid it. And while, as he confesses, their correspondence was a source of comfort for him in prison, it did not bring him as close to her as their frequent writing indicates.[43] As a prisoner, he was restricted in the number of letters he could send out—depending on his prisoner rank, one to four letters a month. He used the privilege to send personal letters, to his wife or other members of his family, including Indira. The letters to Indira that were later published, however, were apparently amassed by Nehru in prison and either given directly to her when she visited him or to his wife or some other visitor; or perhaps they were accumulated until he was released. It is not clear how these missives finally reached his daughter, but it is certain they were not mailed out at each writing. Moreover, their literary style indicates that he wrote them with a view to publication, although one does find personal notes interjected here and there. Perhaps his daughter sensed or knew of this plan; if so it might have diminished their value for her as personal communications. The earlier letters, written three or four years before the second batch, while he was traveling around the plains of northern India and his wife and daughter were spending the summer in the Himalayan hills, were received through the regular postal channels.

All of them were discursive explorations into history, intended essentially to supplement his daughter's education, which, of course, they did admirably well. But they were hardly designed to warm the heart of a sensitive child and adolescent who had experienced a lonely, turbulent childhood and sought, as she says, "companionship and an inner peace in communion with Nature."[44] It is quite understandable that to her, these historical discourses "were just letters at that time." A friend thought she saw a look of utter surprise on Indira's face when she told Nehru that she had read right through the letters and found them impressive. It is perhaps not insignificant that when years later Gandhi was separated from her own children for any length of time, she made a conscious and deliberate effort to make her letters personal and intimate.

It seems that Nehru sensed even in those early years that his daughter was sometimes cold toward him, and it distressed him enough to make him complain to his sister Nan about it. He was peeved because "Indira wrote to him but once in three or four months, and the letters seemed to have been penned out of a mere sense of duty." Yet his reticence and pride prevented him from mentioning this directly to his daughter, and he made sure that no word would get back to her. The fact that he confided his concern to his sister must have injured his daughter's pride when she learned of it years later.

Although Gandhi has freely acknowledged that, as children often do, she took out her frustrations on her mother, I could find no similar admission that she had ever been openly angry with her father—except in one instance. She herself has mentioned without reservation that she and her father clashed over her marriage to Feroze Gandhi. Of course, this acknowledgment of differences was "acceptable" in the context of the "modern" ideal sanctioning interreligious marriages, which were publicly promoted by the official ideology and, more importantly, by Nehru himself. Although Nehru at first expressed reservations about her decision to marry Feroze—who not only was outside her caste but of a different (Parsi) religion as well—the principal reason for resistance within the family seems to have been the difference in socioeconomic backgrounds: Feroze's family was much less socially prominent and well-to-do than the Nehrus. There is a striking similarity here between the social standing of Feroze Gandhi and Indira's mother; in both cases it was a factor in their marriages.

When he seemed unwilling to give his unqualified approval, Indira reportedly told her father that if he did not give his blessing, she would never talk to him again. He relented and later defended the marriage against public opposition, as did Mahatma Gandhi. One suspects that her dominant mood in prevailing over her father's wishes was one of triumph. Commenting on his acquiescence to the wedding, she said: "He had no choice."[45]

Within the family, the only one who sanctioned this union from the start was, somewhat surprisingly, her maternal grandmother, who was in other respects highly traditional. "When it came to my marrying Feroze," said Gandhi, "she was not at all orthodox." The grandmother in fact said that "since neither Feroze nor I were much concerned with religion, she did not see that it mattered."[46] For this, among other reasons, Indira Gandhi has always felt closer to her mother's family than to the Nehru clan, which, for social-status reasons, had been intolerant of her mother and was now opposed to her marriage on the same grounds.

Indira Nehru's decisiveness in this matter seems out of character for that time. During the previous five or six years she had shown considerable uncertainty about whether to remain in England to complete her education and what academic emphases to pursue; and it had taken her nine years to decide to marry Feroze. When her mother was alive, Indira had determined not to marry lest marital commitments interfere with her devotion to the nationalist cause. Yet now, as she firmly told her father while he was still in prison, she had made up her mind to marry and had made her choice. The incident is also interesting as a dramatic demonstration of the quantum change in attitude that had taken place between Nehru's generation and her own. Whereas Nehru had asked his father to pick his wife (then a common practice), his daughter not only did not do so but actually defied her father's wishes in the matter. The decision illustrates the sharp contrast in personality of father and daughter. When it came to challenging paternalistic authority, Nehru preferred to avoid a test of wills between himself and his father—or between himself and the Mahatma, who became his paternal figure in later life. His daughter, on the other hand, was predisposed to confront the problem head on; when she married in 1941, she was prepared not only to defy paternal advice but also to stand by a choice that was highly unconventional by broader social standards. The act took much courage and was a clear indication of the strong impulse toward independence that was to mark Nehru's daughter more and more as time went on. And, although Nehru was forthright in his opposition to *his* father on many issues of importance—particularly those related to the struggle for independence—he confessed that such confrontations made him uncomfortable. His biographers stress that when Motilal died, his son was bereft and that at that point Gandhi became a sort of substitute father.[47]

When Indira's father died, however, she looked for no substitutes. Indeed, soon after she became prime minister, she showed an inclination to put as much distance as possible between herself and the older generation. One of the first "elders" from whom she (as it were) declared her independence was Congress President K. Kamaraj; and Dr. Sarvepalli Radhakrishnan, philosopher, elder statesman, and president of India during the early years of her tenure, also felt her efforts to separate herself from older parental figures. Perhaps too, she associated this political hierarchy of elders with a similar pattern of dominance she experienced within the family—a hierarchy based on age and represented by her grandmother and eldest aunt. Anyone who had followed her life story or who knew her intimately could have predicted that she would no longer tolerate any kind of patronizing attitude or conduct toward her. For someone of her independent cast of mind, it must have been, at times, a stifling experience to live in the shadow of her father during most of her adult life.

The split of the Congress party was, in one sense, an assertion of independence from her would-be fathers. Indeed, many commentators interpreted the event as a struggle between generations; at least two of her younger cabinet ministers told me in 1975 that they had supported Gandhi in 1969 because they felt she represented a new, modern, and forwardlooking generation. From the time she came into office, she encouraged younger elements to assert themselves, whether in the party or the government. Indeed, the younger bureaucrats I spoke with mentioned that she encouraged them to speak up and tried to draw them out when they were reluctant: "it struck me in particular that she was anxious not to bother about hierarchical status of people and that sort of thing. And she would very often go to the younger men at the meeting to find out their ideas, and by-pass some of the senior politicians and Cabinet Ministers there."[48] Such an inclination no doubt alienated many of the "elders" in her party and government.

The more positive identification with her mother also provides further insights into her ambivalence toward her father. Indira Gandhi freely accepts, and even volunteers, the suggestion that she is very much like her mother in personality. Yet, although her political outlook has in the past often echoed her father's, she invariably resists the notion that she resembles him. Although Nehru's love for mountains is well documented by his biographers and himself, she even rejected the suggestion that she inherited this fondness from him: "Yes, he loved them, but also because of me, because I organised his holidays. He quite often went where I liked to go, but I think he liked them."[49]

The contrast in her sentiments for her parents is perhaps most tellingly revealed in her attitude toward the fund her mother set aside for her expenses: "I never took money from my father," she says. "I never took any money from him at all. Even when I was small I was paying my fees out of this fund. Even when I was at Oxford, for my illness, my studies and everything."[50] Again, that tone of triumph and, even more, of pride in her independence from her father—a satisfaction that she did not have to be financially obligated to him.

In the twilight days of his life, Nehru seems to have sensed that, after their long years together, his daughter was once again growing distant from him. In 1962, he said almost plaintively to a friend that he hardly ever saw "Indu" these days. He sounded forlorn, as if deserted, but he evidently never spoke to his daughter about it. As he had said in a letter thirty years earlier, "such has been my training." Sadly for both of them, such had been her training too; and the teacher was not Nehru alone, nor her mother, but the cultural womb and the very conditions of life in their uncertain and anxious times.

Our analysis of Indira Gandhi's relationship with her father has not generated any conclusions about her political personality as either clearly democratic or authoritarian. But three principal inferences can be drawn from it regarding her early experiences with authority—as a family and a political phenomenon—and they may be relevant to her personality development and political behavior. Looking at the political education she received from her father (particularly with reference to democracy and socialism) and her early basic character training, we notice that her ambivalence toward him as an authority figure is paralleled by an ambivalence to authority in general and political authority in particular. We can also discern a certain confusion in her mind between her father's paternal and political roles. Finally, we note a marked ambivalence toward the West, which is common to many Indians as a legacy of British colonial domination; in this instance, however, it is also linked to Gandhi's relations with her parents and other members of the joint family in which she grew up and with her nationalist sentiments and experiences. The pattern is an extremely complex one, with its many crisscross and knotting threads.

First, it should be understood that Indira Nehru's experience with familial and political authority was quite irregular. There were no clear-cut, stable symbols of legitimate authority—either personal or political—to serve as models during her childhood and youth. Like other traditional Indian families (and the Nehru joint family was in many respects traditional, principally in its jointness), it contained a number of authorities that not only provided models of behavior and sources of affection but also exercised control over the child and shaped her behavior and attitudes. Among these, her father's authority was perhaps the most impersonal, remote, and unemotional; Indira was separated from him by physical distance but also, to some extent, by his reserve and his preoccupation with political concerns. It must have been exceedingly difficult for her as a young girl to disentangle her father's paternal role within the family from his image as a prominent political leader favored above others by the saintly Mahatma Gandhi.

Indira could not help but notice and be elated by the fact that her
father was loved by the Indian multitudes. But she may also have been
affected by the way his public role often required him to shape his
parental authority to the demands of impersonal, political authorities.
He was taken from her by Congress strategies, which often necessitated
extensive travel throughout the country, or by the British authorities,
who simply removed him from circulation for extended periods. As
the two contenders struggled for control of India, private life was
subordinated to the imperatives of the contest. Indira's schooling, as
we saw, became the subject of political debate between her father and
grandfather; at another time, it had to be interrupted so that she might
accompany her ailing mother to Europe while her father remained behind in prison. Thus, Nehru was simultaneously father to Indira—projecting, at times, paternal sternness, distance, or indifference—and
political hero to the Indian masses—projecting love, charm, goodness,
and towering strength. A few years ago, Gandhi herself remarked that
at times she was unable to distinguish between her father as a parent
and as a political leader, or to differentiate between her identity as
Nehru's daughter and her Indian political identity.

One message, however, came to her clearly from her father's activities
and the Mahatma's teachings, and it permeated her whole environment
as she was growing up: the British were the enemy, and while they were
not to be hated, their authority was to be unalterably opposed. Western
clothing, Western products, and the Western ways and life-styles introduced by the British were to be shunned. Moreover, Indira Nehru had
personal reasons for resenting this alien influence and presence; for not
only the British, but also the Westernized Nehru clan, prominently displayed an attitude of condescension toward things Indian (as many
Indians do today). She has said that the British treated Indians as if
they were children, thereby fostering a "dangerous need for dependence";[51] in a similar manner, Kamala Nehru's Westernized in-laws
seemed intent on "punishing" Indira's mother for her traditional Indian
upbringing and bearing. These memories and impressions were reinforced from time to time by other Western actions and attitudes that
predated the tense atmosphere of 1975-1976. Her tendency, when confronted with ideas or persons expressing such condescending Western
attitudes, has been to assume a defensive posture, for particularly
during her early years, such attitudes were very threatening to her
self-esteem. The intensity and quickness of her reaction suggests that

they are threatening still. In these early impressionable years she perceived her mother and India—which are both central to her sense of identity—as victims of injustice caused by Western ideas, systems, or persons that—paradoxically—were part of her own personal and political identity.

Where does her father fit into this pattern of ambivalence toward authority and the West? In his public role, of course, Nehru stood in opposition to them. Yet in his private role as husband and brother, when competing claims were made on his loyalties by the two principal rivals for his affections—his "traditional" wife and his "modern" Westernized sister—it was often the latter who emerged the victor. It now seems clear that this outcome was more the result of indifference than a conscious intention to slight or hurt his wife. Yet, as he himself later conceded, any action would have been better than indifference.[52]

Also reinforcing the young Indira's enduringly negative experience with things Western (in the political realm) were her father's letters, particularly those dealing with the nationalist movement and the "political" West in general. The letters written in 1933 contain strongly antagonistic sentiments vis-à-vis the West, especially in its colonialist garb. It is essential to underline the fact that Nehru identified democratic theory, institutions, and processes quite clearly and explicitly as Western in origin. By contrast, he does not clearly or explicitly identify the concept and philosophy of socialism as primarily or exclusively Western. Even in the earlier (1928) letters, the cooperative and collectivistic ethic is presented as the natural and preferred norm of humanity in general and of Indian civilization in particular. In his later writings Nehru incorporated this view into his discussion of socialism, which he believed to be the most appropriate ideology for India.

Although originally, as we saw, he rejected Western-style democracy, later on he embraced it. It could appear to his daughter that he had again shown his preference for things of Western flavor, just as in earlier years he had seemed to favor his Westernized sister over his "traditional" wife—no matter how much Kamala was hurt by the Nehrus' efforts to squeeze her into a Western mold. Projecting these family patterns onto the larger Indian canvas, one could perhaps argue (without stretching the analogy too far) that Indira eventually believed Nehru had tried to squeeze India into the Western democratic mold—with equally painful results. For ten years Gandhi tried to function within the Western political pattern sanctioned by her father, just as she and her mother had tried to fit into the Westernized Nehru family pattern. In both instances, the price exacted by these alien molds was distress or pain, either for herself or for her mother and India—with both of whom her identity is intimately fused.

By exploring Indira Gandhi's personality for clues about her outlook toward authority, we have found that her training would have fostered a democratic temperament and personal style. However, the political philosophy she learned, as well as her experiences with authority, created a deep ambivalence regarding the proper exercise of power. This ambivalence was put to a severe test in 1975. During the first half of that year, her stubborn streak emerged as she prepared to do battle with those who had taunted and opposed her for many years (many of whom had also fought her father). It mounted in June to a fury few had witnessed before. She saw her self-respect, the esteem of others for her, and all she stood for threatened. Because her sense of personal worth is tied up with her desire to achieve great things for India, the personal threat was perceived as a threat to the achievement of the beneficial national goals to which she was committed; and it resolved for a time her ambivalence about authority and its exercise and enabled her to proclaim Emergency Rule. Even so, the inner conflict created by the imposition of authoritarian rule must at times have been overwhelming.

There is still a good deal of speculation about why she relaxed Emergency Rule and eventually called for elections; for she could have held on to the reins of power. No one was more surprised than her political enemies when she took steps to dismantle some of the authoritarian machinery. Their perceptions of her as a "dictator" and "fascist" who would "murder" to preserve power do not fit her last acts in office. No doubt there are many reasons why Gandhi made certain decisions early in 1977; but in the context of our discussion, I believe her reasons were, in a peculiar way, similar to those which motivated her to establish Emergency Rule in the first place. Throughout her life her self-image had been that of a democrat; indeed her self-respect derives in good part from this self-image. Although she vigorously denied it when I spoke to her in 1978 (see Chap. 9, "An Interview with Indira Gandhi,"), I suspect that she was compelled to prove to the world and, above all, to herself, that she is and always has been a democrat. Since childhood the democratic ideal had been very closely related to her sense of personal worth and, equally importantly, to her sense of India's greatness.

Moreover, she must have come to accept that the national goals she had hoped to achieve were slipping more and more out of her hands. We cannot, of course, be sure how much she knew of what was going on in the country; but however great her isolation—because of censorship, fear, and sycophancy—it is unimaginable that news of the excesses of the emergency (especially those perpetrated by her younger son and his allies) and the dearth of intended results did not eventually reach her. One can even speculate further that, having faced what Sanjay Gandhi was doing, she may have decided that—short of publicly opposing or disowning him—revocation of Emergency Rule was the only way to stop him. It is clear that at that time she could never have brought herself to separate herself from him, even if it meant personal and political ruination.

CHAPTER IV

Overture to Dissent: A Coalescence of Conservative Opposition, 1966-1970

The analysis of the preceding chapters is intended to suggest that Indira Gandhi's early life experiences created a strong desire for achievement, self-reliance, and personal independence. Against the background of her upbringing at the center of nationalist politics, these desires meshed with her parallel ambitions for India; personal and national identity merged in subtle and imperceptible ways, as pride in her heritage was fostered, directly or indirectly, by her father.

Later (particularly under conditions of political stress) these experiences gave rise to increasingly ambivalent attitudes about the exercise of political authority and ideological principles of governance. Nevertheless, it was with a firm, conscious commitment to liberal democratic norms and practices that she embarked on her career as India's head of government in 1966. During her first ten years as prime minister this commitment remained an essential part of her positive self-image. Her direct experience of government gave even more definite shape to her political perceptions, style of conduct, and policy patterns, which increasingly departed from Western liberal conceptions. Her public statements made repeated reference to the notion that the "political democracy" expounded in Western liberal democratic theory, that stresses individual civil rights (political and judicial), is flawed when it does not incorporate prnciples of "economic democracy" that stress the collective good and the social and economic welfare of the underprivileged. During these years, she also expressed a determination to continue the great task initiated by her father—laying the firm foundations of a strong, united, independent, and internationally respected India. At the same time, she manifested some uncertainty about the specific programs and policies needed to achieve these broad goals.

Our main concern is to assess the credibility of the Congress Government's case regarding the emergency declaration. To understand the forces that led to her dramatic actions in June 1975 and the months that followed we must look to these early years of her government. One product of these years was the opposition to Gandhi that surfaced with great intensity in 1974. It had simmered for a long time, for Indira Gandhi had made implacable enemies, many of whom vowed to topple her from power. The reasons for their alienation and coalescence of the opposition forces against her are the subject of this chapter.

The "Island Republic of the Indian Elite"

Apart from the caste system and the sanctity of the cow, the most widely known fact about India is that it is haunted by poverty.[1] Evidence is ample and impinges upon the sensibilities of even the least sensitive visitor. India is perhaps one of the few countries in the world where it is virtually impossible to give one a guided tour through the "better" parts of a city, town, or village, for poverty and riches live side by side. The islands of privilege are more like sandbars in the vast shallow waters of deprivation and degradation. What we call the "middle class" in the affluent world—small businessmen, traders and merchants, and the white- and blue-collar workers—is infinitesimal. And although this "middle-upper" class is easily distinguishable from the very wealthy—with their massive assets and perquisites of luxury— it is nevertheless far closer to the elite—in terms of education, status, satisfaction of basic needs, and enjoyment of comforts—than to the multitudes of the poor. To all intents and purposes, one can say (as Gunnar Myrdal does) that there are really only two classes in India— the upper class and the lower—with shadings of affluence in the one and shadings of deprivation in the other.

While the well-off may live in physical proximity to the poor, they are divided from them by a vast gap in consciousness as well as status and condition and in the cultural symbols and tools of communication available to them. This unimaginable chasm has been carefully nurtured for eons, consciously and unconsciously, by the privileged of each generation. During this century, however, enlightened leaders like Gandhi and Nehru tried to awaken the masses, and the elites became more aware of the need to protect their fortresses. Ideas of equality, dignity, and social justice were propagated through the institutions of a democratic government, socialist preachments, and the growth of education, communication, and transportation. The privileged classes began to strengthen their defenses, even though the poor had shown few signs of challenging their supremacy. Once the mere potential for such a challenge was recognized, the wealthy marshalled all their resources to defend themselves. In one sense, the history of India since independence can be seen as a series of efforts by the better-off sections of Indian society to preserve, consolidate, and extend their status and privilege against the potential challengers. This fact is necessary to our understanding of the events that have convulsed India since independence, especially during the period 1966 to 1975 which concerns us here.

The socioeconomic goals of democratic socialism touch directly on the interests of the privileged classes. Although few publicly voiced opposition to the national credo that, under Gandhi and Nehru, became nearly sacrosanct, the fact is that the actions of many within the ruling Congress elite—and of its opponents too—belied the rhetoric of social justice, equality, and human dignity. An observation made by a foreign visitor to the All-India Congress Committee Session at Bhubaneshwar in 1964 (shortly before Nehru's death) illustrates the gap—sometimes wholly unconscious—between precept and practice. When the leaders and rank-and-file met that year, they approved a resolution (after nearly thirty-five years of resistance) containing the most explicit commitment yet to socialism and the ideals of equality and the eradication of the caste system: "'Socialism' . . . does not merely signify changes in the economic relations in society. It involves fundamental changes in the social structure, in ways of thinking and in ways of living. Caste and class have no place in the socialist order that is envisaged by the Congress. Old ideas about privilege on the basis of birth or caste or money or the hierarchy of office should be discarded . . . Congressmen in their everyday life should become examples of this socialist philosophy." Yet on the very grounds where this resolution was passed was a sign reading: "Upper Class People—Waiting Room."[2]

The lack of commitment to a clear philosophy within parties and, more importantly, disagreement on fundamental political values about the ends and means of government, are reflected in the erratic conduct of most politicians. Discrepancies in thought and action are rooted in the sociopolitical attitudes and relations upon which the nationalist movement was founded and which crystallized further in the years after independence. Most struggles for independence tend to submerge ideological differences under the overarching goal of national liberation;

in India too a multitude of special interests and a wide spectrum of political ideologies were brought together to serve a single aim. During the struggle against the British, the Indian National Congress coordinated the activities of all these groups and spearheaded the nationalist struggle. In 1947, the Congress was converted into a political party, leaving to the future the untangling of the many conflicting strands of interests and values woven into the nationalist organization. Over the years, though numerous groups broke away to form their own parties, many others stayed on, and the Congress retained its inclusiveness. The result was not felicitous. The Congress umbrella shaded from view both the virtues and the sins of those huddled under it and prevented the development of any clear ideological and programmatic polarizations. One Indian political scientist has diagnosed well the malady of the Congress party: "The real dilemma facing the Congress, is that it has ceased to be a 'movement' without really becoming a 'party'. The confusion is worst confounded because it has all the inherited attributes of a movement—organizational amorphousness, heterogeneity of membership composition, all-inclusiveness in terms of divergent ideological accommodation, capability to internalize the conflict and mechanisms of compromise to reconcile opposite view-points and interests, etc.— except its clear direction and unified and dedicated commitment to an objective."[3]

The parties in opposition were in a worse fix. Having rejected the protective cover of the Congress, they were exposed to the glaring light of their own contradictions. In the two decades that followed independence, the opposition parties preserved their old, comfortable identities or formed new ones, but were unable to find a common denominator for a broad-based coalition of political and economic forces. And yet the common ground was there, awaiting cultivation.

There can be little doubt that many if not most members of the upper classes are "closet" conservatives. If so, why have they not openly declared themselves? It may be because, once the Congress party—the "champion" of democratic socialism—was established, the influential, articulate, and well-organized socioeconomic groups were reluctant to openly embrace a philosophy that went against the popularly sanctioned credo and to express this forcefully through the opposition parties. In any case, democratic socialism in India was so broadly and ambiguously defined that it lent itself to a variety of interpretations, both conservative and progressive.[4] Moreover, even before independence, a modus vivendi had been reached between the upper classes and the party in power—especially at state and local levels.

At the same time, the administrative corps of independent India, which was entrusted with the implementation of the ruling party's policies, had been coopted by the socioeconomic elites. Indeed, the bureaucratic "steel frame" constructed by the British had been recruited from the upper classes. Civil servants were trained in the British tradition and imbibed the aristocratic outlook of the British ruling class. The leadership of the Congress at the national level sometimes had to turn a blind eye to administrative shortcomings, for it needed the cooperation of this well-trained and efficient staff. The ruling elite also found itself hamstrung by the need to seek the support of the wealthier communities, especially at the grass roots, in order to remain in power. At the state, district, and village level cooperation between socioeconomic elites, elected officials, and civil servants has been more open and visible.

Such accommodations, in turn, encouraged those outside the halls of power to play down their conservative principles so as not to appear out of step with the accepted political creed. Even the few opposing parties that were wholly honest in expressing their political views and seeking popular backing for them—such as the conservative Swatantra party—did not allow these views to stand in the way of alliances with groups that professed divergent or even diametrically opposed ideas. The parties no doubt felt—and quite realistically—that they would have to establish themselves as viable political entities before seeking open support. (Even so, they did not completely lack backing from big business and wealthy landlords, who took care to put their eggs in as many friendly baskets as possible.)

The landed and business elites in particular were wooed by all because they were well-organized and well-endowed with material and social resources and political skills. They could effectively articulate their demands to government administrators and opposing groups. It did not much matter to these elites what party got into office (with the exception perhaps of radical left-communist parties). While an out-and-out conservative government might have been preferable, the ruling Congress party did not altogether fail them. They felt fairly secure during the 1950s and 1960s, including the period from 1966 to 1970 when Mrs. Gandhi was still in the process of consolidating her power.

But this sense of security began to erode in the late sixties, and was seriously threatened after 1971 by legislation and other government actions that seemed to challenge seriously the favored status of this minority. At first the challenge was trivial or merely symbolic, but it soon became an increasingly concrete threat aimed at a wide spectrum of targets. Nevertheless, the landlords, businessmen, and their supporting elites continued to enjoy considerable favor within the ruling party, belying opposition charges that Gandhi was unduly influenced by the Communist party of India and the Soviets and was leading the country on the path to Communism. Even her archfoe, Morarji Desai, conceded that she was not a Communist.

It must be remembered, however, that the division between the right and left wings of the Congress had existed since Nehru's days as prime minister. A decisive struggle for dominance between the two wings was waged as far back as 1951 when Nehru, representing the more leftist views, had seemed to emerge victorious. The conservative wing was never really defeated, however, and continued to wield tremendous influence. Members from this wing were responsible for Shastri's election in 1964 and and for Indira Gandhi's in 1966. By 1967, the younger and more progressive leaders had begun to reassert themselves and rallied around Gandhi, though she was still politically weak. After the 1971 general elections, in which the Congress under Indira Gandhi's leadership swept the country, various conservative strongholds came under attack. The judicial system, upon which the upper classes had always depended for their ultimate defense, was among the important targets of assault in the offensive against vested interests; even before then the relationship between government and the courts had been severely strained. The Indian judiciary—and members of the British-trained or British-inspired legal profession—was (and remains) the bulwark of the aristocracy; but after 1971 its supremacy was seriously challenged. As the economic situation deteriorated in 1972-1973, the government found it necessary to mobilize all the resources at its disposal to meet the growing needs and expectations of the under-privileged classes whose standards of living had been further eroded by natural disasters. At the same time, it tried to salvage something of its planning targets. In the government's effort to stabilize the economy, the landed and business interests were squeezed somewhat, along with the organized working classes and the professionals; the middle-upper classes in particular were severely affected by inflation and unemployment. Discontent stemming from the worsening economic situation impelled disaffected groups to seek strength in cooperation; and from this time on attacks on Gandhi's regime from the Right became more concerted.

The issues that began to emerge out of the increasingly bitter confrontation between the Congress government and the opposition parties were those of development, integration, and democracy—issues that have been considered in a broader context by numerous studies on the politics of India and other underdeveloped countries. Before considering them, we should understand that the party system in India can be described, broadly speaking, as "reconciliational" and competitive; that is, in principle, it is the type of party system functioning in the Western liberal democratic states from which universal suffrage, parliamentary rule, free speech, free association, and a free press were adopted at independence. Such a party system should act as a two-way communications link between the government and the people, the electoral process providing the medium through which alternative leadership and programs can compete for, and mobilize, broad-based political support. This process, as an expression of the popular will, legitimizes the government subsequently formed. Ideally, such a system ensures stability by providing for an orderly, open, and peaceful process of ascertaining the popular will and bringing about a change of leadership when voters decide that it is necessary.

The principal role of the opposition is thus to provide a credible and practical alternative to the ruling party's leaders, policies, and programs. Toward that end, the opposition must be able to act as a potential government, placing national above party duty and reinforcing among its followers a commitment to national values about the ends and means of government. In a transitional society an additional function of political parties is to impart political education to a people steeped in traditional political values and behavior, encouraging civic consciousness, participant values, and a sense of national purpose. Such tasks are difficult in the best of circumstances, but they can become nearly impossible in the volatile climate of Indian politics. Before we can assess the conduct of opposition parties, we need to survey some aspects of the social and economic setting within which all the political forces interacted in the period between 1966 and 1970—when shifting alignments and coalescence among opposition forces began to appear in embryonic form.

Violence Amid Poverty

The five-year period from January 1966 until the end of 1970 was a seething prelude to the tumultuous years that climaxed in the establishment of Emergency Rule. Serious social, economic, and political unrest swept the country, weakening the sense of national unity and retarding the achievement of developmental goals. India was probably spared a violent revolution only because the most aggrieved classes—the poorest peasants, landless laborers, and urban rejects—remained, except in a few pockets, largely quiescent.

Most of the problems were in good part the result of human shortsightedness by Congress and opposition leaders—and by many of the led. But they were also caused in part—and in part exacerbated—by natural disasters, which have been an enduring companion of human existence in Asia. The unpredictable monsoons command the destinies of millions, sometimes inundating the parched earth with overabundant rains, at other times withholding their bounty altogether, and in more propitious times filling the great earthen basins of the north and south with just the proper measure of life-sustaining water.[5]

The failure of the southwest monsoon in 1965 and again in 1966 wrought havoc on Indian agriculture and obliged the government to postpone the fourth five-year plan, which was due to come into operation in April 1966.[6] It was estimated (fairly accurately) that it would be three years before it could become operative. This clobbering blow of nature produced serious food shortages throughout India and famine conditions in several states. Food reserves were exhausted and large shipments had to be purchased from abroad, depleting the government's foreign exchange reserves (out of which imports for industrial production were to have been financed). In September 1965, following the outbreak of war between India and Pakistan, the economy was further hurt by the suspension of U.S. economic aid. The depletion of foreign-exchange reserves and depressed agricultural production, which provides important raw materials for industry, brought about a serious industrial recession. Adding to the misery was the climate of pervasive political instability and the ensuing social and economic unrest.

Throughout the late 1960s much social violence was generated by religious, linguistic, and other communal issues. It peaked in early 1968, declined somewhat, then reached new and more terrible heights in 1969; its echoes were still reverberating in early 1970. The springs of anger, frustration, and hatred are deep and plentiful, and they are easily tapped; the slightest provocation causes them to gush forth. The well-known animosity between the Hindus and Muslims has historic and religious roots, but the economic causes are perhaps no less important. In November 1966, several thousand people led by Hindu Sadhus (holy men)—naked or in saffron-colored robes—marched on Parliament to demand a national ban on cow slaughter. Push led to shove and fighting broke out. Many were killed. In September 1969, horrific riots broke out in Gujarat. Stores were looted, property was destroyed, and people were beaten senseless or burnt alive. This was one of the worst Hindu-Muslim riots in the history of independent India (almost as bad as the massacres that accompanied independence). The riots were triggered by a Hindu attempt to block a Muslim religious procession by driving 200 cows across its path. The violence spread from the state capital, Ahmedabad, to other regions of the state. During this five-year period communal disturbances were endemic, especially in northern India, which has the largest concentration of Muslims.[7] Apart from religiously inspired confrontations, there were linguistic riots and barbarous outpourings of hate among upper- and lower-caste communities. The widespread violence brought mutilation and death to some and financial havoc to many others.

There was also much specifically political violence, most of it arising out of separatist demands in the eastern-most regions and from a political agrarian movement of subversion and terror led by rebels known as "Naxalites." The latter claimed ideological allegiance to the Maoist philosophy of revolution and were said to be encouraged by China and, to a lesser extent, by Pakistan. The movement stemmed originally from the conditions of extreme poverty and destitution endured by peasants in West Bengal, a state distinguished for its industry, its port, and its chronically turbulent politics. The Naxalites were also believed to be responsible for the revolt of another group of tribal peasants in Andhra, the Girijans, and for disturbances in the southern state of Kerala.

The cultural diversity of India is legendary. Out of it spring distinct social, political, and economic identities, all vying for expression, some more shrill, some more violent, others yet more desperate but too weak even to shout and seemingly resigned to their fate. The claims of the poorest and most downtrodden are lost in the cacophony of linguistic, religious, regional, and caste voices of rural India and of the more refined cadences of the urban upper classes. The feudal remnants of the old aristocracy, along with the nouveau riche, have easily shed the outmoded forms of rulership. They have emerged as the principal proponents of modern political forms and ideologies, such as democracy and socialism, without for a moment relinquishing their domination over the poor, lower castes and outcastes, and the tribals—who are described by the rather antiseptic British term "scheduled castes and tribes" or, more condescendingly, as the "backward classes."

According to one respected Indian economist, the annual per capita national income during 1931-1932 (in undivided India) was Rs. 65 (or about $19.50). (The average personal income in the United States at the time ranged between $401 and $531.) In 1949, a United Nations estimate placed the figure at about $57; and Indian government calculations put it at $64 in 1966-1967 and $76 in 1969. (Equivalent figures in the U.S. ranged from $3,000 to $3,700.) Even more revealing of the widespread destitution are some estimates of income distribution in India. For example, in 1968, the poorest 60 percent of the population (that is, about 330 million people) averaged only $58 per person per year. Their share of the aggregate national income was thus 36 percent, while that of the top 20 percent was 42 percent.

Out of such conditions food riots and demands for land erupted from time to time. But these outbursts were all too often overshadowed by the demands of those who, though far from rich, were infinitely better off than the poorest 60 percent of the population—not to mention the poorest 20 percent who were left with only 8 rupees out of every 100. (The top 20 percent commanded 42 out of every 100 rupees of income.) The poorest work as landless laborers, small tenants, or sharecroppers in India's nearly 600,000 villages; or they eke out a living in urban centers as domestic servants, low-paid temporary workers, or just as beggars, roaming the streets and inhabiting the slums.[8]

Among the better off—government employees, organized workers in the private sector, and students—the latter showed the most unflagging enthusiasm, year after year, for strikes, demonstrations, and violent activities; these were mostly inspired by academic grievances rather than sympathy for the poor. Government employees successfully pressed their demands for higher wages or dearness allowances (cost-of-living increases) on several occasions. They consistently defied bans on strikes, particularly during 1967 and 1968, when numerous agitations were launched by state-government employees; unionized central government employees—especially those in the postal and railway systems—stopped work periodically.

During this period, violence accompanied demands for greater autonomy by Mizo tribal rebels in the strategically sensitive easternmost state of Assam, and agitations by people of the Telengana region rocked the southern state of Andhra Pradesh—one of the surplus food producers. The state of Punjab was divided into two after fierce confrontations between Sikhs and Hindus. Territorial disputes with linguistic overtones led to serious rioting at borders between the states of Maharashtra and Mysore in the Indian peninsula. Finally, there was a continuation of demands for independence by the Naga rebels, who in 1962 had been granted their own state. The Naga and Mizo rebels, along with the tribal peasants of Naxalbari in West Bengal, live in politically sensitive and highly strategic areas. They border on China, where many of the rebels, according to the Indian government, go from time to time to seek aid—military and financial as well as diplomatic.

These were among the principal features of the Indian setting between 1966 and 1970. There was open and repeated defiance of central and state authorities by many religious, regional, and linguistic groups, student and trade-union organizations, or militant political factions. The opposition parties often aided and abetted, if they did not actually instigate, the activities of the groups. Thousands upon thousands of workdays were lost in industry; government activities were disrupted; the movement of food to scarcity areas and of materials to industrial plants or docks was delayed or blocked by sabotage, strikes, or other disruptive tactics. All this had adverse effects not only on the harried Indian consumer but also on the vital export trade and, thereby, on the already-precarious foreign-exchange position of the government. After the agricultural disaster of 1965–1966, the government, having depleted its foreign-exchange reserves, had to incur further debt to import food.

These events were clear signs of the erosion of legitimacy not only of the political leadership but even more of India's institutions. The hydra-headed challenge to the Indian polity pointed up the fragility of the country's political and social unity, which sorely needed steady and powerful infusions of national consciousness and of confidence in the institutions and leaders to immunize it against the overpowering effects of parochial, sectional, and factional loyalties. These events were, moreover, indicative of the issues that would have to be tackled if development programs were to be successfully devised and implemented.

Problems of national integration—of unity, order, and stability—overshadowed those of development, or rather they appeared to be in need of more urgent attention. And few leaders, on any side of the political fence, betrayed in action or word an understanding of the powerful link between development and integration. Some politicians were perhaps immobilized by the scale of the disruption; but the deeper problem lay with their philosophies, programs, and public pronouncements. These gave obeisance to high-sounding ideals, attractive catch-words and slogans, but betrayed a lack of reflection on their meaning, particularly over the long run. Their vision seems to have been clouded by short-term considerations of political gains or narrow political and social identities and interests. The Congress, as the party at the helm of the government, had a special obligation to broaden its vision, yet it did not live up to its promises. The opposition parties were, if anything, even more remiss, for they failed to take up the challenge thrust upon them by the government's lapses. The worth of competitive political parties must be assessed by their contribution to the goals of national integration and development within a democratic framework. All share the responsibility of providing realistic choices of leadership, policies, and programs. The burden of this responsibility falls somewhat more heavily on the shoulders of opposition parties, since they must persuade the electorate that they can, individually and collectively, do better than the incumbents. They must be able to effectively mobilize political support of a broad-based nature and, when necessary, enlarge the bases of political participation. Assessing opposition parties and their leaders on the basis of these criteria, let us see how effectively they fulfilled their functions during 1966–1970. In particular, we should assess their role in preserving and promoting order and development within a democratic framework.

Observers of Indian affairs cannot help but be awed by the colossal task of social transformation that has been undertaken. It is inevitable that in such a transitional society, the main political struggle must be—and so it has emerged more and more clearly over the years as—a struggle between the forces for change and those for preservation of the privileged existence of the few. Where have the opposition forces ranged themselves in this struggle? As arbiter between these awesome forces, where has the Indian judiciary stood and why?

The Opposition in Disarray

The period between 1966 and 1970 was the first phase of a winnowing process—within the opposition and the Congress—that reflected an effort to sort and sift the forces of the Right and Left according to economic and political views. The conservatives represented the privileged classes and those who stood at the gates of privilege. Their interests oriented them toward the preservation and consolidation of the status quo in social, economic, and political matters. They were prepared to countenance only such changes as would further protect their privileged position or restore the status quo ante where earlier legislative or government action had encroached on it. Almost all the remaining forces were, in varying degrees, left of center insofar as the pace and targets of change were concerned. The Congress, the two socialist parties, and the two communist parties were committed to some variant of democratic socialism; they were prepared to work within a broadly defined democratic parliamentary framework to achieve their varied socialist goals. With the split of the Communist party–Marxist in 1969, the breakaway faction became a more revolutionary party that rejected the parliamentary road to socialism— although it was divided on the precise details of revolutionary strategy.

Starting in 1967, a new dynamism suffused the opposition forces, particularly those on the Right. Their first efforts at electoral cooperation, meager though they were, bore some fruit during the elections that year and encouraged additional, but still tentative, efforts toward unity. By 1970, following the split of the Congress party, the lines of convergence among conservatives had become clearer, as had those of divergence between the clearly conservative forces and those of the, as yet, inchoate Left.

The philosophies embraced by the opposition parties, as well as the programs offered and actions undertaken by them, seemed to work at cross purposes vis-à-vis the goals of national unity and development. Nor did they reinforce the values of democracy. Sharp differences among the major opposition parties were readily detectable in the 1967 election manifestoes and in other policy statements. Although it was still hardly perceptible, the nucleus of agreement that made possible the movement for "total revolution" in 1974 and the merger of 1977 was evolving.[9] Between 1966 and 1970, however, the differences dominated their relationships.

In retrospect, it seems clear that the major opposition parties had an extraordinary opportunity to vanquish the complacent, corrupt, and cumbersome Congress. It was a wounded lion, its mane clipped by Nehru's death and repeated blows from various quarters. The staggering impact of the food crisis (along with the 1965 war with Pakistan) was borne by a much weakened and groping leadership during Shastri's short rule and Gandhi's first year of initiation into the "fire and brimstone" of politics. Border states were rebelling, Punjabi Hindus and Sikhs were rioting for or against the establishment of a separate Punjabi Sikh state, sadhus were demanding a national ban against cow slaughter; in general, the country was approaching a state of near-anarchy as the elections approached. A custom-built club was handed to Congress opponents in the form of Gandhi's devaluation decision, which even Congressmen privately decried.[10] Despite the conviction of World Bank advisers, government economists, and certain political leaders, who agreed that such an action would alleviate India's grave foreign-exchange problem by stimulating exports, devaluation had the opposite effect. And finally, just two years after Nehru's death, a process of disintegration within the Congress party seemed under way; factional struggles became more intense than ever on the eve of the national elections. In the last half of 1966, a "mini-split" began at the state level and continued into 1967. In West Bengal, Orissa, Bihar, and Rajasthan four new parties were formed by dissident Congressmen.

Here, then, was a chance for responsible opposing parties to come together to forge an electoral alliance or even a merger. All the opposing political parties in Parliament had jointly raised their voices against the prime minister's devaluation decision and the Congress party's economic policies. There had been overwhelming support among opposition members for a motion of no-confidence charging the government with corruption and responsibility for the orgiastic violence that had seized the country. Apparently, the breakdown of law and order was so critical that Congress President K. Kamaraj had hinted at the possibility of a military takeover. Opposition leaders claimed to be appalled by the national pandemonium; yet, as we shall see, they themselves bore some of the responsibility for the violent agitations.

Despite the intensity of rancor toward the Congress, the leading members of the opposition were unable to devise an alternative program and leadership slate for the 1967 elections. Those who a few years later would be drawn together were now marching on separate paths. In December 1966, much activity had been afoot among the conservative opposition to search out common grounds for political cooperation. Acharya Kripalani, a former president of the Congress party (now elder statesman of the Janata party) chaired a national convention of former Congressmen in New Delhi; they pledged to "revive the basic values of the pre-independence Congress but modify the programmes in the light of the experience of the last 20 years."[11] Toward this end, a new all-India party was formed, adding one more to the many "unrecognized" parties and to the twenty-six recognized parties that contested the elections in 1967.[12] Jayaprakash Narayan, the now nearly forgotten leader of the 1974 movement and respected voice of the opposition during and shortly after the end of Emergency Rule, in December 1966 presided over a convention that proposed a nonparty system for Parliament and the legislative assemblies.

The most broadly based efforts toward political cooperation were made at the end of 1966 by opposition leaders, who met to discuss the possibility of forging electoral agreements at the national level. No agreements could be reached for contesting parliamentary constituencies, although at the state level some parties did combine to contest for seats in the legislative assemblies. These local alliances were clearly not the result of any coherent political strategy; nor were they inspired by common programs or principles. Not only did rightist candidates link hands with leftists in some states, but parties aligned in some constituencies were fighting one another in other constituencies in the same state. Neither at the state level, then, nor at the center were opposition parties able to submerge their differences enough to offer to the electorate a responsible and clear alternative of policies and leaders; they could not even reduce the choices offered to the voter to a manageable number.

The opposition must thus be held accountable for betrayal of an important responsibility imposed by democratic convention and logic. The obligation to offer a sensible choice ought to have been honored by those who had accepted, implicitly or explicitly, the principle of electoral competition. Alas, it was not. The alternative to the Congress party was twenty-five other parties, only seven of which challenged the Congress as "national" parties. Such a plethora of candidates and parties negates the principles of "free choice" nearly as much as the "yes" or "no" vote for a single candidate allowed in a one-party system.

Prior to 1977 many opposition leaders attributed Congress victories to its special advantage as an incumbent party and blamed their defeats on such factors as the system of voting (single ballot–simple majority rule) and Congress rigging of elections. But 1977 proved beyond doubt that the opposition, when united, could overcome far greater obstacles than any they had claimed to encounter before. It took a threat of such a magnitude—and Emergency Rule clearly presented this threat to their very existence—to accomplish something that could have been accomplished long before. In spite of the momentum created by the 1974 movement, and even though things were clearly coming to a head in 1975, the president of the Opposition Congress, Asoka Mehta, made the following comment about the obstacles to unification:

> Some want the opposition parties to disband and form one party. Others take another stand and suggest the formation of a federal structure but are opposed to disbanding the parties. They feel they don't want to disband until they are able to pull together. *Then of course there are long histories and traditions with each party.* If they are stamped out by a premature merger, then those who have supported the parties may lose interest. *I am not saying which is right and which is wrong.* Both are valid.[13]

Thus, even at such a crucial period, there was bickering among party leaders who were still concerned with their special political identities. Exactly two months after these comments, a state of emergency was declared; and within twenty-one months after that (and two months after the relaxation of the emergency), these very same parties *had* merged.[14] Nearly a decade earlier, the chances for merger must have seemed not only very dimly conceivable but probably quite out of the question.

So in 1967, owing to the proliferation of parties, not one of them could win even the 10 percent of the parliamentary seats needed to qualify as an official opposition party. Swatantra, the second largest parliamentary party after the Congress, got less than 9 percent of the popular vote and about 8 percent of the seats, while the third largest, the Jana Sangh, got just over 9 percent of the popular vote and nearly 7 percent of the seats. Even so the share of the popular vote (35 percent) obtained by the combined national opposition parties was only five percentage points below that of the Congress. However, as seven parties had shared this percentage, and another nearly 25 percent was split up among independents and small state parties, the opposition forces had clearly failed in their major task.

Had they the will and the foresight, some opposition parties could have devised a workable alliance at the national level, for there were several issues on which they held congruent views. The Swatantra and the Jana Sangh, in particular, had similar conservative ideologies and were closest together on matters of economic and foreign policy. In international affairs, both advocated abandonment of the nonalignment policy and formation of alliances with Western democratic countries.

In economic policy, the Swatantra advocated abolition of the Planning Commission and the fourth plan. It opted instead for "democratic planning" along the lines of the British, French, or Scandinavian models. Although the Jana Sangh did not explicitly support such measures, it indicated it would not be guided by "doctrinaire socialism" in developing new industry and would oppose further expansion of the public sector, except in such basic industries as power, mineral oils, and defense. In embracing the principle of "micro-economic planning," the Jana Sangh was essentially proposing that centralized planning (the function of the Planning Commission) be done away with. Instead it supported "region-wise and project-wise" planning, without indicating the size of the regional or project unit. Like the Swatantra, it rejected the "totalitarian methods" of planning relied on by countries like the Soviet Union and China (and compared the Indian planning model to those models). Existing private-sector industries would not be touched by the Jana Sangh, and all foreign trade would be left in private hands. Instead of planning targets, the private sector would be subject to the "laws of market economy." The Swatantra was even more enthusiastic and explicit in its espousal of free enterprise.

Thus both parties accepted, in principle, a "mixed economy," but with the mix definitely favoring the private sector. Nationalization of banks and joint or cooperative farming were definitely opposed. M. R. Masani, prominent leader and president (1969–1971) of the Swatantra party, wrote in 1961 that the party's principles included "maximum freedom for the individual and minimum interference by the State." The party, held that the "progress, welfare and happiness of the people depend on individual initiative, enterprise and energy."[15]

Common points between the Jana Sangh and the Swatantra could also be found in their views on fiscal and monetary policy. Both parties were critical of deficit financing and control of prices, wages, and profits. They also railed against heavy taxation and other government fiscal policies that, they said, had "crushed the middle class." Both proposed to implement a drastic economy in government expenditure and to reduce reliance on foreign resources to a minimum. The Swatantra put forth the view that India's foreign-exchange problem would be alleviated if foreign capital, in the form of government-to-government loans, were diverted away from the government and toward private enterprise. No indication was given, however, of how deficit financing could be avoided by, on the one hand, drastically reducing government expenditure, taxation, and foreign borrowings, while, on the other, introducing an extensive social-security program, raising workers' wages, offering agricultural incentives (in the form of credit, fertilizer, irrigation projects, etc.), and setting a minimum wage of Rs. 125 (approximately $17 a month), even for agricultural laborers.

In the agricultural sector, the programs and policies of the two parties on the whole favored the established or better-off farmer, although both made perfunctory gestures of sympathy toward the poor farmer and the landless agricultural laborer. The Swatantra pledged, in effect, to dismantle the whole constitutional and statutory structure underpinning the land reforms effected under Nehru in an attempt to further social justice in the agrarian sector. The Jana Sangh's official views, on the surface, were slightly less conservative; while advocating "peasant proprietorship" as the basis of the land system, the party also acknowledged that the "right to property is subject to social sanction," and noted that "there is no such thing as an absolute and immutable right of property." Its overall position on agrarian reform, however, was by no means clear. On the one hand, it stated that "the present system of land tenure requires to be changed" and acknowledged the problem of absentee land-holders: "Legally they are agriculturalists and whatever facilities are provided by the government to agriculturalists are in most cases appropriated by these people. The result is that the actual tiller lives in a precarious condition, impoverished and famished. The tiller must become the owner of the land and get all the benefits due to an agriculturalist." On the other hand, it was prepared to make exceptions for some farmers who, under certain undefined conditions, could not till their land. Under such vague conditions, the absentee landlord would be able to function as he always had. Specifically exempt from the ban on absentee leasing were "minors, widows, infirm and disabled persons, or army personnel";[16] in the past landlords have displayed great ingenuity in finding shelter under just such conditions. Moreover, it would be quite unlikely that the courts would interpret such criteria in favor of the poor tenant—especially the Supreme Court, which tends to be very protective of the property rights of absentee landlords. Ways could be found to subvert the social and economic purposes of such an agrarian policy, and it seems unlikely that that possibility wholly escaped the notice of the highly astute political leaders and ideologues of the Jana Sangh.

Both parties also made strong political overtures to government employees; teachers, especially at the primary level (where they were seen as molders of the political views of the future electorate), were also singled out for favorable attention; and the rights of organized labor were respectfully treated. The appeal of these two parties, therefore, was basically to the upper (or, in the preferred terminology of the two parties, the "middle") classes, rather than to the poor: to the urban voter and the upper crust of the rural areas; to the white-collar worker, especially government employees, professionals, and intellectuals; and to former princes and ex-zamindars. The composition of the party membership and the size of the organization alone suggests that the recruiting activities of each party were directed to these smaller classes and to urban centers.

On certain cultural questions too, their policies were highly compatible and stressed traditional and religious values. The Swatantra, for example, saw religion as a "dynamic force for strengthening moral and spiritual values" and believed that "the role of Dharma a God-oriented inner law" ought to be "resuscitated and welcomed and fostered by the Government of the country." Jana Sangh philosophy placed even greater emphasis on this concept, according to which, "absolute sovereignty vests in Dharma alone." Dharma has always been a vaguely defined concept, and, according to the Jana Sangh's official definition (which did not illuminate it further), it refers to "those eternal principles which sustain an entity—individual or corporate—and abiding by which, that entity can achieve material prosperity in this world and spiritual salvation in the next."[17] In essence, dharma seems to denote a set of transcendental, spiritually derived ethical and moral principles of conduct, a sort of ultimate "rule of law." It is just such a principle, stressing acceptance of the existing order and rewards in the after-life, along with the emphasis on nonviolence, that has kept the lower castes and classes in thrall to the upper social strata over the centuries. As moral dicta, the eternal rule of law and the principle of nonviolence have been observed more in their breach than in their practice.

Although the Jana Sangh was generally identified as the representative of "political Hinduism," the party assiduously avoided this image in its official documents. Its basic philosophical statement does not mention the term *Hindu* or *Hinduism;* the emphasis was rather on *Bharat,* a more generic Sanskrit term for India. There seems little question, however, that by "Bharatiya Sanskriti" (Indian culture) what was really meant was Hindu Aryan culture—the major indigenous component of Indic civilization. This may be surmised by, among other things, the status given to the ancient and now dead language of Sanskrit, which, according to the Jana Sangh, "has always been India's National Language" and "should be recognized as such."[18] This status was symbolic, however; it was proposed that Sanskrit be used only on ceremonial occasions. Hindi, on the other hand, which is derived from Sanskrit, was given a central place "as the Centre's Official Language." A strong stand was taken, moreover, in favor of the eventual abandonment of English as a medium of instruction and official communication. Were such a policy adopted, the speakers of Dravidian languages in the southern peninsula (numbering about 25 percent of the total population), Urdu speakers (another 11 percent if we include most Muslims), and tens of millions of other non-Hindi speakers would be at a disadvantage in the educational system, as well as in the governmental, and political systems, which now conduct their affairs in English, particularly at the central level. While the Swatantra party's manifesto remained silent on the language question, it seemed to agree with the Jana Sangh when, in 1962 and 1967, it criticized Congress policy as encouraging "linguism" and thus separatism.

The principle of decentralization of political and economic power was another theme common to both party platforms, although since its inception in 1951 the Jana Sangh also advocated the dismantling of the federal structure and its replacement by a unitary system of government (a suggestion which Jayaprakash Narayan thought betrayed "fascistic tendencies"). The need for greater decentralization runs through the arguments offered by almost all of the opposition parties, particularly those that promoted regional or linguistic interests. Here, drawing some support from the Swatantra, the Jana Sangh parted company with most other parties; it firmly opposed any and all "separatist demands" that claim "special privileges and protection on the basis of province, religion, caste or language."[19] While acknowledging (in its 1967 manifesto) allegations of discrimination (which it pledged to end forthwith), it refused to recognize the right of the untouchables and other depressed castes and tribes to special treatment or opportunities, which would allow a "vested interest" in backwardness to develop. The Jana Sangh also rejected all concepts that would "seek to perpetuate artificial distinctions amongst the one people that inhabit this land"; in particular, it would "put an end to the concept of minority or majority on the basis of religion."[20] Carried to an extreme, such an idea sharply conflicts with the pluralistic credo of democratic philosophy. In 1967, the Jana Sangh proposed a "law of treason" to which groups considered separatist and others "threatening India's integrity and sovereignty" would presumably be subject. Further restrictions were to be imposed on "fifth columnists" and "disruptionist elements" (neither of which are clearly defined).

On the Left, the most moderate parties were rather similar to the two right-wing parties; both accepted the principle of mixed enterprise, with the Samyukta Socialist Party (SSP) advocating more selective and gradual nationalization. The Praja Socialist Party (PSP), along with the Jana Sangh, urged the development of atomic energy—for military as well as peaceful economic purposes—and the total integration of Jammu and Kashmir. Like the Swatantra, however, the PSP and SSP remained largely silent on the specifics of the language question, leaving this policy area blurred and open to possible dispute. In foreign policy, the PSP echoed the conservatives' stand on the Middle East by pleading for friendly relations with Israel, although it did voice opposition to a strategy of military alliances advocated by the Swatantra and the Jana Sangh.

As might be expected, the widest differences between the conservative and leftist parties were over economic policy, particularly bank nationalization, which was supported by all the leftist parties and vigorously opposed by all conservatives. The leftists, however, were divided on the degree and rate of nationalization of business, industry, and trade. Nor would the moderate leftists commit themselves to a radical land-reform program, as the Communists did.

One last notable difference in outlook among the parties in opposition concerned defense and the military. The highly militaristic Jana

Sangh party manifesto not only favored a hard line toward Pakistan and China and (with the Praja Socialist Party) the development of nuclear weapons, it also stressed a powerful, well-financed military establishment. Several times the military were given special mention, and an entire volume of their basic party documents was devoted to defense and external affairs. The Jana Sangh's military-defense posture differed markedly from most other opposition parties on both sides.

At election time, differences on policy and ideological questions were compounded by personal rivalries in the various state constituencies and by clashes resulting from caste, linguistic, and regional animosities. Because of the inability of candidates to reconcile their differences once they had been elected to legislative seats and offices, many of the coalition state governments headed by opposition parties fell. In terms of ideology, programs, or action, these parties contributed nothing positive to the goal of political unity and stability; nor, while in office, did they uphold democratic values in the pursuit of their political strategies. Opposition governments were characterized by political indiscipline and cabinet instability time and again as legislators crossed from the government side to the opposition Congress in various state legislatures. More often, they defected to form their own parties. By the end of 1967, one out of every ten state legislators had changed party loyalties since the general elections ten months before. Some had done so more than once, and at least one had the dubious distinction of having done so five times in forty-eight hours. Although numerically the largest number of defectors were from the Congress party, the proportion of non-Congress legislators switching loyalties was about the same.

Typical of the problems faced by the newly elected state governments made up of opposition parties were those arising in the states of Uttar Pradesh (U.P.), Bihar, and West Bengal—respectively, the first, second, and fourth largest states in the union and the three largest in northern India: they contain 35 percent of the total population. The U.P. and Bihar are among the poorest, and West Bengal is one of the most highly industrialized states in India.

In 1967, the ruling party in New Delhi lost the largest state in the nation; Uttar Pradesh was the home state of Nehru, Shastri, and Indira Gandhi and had always been a Congress stronghold. It is a pivotal state in Indian politics; by virtue of its population (in 1971, 88 million) it returns the largest number of legislators to Parliament. Thus, to the extent its members act as a unit, it can substantially weaken or strengthen the ability of the ruling party to crucial legislation, especially in the area of agriculture. Although it is by far the largest producer of foodgrains in the country, and an exporter of some products, it is also among the poorer states, and thus its politics are potentially volatile. The turbulent nature of U.P. politics is exacerbated by the communal problem. Its Hindu community is known for its strong attachment to religion and language; and the presence of a large Urdu-speaking, Muslim minority means that Hindu-Muslim confrontations are frequent.

It is not wholly surprising, then, that within a few months of taking power, dissensions erupted between and within the constituent parties of the U.P. United Front government. Some members of the Swatantra resigned to protest their party's anti-Arab stand (during the six-day war between Israel and the Arab states).[21] Subsequently the Swatantra withdrew from the government, charging it lacked unity of purpose. Just three months later (in January 1968), it returned, in support of the chief minister's firm handling of student lawlessness over recognition of Urdu as a second regional language. On the other hand, the Jana Sangh supported the students' opposition to the measure and threatened to withdraw from the coalition if such a language policy were implemented. Leftist elements in the coalition created further discord by demanding the reduction or abolition of land revenue on small holdings.

These dissensions soon led to the resignation of the chief minister, Charan Singh (later home minister in the Janata party government and reportedly one of the more powerful members of the party). Among the reasons for quitting, he cited his knowledge that some constituent parties were planning to seize public lands illegally; he also noted that some members of the United Front were openly condemning the administration of which they were a part. With his resignation in February 1968, the United Front broke up, and Uttar Pradesh came under the rule of the central government.

Similar instability characterized the United Front government of Bihar—the second largest state of the union (population then roughly 56 million) and the poorest of all. This state spawned a number of the leaders who led the opposition to the Congress government in 1974–1975. Jayaprakash Narayan, the former Socialist leader who, in 1974, called for "total revolution," hails from Bihar, as does the present minister of defense. Jagjivan Ram (who almost became Prime Minister in 1977). In 1967, Bihar was the only state in which most of the national opposition parties had enough strength to be represented in the coalition.

In Bihar too, the opposition parties were hopelessly divided. One of the major issues (as in the U.P.) was the status of Urdu as a second language. The Jana Sangh took up its usual role as an opponent of Urdu; the deputy chief minister refused to attend United Front coordination committee meetings unless the Jana Sangh gave up its anti-Urdu policy. During the first quarter of 1968, Bihar was engulfed in one of its worst episodes of communal rioting, and most of the people killed were Muslims. The army had to be called in when it became evident that organized attacks were being carried out against Muslims. In June 1968, President's Rule was introduced after the fall of three successive governments in six months. That same month, after the disorders had spread to several states, the National Integration Council was revived and met in Srinagar, Kashmir, to review the situation and recommend action.

Unlike Bihar and Uttar Pradesh, which were preoccupied with communal issues after the 1967 elections, West Bengal—one of the most industrially advanced states—experienced massive economic unrest. It was governed by a coalition that brought together both right- and left-wing Communists in a government led by a former Congressman who had formed his own party. After prolonged and sharp internal dissensions over industrial and agrarian issues, this ministry fell. Its Congress successor was beset with political and socioeconomic disruptions led by the former United Front parties.

The year 1968, then, was marked by debilitating dissent and schisms in the United Front governments—in the three important states discussed here and in the remaining five that had come under non-Congress rule. The conduct of both rank-and-file and leaders in the various coalition parties was hardly designed to either uphold democratic values or promote the cause of unity and stability. Merger negotiations among major opposition parties, which had been opened again in the spring of 1969, broke down by summer. Further impetus to such negotiations was furnished in the latter half of 1969, when the split between the right and left wings of the Congress party afforded the opposition another promising opportunity to forge a well-polarized system of two or even three parties. But once again, leaders failed to do so. Disillusionment engendered by the events of 1968 had by now taken deep root among some leaders who had become skeptical about the viability of the party system itself. Mistrust of one another led to cynicism and made negotiations futile. The founder of the Swatantra said in 1968: "We have had enough of political parties. Wherever else this system may have done well, it is not doing well in India, and will not do better as time goes on but will get worse and worse."[22] In the same year, Jayaprakash Narayan repeated his earlier exhortations for a partyless democracy. A decade earlier, he had expressed his firm belief in the possibility of a partyless democracy. Beginning with a system of indirect elections for local village and district bodies, the system would be extended to the state and finally to the central level. He pleaded with all the parties to "agree that as far as the village panchayats (councils) are concerned, as far as local boards and district boards are concerned, as far as municipalities are concerned—including the biggest municipalities . . . there shall be no party system introduced."[23]

Such was, in 1968, the judgment of respected leaders about the working of the party system in India—Congressmen as well as opposition leaders. None of their programs were suited to advancing the goals of social justice or economic growth; if anything, the parties of the Right (particularly the Jana Sangh and Swatantra) were headed away from such goals. In spite of their many divisions over a great variety of issues, we can begin to see early signs of a coalescence of conservative leaders and parties. Most of the parties that were later to come together joined hands in 1967 to propose Jayaprakash Narayan as president of India. Eight years later, he was one of the principal spokesmen of a conservative coalition (although, paradoxically, he would be the first to disavow any claims to a conservative outlook). The only party that opposed Narayan's candidacy was the Jana Sangh, whose belief in a unitary system of government had been sharply and consistently criticized by Narayan as "fascistic." No doubt he was also thought to be too sympathetic to the Muslims and inclined toward friendship with Pakistan. (The Jana Sangh also opposed the nomination of a Muslim candidate for vice-president.) In the end, the compromise presidential candidate, on whom all noncommunist opposition parties agreed, was a man who, until shortly before, had been chief justice of the Supreme Court and had led the majority judgment in a ruling that decreed that Parliament had no authority to take away or abridge by constitutional amendment any of the fundamental rights guaranteed by the constitution, particularly the right to private property.

The nomination of the justice is indicative of the conservative opposition's paramount concern for fundamental rights, by which it meant, in particular, property rights. There was no ambiguity about this position, nor about the class interests represented when the Swatantra election pledge singled out for repeal the seventeenth amendment (passed in 1964), according to which land reforms were not to be deemed void on the ground that they were inconsistent with the fundamental rights provision protecting the right to private property.[24]

This emphasis on fundamental rights by conservative parties and on the "fostering of individual interest" is akin to early English liberal theory, which had propounded that the state's only function was that of policeman among conflicting interests. But the Swatantra did not claim to derive its theories from Western philosophy. Rather, it sought sanction for its ideals in the Gandhian principle of "trusteeship," which was basically utopian, paternalistic, and feudalistic in nature. As perceived by the Swatantra, the state's main function was to "foster and utilise the sense of moral obligation, the pride, satisfaction and fulfillment felt by individuals in serving others."[25] It is true that Gandhi shared the anarchist's fear of the violence inherent in state power. "The state," he said, "represents violence in a concentrated and organised form." Hence, he preferred to accommodate himself to the violence inherent in capitalist exploitation, which was, presumably, not so concentrated nor so well organized. Believing that the use of violence by the state would only recoil in violence, he sought to achieve his goals by persuasion. If the capitalist could be re-educated, it would not be necessary to destroy him; for the evil was not in the accumulation of capital as such but in the manner of its use: "The rich man does not keep back meat from the poor by retaining his riches, but by basely using them. Riches are a form of strength; and a strong man does not injure others by keeping his strength, but by using it injuriously. . . . The fortitude and intelligence which acquire riches are intended, by the Giver of both, not to scatter, nor to give away, but to employ those riches in the service of mankind."[26] Sentiments such as this greatly endeared Gandhi to the conservatives.

But the Swatantra cited only a small part of Gandhi's formula of trusteeship, which was in essence an attempt to deal with the injustice, inequalities, and violence attending the ownership of property and capital. Though committed to nonviolence, Gandhi was equally persuaded that the ownership of capital represented a form of violence and exploitation and that, ultimately, capitalist institutions would have to be abolished. Believing in the infinite malleability of people and their ultimate goodness, Gandhi said back in 1934: "Those who own money now are asked to behave like the trustees holding their riches on behalf of the poor." In 1940, his last and most authoritative conception of the trusteeship theory, however, again explicitly rejected capitalism. While reaffirming his faith that "human nature is never beyond redemption," he went on to say that trusteeship "does not recognise any right of private ownership of property except so far as it may be permitted by society for its own welfare." Here, for the first time, Gandhi accepted the need for state-regulated trusteeship and recognized "social necessity" rather than "personal whim" as the prime determinant of the character of production. While he did not want to acknowledge in principle the propriety of violence, he understood that such violence was a reality and, under certain conditions, inevitable. Thus he said: "A non-violent system of government is clearly an impossibility so long as the wide gulf between the rich and the hungry millions persists." It was in this context that he predicted a "violent and bloody revolution."[27] Clearly, he subscribed to the socialist goal of a classless egalitarian society but not to the Marxist formulation of the philosophy. His brand of socialism was to be found in the *Gita*, he said: "It means that we may not own anything beyond our strict requirement but should share equally with all god's creatures the means of subsistence. ... To have a personal bank account would thus be incompatible with this ideal."[28] Such ideas were a far cry from the brand of "Gandhism" parties like the Swatantra promoted.

Nor did the conservatives' emphasis on the individual accord with their own emphasis on dharma as the superior moral law guiding man and giving primacy to the social good over that of the individual. Indeed, one of India's founding fathers, commenting during the constitutional debates on the right to property and its relation to the concept of dharma, remarked that: "Our ancients never regarded the institution of property as an end in itself. Property exists for *dharma. Dharma* and the duty which the individual owes to the society form the whole basis of social framework. *Dharma* is the law of social well-being and varies from *yuga* to *yuga* (i.e., age to age). Capitalism as it is practised in the west came in the wake of the Industrial Revolution and is alien to the root idea of our civilisation. The sole end of property is *yagna* and to serve a social purpose."[29] The "Gandhian" politicians, therefore, who challenged Indira Gandhi as self-proclaimed successors to the Mahatma bear little resemblance to the man or his philosophy.[30]

Whether Gandhian or not, conservative elements opposed several of Indira Gandhi's efforts to erase vestiges of feudatory rights and to regulate capital and landed property resources. In this, they found a staunch ally in the judiciary. But the weak link in the government's armor was the presidency, which became a prime target of the conservative opposition's strategy (both inside and outside Congress) to block the efforts of the prime minister and her allies, which might undermine conservatives' interests and those of their constituents.

Opposition Strategies—A Blow to Socialism

The issues discussed during the 1967 election campaigns for Parliament, the state legislatures, and the presidency had much in common with those raised by the Supreme Court decision of February 27, 1967 (the Golaknath decision). It stated that Parliament was not empowered to revoke or abridge by constitutional amendment any of the fundamental rights guaranteed by the constitution. (The right in question was that of private property.) This decision and the issues debated in the presidential elections that followed it had ramifications for economic policy, especially for a leadership committed to economic change. They also raised questions about the political supremacy of the president and the judiciary, on one side, and the prime minister and her government, on the other.

Similar issues had surfaced many years earlier when Nehru was prime minister. Like his daughter, Prime Minister Nehru's efforts to implement economic and social reforms were constrained by the courts. But unlike his daughter, he took no firm measures to break loose of the courts' constraints, although he did try to assure his supremacy vis-à-vis the president. He was concerned enough about this question to discreetly ask his attorney-general for an opinion; but, so as not to magnify a touchy issue, he chose not to discuss it publicly.[31] Nehru and other interpreters of constitutional powers viewed the president as a nominal head of state—analogous to the British monarch. Others, including the first president of India, Dr. Rajendra Prasad, believed that the president did in law, and should in fact, enjoy substantial powers. This tug-of-war continued during the two five-year terms of the first president and was intensified during the term of the second president, the well-known philosopher Dr. S. Radhakrishnan. He was still in office when Indira Gandhi came to power. In those earlier years, however, the power and popularity of Nehru and the Congress party were great enough to act as constraints upon the Supreme Court and the president. By the time Gandhi became prime minister such constraints had been considerably weakened.

Other important political events preceded and followed the Golaknath ruling. Although it cannot be said that the decision was influenced by the results of the general elections (held just a week earlier), it certainly did sharpen the political and economic issues raised by the defeat of the Congress party in the states and its weakening at the center. The Congress was debilitated not only by its electoral reverses but also by the wrangling that, as bad as it was before the elections, now became even more intense as leaders argued over the causes of the debacle. A short time later presidential elections contributed still further to the political strains—both within the party and with the opposition parties. These developments made it inadvisable for Gandhi to risk confrontation with the courts over the issue of supremacy. (Later she was prepared to confront the judiciary and the other forces she perceived as obstacles to her programs.)

By the 1960s, it was clear to most impartial observers that the Supreme Court was the most effective shelter of businessmen and big landlords.[32] Nearly as many reforms had been declared invalid by the Indian Supreme Court in a decade and a half than in all of American constitutional history. One study indicated that in a majority of cases involving land reforms, business regulation, and expansion of the public sector the business classes and the landlords (rural and urban) were in litigation with the government; and over 40 percent of these cases were decided in their favor.[33] It has been suggested that the conservatism of the court's decisions stemmed from the nineteenth-century economic philosophies of most of the judges, which closely resemble the political and economic outlooks of the conservative Jana Sangh and Swatantra parties. Chief Justice K. Subba Rao, who expounded the majority view in the controversial decision, has been described as "the most inveterate, intractable libertarian on the Court" and an "archetype classical (19th century) liberal."[34]

It is difficult to refute the contention that since independence the courts' tendency has been to defend the status quo in the name of fundamental rights. However, the language of the constitution itself has probably made possible the conservative interpretation of the provisions pertaining to the government's economic and social power, on the one hand, and the individual's fundamental rights, on the other. Though citizens can seek relief through state and federal courts in cases involving their individual fundamental rights, they may not do so in cases that involve more general conditions of social justice—such as the right to work. A separate part (Part IV) of the constitution enumerates the latter rights under the title "Directive Principles of State Policy." These instruct the state to "direct its policy toward securing—(a) that the citizens, men and women equally have the right to an adequate means of livelihood; (b) that the ownership and control of the material resources of the community are so distributed as best to subserve the common good; (c) that the operation of the economic system does not result in the concentration of wealth and means of production to the common detriment," and, in general, toward securing benefits for the social welfare. The state is also enjoined to secure for its citizens the right to work, education, and public assistance, "within the limits of its economic capacity and development." In short, this chapter is as close to a complete statement of socialist goals as the founding fathers were prepared to make.[35] Though Nehru himself favored a less ambiguous espousal of socialist doctrine, he was, as usual, more concerned with achieving harmony and consensus among members of the Constituent Assembly that shaped India's constitution between 1947 and 1949. Thus he said: "If, in accordance with my own desire, I had put in that we want a socialist state, we would have put in something which may be agreeable to many and may not be agreeable to some and we wanted this Resolution [the Objectives Resolution] not to be controversial in regard to such matters. Therefore, we have laid down, not theoretical words and formulae, but rather the content of the things we desire."[36] On the other hand, the chairman of the committee that drafted the constitution rightly foresaw (as did others) that there would be difficulties if a clear statement of India's economic and social ideology was not made. He noted during the debate that he expected the Objectives Resolution (and by extension the constitution) "to state in most explicit terms that in order that there may be social and economic justice in this country, there would be nationalisation of industry and nationalisation of land. I do not understand how it could be possible for any future Government which believes in doing justice, socially, economically, and politically, unless its economy is a socialistic economy."[37]

Nonetheless, neither the preamble to the constitution nor the Directive Principles of State Policy contain a clear statement of socialist goals; and political and judicial neglect of the high-sounding ideals embodied in the directive principles was further assured by an article directing that these principles "shall not be enforceable by any court" (Article 37). The framers' efforts to ensure the respect and implementation of these social goals included a phrase sanctioning them as "fundamental in the governance of the country" and directing the state, as a matter of duty, "to apply these principles in making laws."

Nevertheless, at the very first test of their "fundamental" nature, the Supreme Court held that these principles were "subsidiary" to the individual's fundamental rights. In the 1967 decision, Chief Justice K. Subba Rao went further and vested the fundamental rights with a "transcendental" nature that, in effect, rendered them entirely beyond the reach of the amending power of Parliament. Elsewhere he said that "the concept of fundamental rights is rooted in the doctrine of natural law."[38] This accorded closely with the view expressed by Swatantra and Jana Sangh leaders during the 1967 election campaign—that dharma, as the law of God, is superior to manmade laws. It will be recalled that the Swatantra had specifically singled out for repeal amendments that had "abridged or taken away" the fundamental right to private property.

Other interpreters of the constitution have challenged such a conservative view, noting that the "natural-law" theory, which is derived from religious philosophical principles, contradicts the logic of the constitution (particularly Articles 27 and 30). The latter affirm the secular nature of the Indian state and proclaim its duty to abolish manmade injustices (such as untouchability) through manmade laws.

Given the views of Chief Justice Subba Rao, we are not surprised that the leaders of the conservative opposition chose him as their candidate for president of India in 1967 (even though the Jana Sangh's election manifesto pledged that retired judges would "not be eligible for appointment to any governmental post"). The presidency, though an elective post, was vested with great political significance; and Rao's resignation from the Supreme Court less than a month before the presidential election (and three months before he was due to retire as chief justice) marked a departure from the tradition that barred former members of the judiciary, especially chief justices, from politics.

Although it appears that the concept of a socialist state was not agreeable to some members of the original Constituent Assembly,[39] there seems to have been considerable agreement about the meaning of "socioeconomic justice." For almost all, it meant rejection of the existing social structure, the "remaking" of material conditions, and the transition from "serfdom to freedom." However, the effect of the 1967 decision was to strengthen the economic status quo, especially in the rural areas, and to hinder Parliament's efforts to remake material conditions. Thus were all the economic rights guaranteed to the individual as fundamental rendered meaningless to the poor. For a new social order could only be brought about peacefully through the legislative process— by means of the kind of laws and amendments that had been enacted since independence. By denying the government the safety valve of legislation and amendment with reference to fundamental rights, the Supreme Court rendered change incompatible with democratic procedure.

Once it had been decided that the fundamental rights were transcendental and thus eternal, it followed inevitably that all the land-reform legislation passed since the early fifties was null and void, along with the amendments that had given them legal sanction. Indeed, Chief Justice Rao ruled specifically that the first, fourth, and seventeenth (land-reform) amendments were in principle unconstitutional. He recognized, however, that a retrospective ruling would have a chaotic impact on society and the national economy; he therefore declared that "our decisions will not affect the validity of the Constitution (17th Amendment) Act, 1964 or other amendments made to the Constitution taking away or abridging the fundamental rights."[40] The ruling would have only prospective effect. Of course, the chief justice contradicted his own logic and the principle on which he based his decision; for if fundamental rights are eternal and transcendental (and may not be violated under any circumstances), the "spurious" first, fourth, and seventeenth amendments which give sanction to wrongful actions, ought to be struck down.

The decision thus brought into high relief the conflict between individual liberty (guaranteed by the fundamental rights) and the welfare of the common man (sanctioned by the directive principles). The efforts of the framers to place civil and economic liberties on the same plane were thwarted: (1) because they were not prepared to make the directive principles subject to the judicial process, as were the fundamental rights; (2) because the Supreme Court's judgment ignored the Constituent Assembly debates, which made clear the framers' intent that both the fundamental rights and the directive principles should be of equal weight; and (3) because it ignored its own construction of the provisions in the fundamental rights and directive principles chapters—that is, that they constituted an "integrated scheme," which implies that the fundamental rights ought to be read with reference to the directive principles (and vice versa).

The significance of the various arguments made by the justices who concurred in the majority opinion was that the rights of the common man and the public good were rendered subservient to the liberties of the individual. One of the basic principles of socialism was thereby nullified. Henceforth, by judicial sanction, the rights of the few would be protected against those of many; for it goes without saying that the poor and largely illiterate masses could not afford the fees of lawyers to defend their cases (or even to advise them), nor the expense of traveling to the state or national capital to be present at the defense of their cases. Even if they could, they would understand very little, for the proceedings in the highest tribunal of the land were carried on in English. Finally, the Golaknath ruling signaled to all concerned that such crucial matters of public policy would henceforth be left in the hands of the appointed judiciary, which had shown itself insensitive to larger public needs. The only recourse left to the poor to bring about social and economic reform was thus the political process, through which they could at least express their displeasure with their elected leaders. We have noted, however, that the political process has lent itself more easily to manipulation by the privileged classes than to the pinpricks of a poverty-stricken electorate whose common economic and social interests are diffused among a myriad of group identities.

The Conservatives Emerge from the Shadows

Only about two years after the Golaknath ruling, almost the same scenario was enacted; the result was a further coalescence of conservative forces as the right wing of the Congress party joined the opposition. Also in 1969, the Supreme Court once again challenged Indira Gandhi's social- and economic-reform policies; and, yet again, the issue of presidential/prime ministerial supremacy was raised. What finally precipitated the party split was the scheduling of another presidential election, necessitated by the sudden death of President Zakir Husain (who had been elected in 1967). The dimensions of this conflict were most visible during Nehru's tenure, when, significantly, Gandhi was, as her father's confidante, privy to all the "palace intrigues."

The president's boldest effort to weaken the prime minister came in 1963, according to an "inside story" written by an aide-de-camp of President Radhakrishnan. According to this account, the president attempted to secure Nehru's resignation through a plan sponsored by the Congress president and later implemented by the prime minister (minus one important segment). The Kamaraj Plan, as it was informally dubbed after the Congress president, called for all cabinet ministers (including the prime minister) to resign and undertake organizational work among the people—in order to strengthen the Congress, whose image had been badly mauled by the nation's defeat at the hands of China in 1962. The scheme was reportedly concocted at the president's instance. According to the scenario, Kamaraj would tell Nehru that Radhakrishnan would accept all the resignations except that of Nehru, who would be asked to form another government and carry on. This plan, however, was to be only a ruse to get Nehru out: "as soon as Nehru tendered his resignation, the President would accept it, thus ejecting him from the seat of power."[41] It is a fantastic tale, and it strains credulity, given the reputations for integrity of both Radhakrishnan and Kamaraj. All that can be said about it for certain is that, after this time, the relationship between Nehru and Radhakrishnan was very, very strained. On the other hand, Kamaraj, who reportedly revealed the plot to Nehru, became quite close to the prime minister.[42]

Even though all the details of the story may not be true, it is well known that strains existed between Nehru and both the presidents who served during his years as prime minister. Although to date there have been no open confrontations between the holders of these two positions, there has been prolonged debate about the constitutional question. Opposed to Nehru's view (which he shared with many others) that the president is a figurehead required to act on the advice of the Council of Ministers, is a second position that the president's oath to "protect and defend the Constitution" vests in him the "Executive power of the Union." According to this view he is the guardian of the constitution and may, if he so chooses, assume great powers within the broad limits set down by the constitution.

A book by the late K. M. Munshi,[43] an erudite member and ideologue of the Swatantra party, expounded the conservative view that the president was not bound to accept the advice tendered by the Council of Ministers and argued that some of the president's powers are in effect supraministerial. They can be exercised at the president's discretion to dismiss a ministry that has lost Parliament's confidence, dissolve the lower house if he thinks it has lost the people's confidence, and serve as the supreme commander in an emergency—in the event that the Council of Ministers has not acted to defend the country.

Such an interpretation clearly allows great discretionary powers for the president—indeed it makes him something of a potential autocrat. A president inclined to assert his position in the manner outlined by Munshi could create a grave constitutional crisis. The office of the president, then, is a political powderkeg. Its incumbent can be a strong alternative source of power, but any attempt to exercise such power could lead to a political explosion between the president and the prime minister. Moreover, it is safe to say that in the present system any prime minister so challenged would use all the many resources of the office to squelch defiance on the part of the president.

The presidency and the split Against this background, we can view the 1969 struggle over the presidential nominations. Cracks in the Congress structure were already evident in 1967, and these had deepened in 1968. The Congress had approached the February 1967 elections in a state of disharmony, and many Congressmen had defected right after the elections. Members of the Congress high command blamed each other for the electoral failure while disagreeing about whom to nominate for president when Radhakrishnan's term expired in May. For the first time, the Congress could not be sure that its candidate would be elected, as the recent elections had earned it only a 2 percent majority in the electoral college. With opposition governments in several states and factions rending the party, Gandhi could not afford to have a president whose loyalty was in doubt.

Normally the vice-president would have been selected as the Congress nominee without any fuss; he was Zakir Husain, a Muslim. Gandhi felt that he was the best candidate, but the old guard, according to her, thought people were not yet ready to accept a Muslim. It was reported elsewhere that Radhakrishnan himself stressed the element of risk in nominating a Muslim. He suggested a plan (suspiciously like the 1963 scheme) in which he would be nominated again but would resign after six months, enabling Husain to step into the office without having to face a risky contest. But Gandhi refused to fall in with this plan. (She was convinced even then that the old guard wanted her out; and "when Dr. Husain died, they decided to take this as their opportunity to oust me.") She claimed they baulked her all the way and talked against her behind her back; she said that Kamaraj (like Radhakrishnan, a southerner and a Hindu) held evening press conferences to criticize her. She stuck to her decision, in spite of considerable pressure, and won out in the end; Zakir Husain became president of India. But he died two years later, and the old controversy flared up once again.

Another source of contention in 1967 was a resolution adopted by the Congress in June. Morarji Desai and other conservatives had been unhappy with a program that, as originally proposed by the left wing, sought to nationalize large commercial banks. Desai threatened to resign then if the party adopted or tried to implement any program of bank nationalization. Later in 1969, he did resign from the cabinet—immediately after Indira Gandhi had unceremoniously dismissed him as finance minister and three days before she announced her bank nationalization policy.

Desai's resignation was but one event in a mighty struggle for power among rival policy groups in the Congress. No doubt to some extent the split reflected the clash of personalities—in particular those of the prime minister and her finance minister. But interpreting it as merely a personal spat or as a naked struggle for power, slights or ignores altogether the philosophical outlooks of the two sides. Nor does it do to say that Gandhi had no philosophy whatever—that is mistaking the lack of a clear and specific *articulation* of philosophy with no philosophy at all. To appreciate the conflict it is necessary to look briefly at the sequence of events that led to the party split.

In the spring of 1969, signs of the impending division were clearly evident. At the seventy-second session of Congress, the president of the party, S. Nijalingappa, made a speech in which he publicly criticized (by implication) long-standing policies of the government and the prime minister. His stand on some issues was similar to those of the conservative opposition parties. For example, he echoed the Jana Sangh's position on linguistic policy: "We should *do away with these linguistic states* and reorganize the country on an essentially economic basis." More important, his economic position was decidedly at variance with that of the government and paralleled the views expressed by Swatantra and Jana Sangh spokesmen. Even as he spoke, the government was preparing a bill to curb the concentration of economic power in monopolies and prohibit restrictive trade practices. Yet the Congress president averred: "it is a fact that monopolies in industry are growing. It is no use our crying hoarse against these monopolistic tendencies. What we have to consider is how best we can control the growth of monopolies without detriment to industrial development. . . . *I believe that industries, by whomsoever established, should be encouraged.* If private industries misbehaved or made undue profits, they can both be punished and controlled *through fiscal measures.*" He went on to criticize the management of some industries in the public sector. Finally, he was critical of the practice of granting licenses for production or import, a system on which the Government had long relied to regulate production and external trade, with a view to encouraging some domestic industries and discouraging others. The Congress President, however, said: "Where there are controls and licensing, there is always corruption and the sooner we do away with licensing and controls the better it would be."[44] In recommending (as the Swatantra and Jana Sangh parties did) that "fiscal measures" be used to regulate private industries if they "made undue profits," he was saying in just so many words that the government's bill was improper and should be dropped. None of these policy statements had been cleared with the head of the government. Indira Gandhi's speech at the same session was in direct contradiction to the policies enunciated by the party president.

This skirmish between the prime minister and the party president was vested with greater significance by the death of the Indian president on May 3. Barely a week afterward, Syndicate leader S. K. Patil won a by-election in Bombay and promptly announced his intention to start "doing things" and "turning a few tables."[45]

The stage was now set for the fateful All-India Congress Committee (AICC) meeting, held in July 1969 in the provincial capital of Bangalore. The prime minister arrived a day late, but she had sent all members a note setting forth a ten-point program of economic reform—an extended version of the 1967 Ten-Point Programme. In her economic message, Gandhi asked members to consider, among other things, the nationalization of "the top five or six banks or issue directions that the resources of banks should be reserved to a larger extent for public purposes."[46] Her suggestions were approved by the Working Committee of the party on July 11 and by the AICC on July 13. (This was a much milder program than the one she undertook just twenty days later, but other events had transpired in the interim.) On July 12, three days after her economic note was sent to members and one day after the Working Committee approved it, the Congress Parliamentary Board (the highest nominating body), which was controlled by members of the Syndicate, named Sanjivva Reddy as the party's candidate for president.[47]

This was a significant action in the larger context because of rival political leaders' expectations that after the next national election (in 1972) the presidency would become a particularly strategic post— giving the party or faction whose candidate was elected to it a distinct advantage. The defeat suffered by the Congress party in 1967, if re-peated in 1972, could change the composition of the Lok Sabha enough to provide an opportunity for the president to act independently or ally himself with the opposition (a Congress faction or an opposition party). The fear of some (and the hope of others) that he might bypass the Council of Ministers (and the prime minister) was fed by the uncer-tainty about the president's constitutional prerogatives—especially in a political crisis. For the prime minister the reality of such a danger was signaled, perhaps inadvertently, by a younger and less experienced Member of Parliament, Tarkeshwari Sinha, who was said to be a sup-porter of Morarji Desai. In a news article she hinted quite broadly that once Reddy was in the presidency, efforts would be made to oust the prime minister.

Gandhi acted swiftly. On the following day (July 13), Acting Presi-dent V. V. Giri, who had been persuaded to support the prime minister, announced his candidacy for the presidency as an independent. On the sixteenth, Gandhi stripped Desai of the Finance portfolio. Three days later, she announced the nationalization (by presidential order) of four-teen top commercial banks; and within two more days, a bill had been introduced for the nationalization of the banks.

Although Gandhi had earlier assented to Reddy's candidacy and re-frained from publicly supporting Giri, she indirectly indicated Giri as her choice by asking members of the Congress parliamentary party to "vote their conscience." Had she not done this, her position would have been untenable. The parliamentary strength of the Congress had been considerably whittled down by the 1967 elections; and her leadership of the party was now under siege. With a hostile resident ensconced in the president's house, any number of situations could arise (or be fabricated) whereby the president, guided by the Syndicate, could engineer her downfall. Just such a plan had already been reported in the press. Moreover, it was common knowledge that secret negotiations were being held between Syndicate leaders and top figures in the major opposition parties; their purpose, it was rumored, was to work out a scheme of collaboration during the elections for president and vice-president.

If indeed Syndicate members had made a deal whereby, for example, the Congress candidate for vice-president would yield to his opposition counterpart in return for opposition support of Reddy, they would be in violation of two counts of party discipline: (1) "deliberately acting or carrying on propaganda against the programmes and decisions of the Congress"; and (2) "deliberately acting in a way calculated to lower the prestige of the Congress or carrying on propaganda against Congress Committees or office-bearers thereof."[48] That there actually was such a breach of discipline seems quite plausible, although the evidence is circumstantial. At least two of the opposition parties (the Swatantra and the Dravida Munnetra Kazagaham) announced their decision to give their second preference vote to Reddy; and indeed an overwhelming majority of those who voted for the opposition candidate, C. D. Deshmukh, gave second preference to Sanjivva Reddy. According to Deshmukh, this was the clear expectation of the opposition leadership: "During the conversations that were held between Charan Singh (BKD leader) and myself, I had made it clear that I had no views or wishes with regard to the second preference votes of my backers. . . . *The expectation was that they would go to Sanjivva Reddy,* but obviously Charan Singh was apprehensive that an appreciable portion would go to V. V. Giri. . . . An analysis of voting made by the Swatantra Party after the election disclosed that there had been betrayals by party members."[49] In other words, although members of the opposition were instructed to give their second preference to Reddy, enough of them went over to Giri to tip the scales in his favor.

On the other hand, if Gandhi had publicly worked against the official Congress nominee, she too would have been in breach of discipline, though this type of political activity is usually carried on "in camera." In any case, the question of discipline became academic by November, when the Working Committee, the body empowered to exercise discipline, split evenly—ten members meeting under the leadership of Gandhi and the remaining ten under that of Nijalingappa, who remained president of the Syndicate half of the Working Committee.

In the meantime, V. V. Giri was elected president on August 20 by a narrow margin. He won the support of a fairly large number of Congress MPs who remained loyal to Gandhi and of most MPs from the leftist parties. (As a long-time trade unionist, he commanded the respect of union-supported parties.) Within less than three months, rival sessions of the Congress Working Committee were meeting in New Delhi. The conservative faction "expelled" Indira Gandhi from party membership, while her faction affirmed their confidence in her leadership. On November 16, the conservatives formed a new party in Parliament, the Congress Organization, and elected their own parliamentary leaders; the prime minister's faction did likewise. The split was now final.

Conservative realignment and the judiciary A virtually parallel development was taking place in the Supreme Court. Decisions invalidating two of the prime minister's policies—one of economic and the other of symbolic importance—were handed down. The conservative opposition, determined to reverse the government's bank nationalization plan, again found in the Supreme Court a staunch confederate.[50] On July 22, 1969, the court granted a limited stay of the president's Banking Ordinance. A short time later (September 8), after both houses of Parliament had translated the nationalization decree into law, a similar stay was issued. In the final ruling in February 1970 the court declared the bank nationalization act unconstitutional.

Prior to this time there had been a good deal of debate in various public forums (and within the Congress) about the lopsided distribution of credit; the banks favored industry, particularly the larger, monopolistic concerns. Desai himself had acknowledged this in a statement to the Lok Sabha in December 1967: "Historically, the banks in our country have been started by industrial and business houses, and they have close traditional links with them. The boards of directors consist of industrialists and businessmen; small-scale industries, agriculture, and other sectors of our economic life have hardly any influence in the overall credit decisions taken by the banks. A good proportion of advances is given to directors and the concerns in which they are interested."[51] Because of the low level of savings in the country—the result of general poverty—it was a matter of vital importance to mobilize scarce capital resources to provide adequate credit to those without the collateral required by the large banks. One economist reported that in 1967 as much as 57 percent of the total credit allocated by the fourteen banks nationalized in 1969 had been allocated to big industrialists;

another 19.4 percent had gone to trade and commerce; and 10.2 percent had been advanced as personal loans. Small-scale industry had received 6.6 percent of the funds loaned by these banks. The smallest proportion—.4 of 1 percent—had gone to agriculture; in 1969 Desai's scheme of "social control" (discussed below) had raised the share of agriculture to only 2 percent. By 1972, following first implementation of "social control" and then bank nationalization, the share of agriculture and other "neglected sectors"—small-scale industry, road transport, and retail and small businesses in the rural areas—had arisen to 26.1 percent of total credit extended.[52]

In 1967, however, Desai opposed the nationalization scheme; he felt that "social control" would accomplish the same purpose and threatened to resign if it was interpreted as nationalization. The latter was the interpretation advanced by more leftist elements in the Congress and was the popular understanding of the term. Desai's alternative proposal—the Banking Laws (Amendment) Act—was enacted in 1968. It reconstituted the boards of directors of banks in such a way as to give representation to specialists in fields like accountancy, agriculture, banking, finance, and rural economy. In addition, a high-level body (the National Credit Council) was set up to "assess the demand for bank credit from various sectors, determine priorities for granting loans and advances, and coordinate lending and investment policies." The banks continued to select their own personnel (subject to appropriate skills) and to make their own decisions on lending and investment policy. The government could issue directives on questions of policy, but they would not be binding.

Desai's scheme was superseded by the nationalization act, which was passed under protest from the Swatantra and Jana Sangh. It brought the banks' assets and policymaking under direct government control. The boards of directors were replaced by an advisory board, which would function until new boards could be constituted.[53]

Since Nehru's time, when Desai had also held the powerful Finance portfolio, he had been known as the strongest proponent of conservative policies. He had often come into conflict with Nehru because of his views and his highly authoritarian style. Later he clashed with the leftists in the Congress who supported Gandhi's election in 1966 and 1967.

The division between right and left wings of the party had first come to a head when the first "Ten-Point Programme" resolution (passed in

New Delhi in June 1967) was discussed at an AICC meeting. It had been ratified under the urgings of younger leftist leaders, who saw it as a means of refurbishing the discredited image of the Congress as a conservative and even reactionary party. However, the best they could do, as far as incorporating progressive content and language, was to accept Desai's formula, "social control of the banking institutions." Another part of the resolution was a decision to "examine and take steps to remove" the "privileges and privy purses enjoyed by the exrulers" as "incongruous to the concept and practice of democracy."[54]

Consideration of the measures to abolish the princes' privileges began with the reversal Congress suffered in the February elections. The defeat was widely interpreted by the press and other nongovernment observers—particularly left-wing members of the Congress—as a repudiation of the Syndicate. In 1966 and 1967, when Indira Gandhi was elected prime minister, Desai and the Syndicate were still at odds with each other. Later, however, as concern with her more radical policies became increasingly pronounced, the two conservative forces were united.

After the Congress party had approved it, the scheme to abolish privy purses was accepted by the cabinet, which then notified the princes and asked for their cooperation in working out the details. The Law Ministry, which was asked to consider the legality and constitutionality of the measure, expressed the opinion that there were no legal or constitutional bars to the step. Yet, despite the resolution of the AICC, the cabinet's endorsement, and the Law Ministry's clearance, Desai, though he accepted the decisions as binding on him as deputy prime minister, stated publicly that he personally felt the princes' privileges and purses ought not to be revoked, as a matter of honor. The promise to maintain them had been made by the Congress to the British and to the princes as one of the conditions of independence. Syndicate leaders like S. K. Patil and others endorsed this view. Following the Congress split, and after the abolition bill had failed to pass the upper house, a presidential order issued September 7, 1970, derecognized the former rulers.

Petitioning the Supreme Court for relief against the government, the princes argued that the presidential order was unconstitutional in that it violated the fundamental rights of property and equality before the law. The right to receive privy purses, it was contended, partook of the character of property.[55] In December 1970, the court ruled that issuance of the president's order was not within his constitutional power and was therefore illegal. Upon hearing the judgment, the Swatantra and the Congress Organization demanded that the government resign and go to the country for a fresh mandate. Within two weeks, Prime Minister Gandhi had done just that.

The power to amend the constitution to effect social and economic policy became a major issue on which Gandhi sought a popular mandate during the 1971 election campaign. In both the bank nationalization and the privy purses cases, the Supreme Court had defended its judgment by reference to the fundamental right to property guaranteed in the constitution. Not that the government, in taking these actions, had ever advocated the abolition of private property; but it did argue the right to restrict it for the purpose of fulfilling the responsibilities enjoined upon it under the Directive Principles of the constitution. One of the founding fathers had said, about the propriety of intervention by the courts in cases involving the property right, that: "the principles formulated by the legislature may commend themselves to a court or they may not. The province of the courts is normally to administer the law as enacted by the Legislature within the limits of its power. Of course, if the legislation is a colourable device, a contrivance to outstep the limits of the legislative power or . . . is a fraudulent exercise of the power, the court may pronounce the legislation to be invalid or *ultra vires.*"[56] It appears, then, that the judiciary was expected to intervene *only* when legislation was *prima facie* a device to take away the right of property altogether, not when it was intended to implement socioeconomic policies prescribed under the constitution.

The call for elections was issued on December 27, 1970. Among the issues on which Gandhi and her government would seek popular backing, she said, were the abolition of privy purses and privileges and bank nationalization. She charged that vested interests had tried to block her policies of economic and social reform. Indeed the forces of conservatism, aided and abetted by the judiciary, had begun to coalesce; they emerged from the shadows, ready to do battle. The stage was set for the dramatic 1971 elections—and for all that followed.

CHAPTER V

A Failure of Leadership: Ideological Vacillation and Incoherence

Steering to the Left

The electoral victories of 1971 and 1972 (in national and state polls) affirmed the immense nationwide popularity of Indira Gandhi, and for a time it seemed that Congressmen were revitalized and united behind their leader. Many expected that the prime minister's resounding electoral triumph would open the way to significant political and economic change, consonant with the election campaign promise to *garibi hatao* (abolish poverty).

For a time these expectations were confirmed. Prime Minister Gandhi seemed determined to introduce more progressive policies. The prime target of her strategy was the Supreme Court. She proceeded to amend the constitution in such a way as to loosen the judicial constraints that had blocked progressive policies for so long. During the 1972 election campaigns she took pleasure in repeatedly reminding the people in state after state that many of the 1971 pledges had been redeemed. The 1972 manifesto stressed the fact that Parliament's power to amend any part of the constitution had been "restored" by the twenty-fourth amendment, which was passed in August 1971. This enactment affirmed the power of Parliament to amend even the provisions dealing with "fundamental rights"—which we have seen was a code term for property rights. Gandhi had thus succeeded in removing the obstacles to amendment erected by the Golaknath decision. Even Morarji Desai's breakaway Congress Organization, which had opposed changes in the fundamental rights section of the constitution during the 1971 election campaign, reversed its position after its devastating defeat. During the August 1971 parliamentary debates, the Congress Organization supported the twenty-fourth amendment, although the Jana Sangh and Swatantra continued to oppose it.

During the state election campaigns the prime minister also availed herself of the opportunity to tell the people that—as a result of the twenty-fifth amendment (passed in December 1971)—Parliament's power to establish guidelines for the amount of compensation payable when the state acquired or requisitioned property was not subject to judicial review. She intended this piece of legislation to deal with the bank-nationalization case, in which the Supreme Court had affirmed to property owners the right to compensation equivalent to the market value of the property taken. Such a ruling would have made the financial burden on government intolerable and effectively nullified reform efforts requiring nationalization. Gandhi's purpose was to empower the Congress-controlled Parliament to specify—in cash or otherwise—the amount to be compensated. In addition, laws of parliament or legislative assemblies aimed at preventing concentration of economic power, in accordance with the Directive Principles, could not be challenged in the courts.

As the 1972 state elections neared, the prime minister took particular pride in pointing out that, as promised, the former princes had been stripped of their privy purses and other privileges deemed incompatible with the government's aim to bring about a more egalitarian society. The twenty-sixth amendment, which fulfilled this promise, was passed in December 1971, in the face of stiff opposition from the Jana Sangh and Swatantra parties.[1] Then, in May 1972, the leftist stronghold in the state of Kerala was delighted by the passage of the twenty-ninth amendment, which protected the Kerala Land Reforms Act, enacted in 1963 and amended in 1969 and 1971. In April 1972, the Supreme Court of India had upheld Kerala High Court rulings that struck down certain vital provisions of the amended act, rendering it ineffective. The 1969 and 1971 amendments to the act were now included in the ninth schedule of the constitution to protect them from any judicial challenge based on infringement of fundamental rights.

Gandhi's sharpest confrontation with the judiciary came in April 1973 when, to further protect progressive legislation from the conservatism of the Supreme Court, she appointed as chief justice a liberal whose constitutional opinions had invariably favored government positions. In so doing, however, she broke a precedent, set since independence, of selecting as chief justice the most senior judge on the bench. Her action provoked quite a storm, and three senior justices resigned in protest. She thereby alienated the influential legal profession, as well as other conservative forces. Many charged her with subverting the independence of the highest court of the land, while she and her supporters defended the action—comparing it to Franklin Roosevelt's appointments to the U.S. Supreme Court during the 1930s—which were inspired by similar progressive sentiments.

The prime minister's second strategic thrust aimed at parts of the private sector. The coking-coal industry was nationalized in May 1972, and the pledge to nationalize general insurance companies was fulfilled in September 1972. On the whole, however, she seemed to proceed gingerly with nationalization. During 1971 and the first half of 1972, relatively small undertakings—in shipping, gold, and copper—were drawn into the government's net. Full control of the coal industry did not come until early 1973, when 464 noncoking mines in the private sector were acquired. By then the management of forty-six textile mills in twelve states had been transferred (in October 1972) to the state-owned Textile Corporation, pending nationalization. The management of the Indian Iron and Steel Company (IISCO), one of the two largest steel-producing companies, was taken over by the government in August 1972 without compensation. The leftist minister of steel and mines, S. M. Kumaramangalam (a former Communist), announced that a single holding company would control steel and associated industries; he also affirmed that IISCO would not be returned to private management. The government would control and supervise steel plants in the public sector and also have a say in the management of the private Tata Iron and Steel Company (the other large steel producer); the latter was part of the Tata conglomerate, the largest business house in the country. Two more large companies (in steel and railway-wagon construction) were nationalized in December 1973.

These bold steps provoked the ire of powerful vested interests. IISCO was the largest company in Martin Burn, the third largest business house in the country, and one of the largest shareholders in the influential English-language newspaper chain, Statesman Ltd. N. A. Palkhivala, who was known as the brains of the Swatantra, was deputy chairman of Tata Iron and Steel at the time. He was also chairman of Associated Cement Companies Ltd., the leading company of ACC, the fifth largest of the seventy-five business houses listed in the 1965 Monopolies Report. One of the Tata firms is one of the two largest shareholders in Statesman Ltd.

The prime minister also incurred the wrath of powerful agricultural interests when it was decided in 1972, following food riots in the summer and autumn, that public agencies would take over the wholesale trade in wheat, starting with the winter crops, and in rice, starting with the next summer. Her food and agriculture minister obtained this commitment from state representatives and urged them to fix a time schedule for its implementation. A few months later, the takeover decision was confirmed at a conference of the states' chief ministers, presided over by Gandhi. Rich peasants were also angered by the 1972–1973 budget, which taxed fertilizers and power pumps, items used almost exclusively by wealthy farmers A parallel move to the left in foreign economic relations was discerned in the 30 percent increase (over the 1970 level) in trade with the Russians.

Such leftist policies generated deep anxiety among business and landed interests and renewed conservative opposition to Gandhi and her government. The Jana Sangh resolved "to organize mass unrest" and demanded the prime minister's resignation.[2] The breakaway Congress Organization claimed to perceive a widespread desire for a "national front of some opposition parties who, with all their ideological differences, are able to have a common mind on the basic problems of poverty, unemployment," and other economic problems.[3] No such national front could be forged, however. The Socialist party, for the time shunning alliances with conservative parties, entered into agreements with the Communist party of India-Marxist and several other smaller leftist parties. It refused, however, to have anything to do with the Soviet-oriented Communist party of India, which had been supportive of Gandhi. Moreover, instead of mending its own fences with former cohorts from earlier socialist incarnations, the party split again in 1972; some members walked out to form the "real" Socialist party, announcing at the same time that they would work for socialist unity. The Swatantra leaders were dealt a serious blow by the death of C. Rajagopalachari, the party's founder, at the end of 1972; during early 1973 their tone betrayed frustration, fatigue, and resignation. On the whole, the opposition remained divided and plagued by internal defections; and it missed yet another opportunity to come together at the national level and for the early 1972 elections in the largest state, Uttar Pradesh.

Economic Crisis

Through 1973, then, the difficulties confronted by the Congress did not stem from the activities of opposition parties. The main crisis, which began in 1972, was economic. And it was destined to become the most serious one faced by any Indian government. Later, political discontent fed on this crisis and assumed grave proportions. Unlike the earlier period of tumult, when some rays of light from the economic sphere illumined the political gloom, the full force of political disruption had to be confronted during the toughest period of economic stress. Although in 1971 the weather in the country as a whole was good, some food-producing states (Uttar Pradesh, Bihar, and West Bengal) were hit by extraordinarily severe floods, and parts of others (Maharashtra, Mysore, and Andhra Pradesh) were plagued by droughts. The following year's crops were bound to be affected. After five successive years of good monsoons, the elements began to work against Indira Gandhi. The summer monsoon of 1972 was very poor; extensive drought conditions starting at this time lasted through the spring of 1974. By mid-1972, as agricultural production began to slacken and prices started to rise, the economy inevitably felt the strain of the 10 million refugees who had fled East Pakistan during the Pakistani civil war in 1971. Almost all of them had been repatriated by April 1972, but in the meantime they had had to be supported from India's food reserves.

By this time the tremendous financial burden of India's war with Pakistan was also increasingly felt, and the inflationary impact of the looming oil crisis, reverberating throughout the world, dealt yet another enervating blow to the ailing Indian economy. During the summer and autumn of 1972, as economic conditions deteriorated, there were disturbances in several states. One of the most serious took place in Bihar. According to press accounts, it reflected the people's disillusionment with the government's handling of the problems of food shortage and rising prices. In September, a mass demonstration was held in Patna, the state's capital. The Congress president charged the opposition parties with aiding and abetting demonstrators throughout the country, and no doubt some opposition leaders did exploit the worsening situation. But the prime cause of discontent was the economic slump.

In October 1972, as the crisis deepened, Gandhi struck an optimistic note at the All-India Congress Committee session at Gandhinagar, Gujarat. However, a resolution passed by the AICC revealed the prime minister's and the party's preoccupation with the critical food situation: the party resolved to advise the government to assume control over the wholesale trade in various essential commodities, including wheat. The intent was to establish a public-distribution system that would make food available to the poorer sections of the population at fair prices. Another resolution on economic policy passed at AICC took note of the slow rate of growth in both agriculture and industry and attributed it to bad weather and shortages of key materials. The difficulties, however, were termed "temporary."

The following year revealed that this assessment was woefully premature. Another long spell of drought, relieved only briefly by a favorable winter monsoon, was in store for India. By late 1973 the mounting problems were reflected in the level of deficit financing, which had risen to almost four times the amount estimated in the 1972–1973 budget. Responsible for the sharp increases in government borrowings from the Reserve Bank of India was the additional money spent on drought relief. But the upward trend in government borrowing was also due to pay raises for government employees at the center and in the states. Increased government spending was inevitably reflected in spiralling prices, especially of essential commodities, and the inflationary conditions were a sign of lower agricultural production as well as the increase in demand created by larger government spending. Another factor in the price rise was the failure of government to procure enough food for distribution. While this failure was to some degree the result of slipshod administrative action, the main reason for the inadequate procurement was the tendency of rich farmers to hoard surpluses in order to benefit from consequent price increases. During 1973 the decline in agricultural production necessitated the distribution of all of the 7 to 8 million tons of buffer stock held at the beginning of the year. In spite of assurances in 1971 and 1972 that no more food would have to be imported, by the end of 1973 2.2 million tons had to be bought from the United States. The crisis was further aggravated in May 1973, when a strike by railwaymen prevented the movement of foodgrains to scarcity areas and other outlying regions. In some states unruly crowds forced foodgrain shops to sell at reduced prices. The summer of 1973 brought riots and other disturbances, largely caused by the severe food shortages.

Her Clouded Ideological Horizon

The economic crisis of 1973 laid bare the weaknesses of the Congress administration and Gandhi's own ideology and policies, which, by

1974, began to buckle in the face of burgeoning political unrest mobilized by the "J. P." movement. Gandhi and her government limped into 1975. The last straw was the party's electoral defeat in the state of Gujarat and, more importantly, the Allahabad High Court's decision against Gandhi in the election petition case brought against her by her political enemy, Raj Narain. By midyear, unable to withstand the sustained economic and political pressures, the prime minister had declared a state of emergency and begun to build an authoritarian structure.

While in 1974–1975 the movement provided the prime minister with ample grounds to retaliate against its leaders, in a way it was her own policies that provided the soil upon which it could grow. Indira Gandhi and the Congress must be held accountable for abandoning the progressive course toward which she had steered the state in 1971–1972. Perhaps, given the weak ideological underpinnings of her policies, this was an inevitable lapse. Nevertheless, her reversal of economic strategy in 1974 contributed to the conditions that fueled the opposition engine and set her on a collision course with the forces contending against her.

Of course it is acknowledged that the economic ills visited upon the country after 1972 had multiple causes—many of them external. The Indo-Pakistan War of 1971 and the refugee problem that foreshadowed it, contributed, as did the ongoing drought and the worldwide inflationary trend that preceded, and was exacerbated by, the oil crisis of 1973. The severity and pervasiveness of the economic distress, however, must also be recognized as a long-term failure of leadership on the part of Indira Gandhi—a failure to act prudently enough to forestall or alleviate the food crisis and runaway inflation, or consistently enough with reference to agrarian and other social reforms for radically redistributing economic wealth and power. It was also a failure to live up to the promises of self-reliance the government had repeatedly made to the people.

Principal among the internal limitations of leadership were the contradictions inherent in Gandhi's ideology of democratic socialism. These were reflected in the prime minister's gradualist strategy of change and aggravated by her personal style of decisionmaking, which, in domestic matters particularly, was excessively slow. The duality of political and governmental roles gave rise to countervailing pulls on her strategies and thought processes. The conflict between them was most clearly reflected in her reluctance (1) to cleanse the Congress government and party organization of conservative and corrupt elements inimical to socialist reforms; and (2) to otherwise streamline the party so as to make it a more efficient agent of social and economic change. In and of themselves, each of these was a serious enough shortcoming; but inextricably intermeshed they formed a larger pattern of near-inertia that rendered them grave failings of leadership.

The tendency to move with caution when faced with particularly difficult or critical problems was repeatedly singled out as characteristic by many of her colleagues, friends, and others I spoke with. One cabinet minister described her decisionmaking style in words echoed by others: "She never takes a decision in a hurry. She likes to have a series of options available. That is her style of coming to a decision. . . . She will give the impression to others that she does not know what she is going to do or what she wants to do. As events develop, one or the other options closes by itself. Then she ultimately works up to a situation and sees what is the most desirable."[4] Her foremost critic, Jayaprakash Narayan, echoed this view: "My impression has been that one of her favorite methods of dealing with issues has been to put them on the shelf and let them be forgotten for a while and let events find their own solution."[5]

This style of decisionmaking served her well in the midst of the Bangladesh crisis. In 1971 she was under tremendous pressure to act, and act quickly, as the refugees began to pour into India. The Jana Sangh and other "super-patriots" urged immediate retaliation against Pakistan. The popular mood was anxious: "People at the time were saying, 'What is she doing? We will be destroyed.' And she was waiting. Then, just at the right moment, she acted, and within 15 days it was over."[6]

In certain domestic matters, however, the caution was overdone. As regards agrarian and land reforms, little of substance was accomplished after 1966, apart from pious statements in endless Congress resolutions and election manifestoes. The constitutional amendments countering conservative Supreme Court decisions in this matter were, of course, important steps in the right direction, but they were not followed up. When asked about it, Gandhi explained her poor record in the restructuring of land relations by saying that "one can only bully state leaders so much and no more." Since agriculture was a state preserve, there were limits to what she could do. But what about an amendment, I asked, bringing the subject under the legislative jurisdiction of the center? "You need the support of the state leaders for that," she said, "and they will not give it. So my hands are tied. At least now, some of them have passed legislation and a lot has been done in terms of redistribution." Nonetheless, she agreed "more could be done. But these things cannot be done overnight."[7] To my suggestion that perhaps the problem lay not so much with legislation but with its implementation, there was no response.

This brief exchange illustrates clearly the problems of her political personality: the tendency toward very gradual reform; dim awareness of the inherent contradiction between the imperatives of democratic procedure and socialist revolution; and the reluctance to disturb the party organization on which her political and governmental power rested but of whose inadequacies she was painfully aware.

One finds an expression of these predispositions and perceptions in many of her public pronouncements. The inherent contradictions in the ideology of democratic socialism take on an even sharper coloring when filtered through Indira Gandhi's mind. Though she is by no means an original thinker, she has her own style of thinking and speaking; certain political themes run through her public comments like a familiar refrain. These are particularly vivid when she is talking about democracy and socialism. Speaking of democratic socialism, she generally refers separately to each philosophical strand, implicitly assuming that in practice the two distinct modes of thought could be blended into a coherent philosophy. Indeed, the theme of blending, balancing, and harmonizing pervades her speeches; in addresses and public comments, one finds a variant of "in everything that we do, we have to try and find a balance."[8] In coping with conflict, personal and political, she labored to absorb opposing segments of a discordant situation—between her father and mother, between impulses toward independence and dependence, rebellion and submission, or between contradictory conservative and radical views. Instinctively and emotionally a "naysayer," intellectually she opted for the "definite maybe" of the middle-of-the-roader. Even during the 1969 Congress split, she did not exert herself to clearly separate the right-wing elements from the Congress left. After 1969, particularly in 1971–1972, some analysts noted a shift in style from consensual to confrontational politics.[9] This was a correct observation, up to a point She did indeed seem more inclined to stand firmly behind left-oriented policies. But when severely tested, her response to conflict through June 25, 1975, remained typically Indian—

guided by an impulse to synthesize and absorb. She invariably shied away from clear-cut distinctions and, in accordance with the larger intellectual tradition to which she is heir, recoiled from efforts to elicit from her clear definitions of either democracy or socialism. Asked about the apparent lack of a coherent economic and social philosophy behind the Twenty-Point Economic Programme of July 1, 1975, she replied: "This is where I always get into trouble because you know I don't think you can label these under separate philosophical categories—all these things are so interlinked."[10]

Shortly after the emergency proclamation, she indicated that the old style of democratic functioning could not be resumed. In August I tried to get her to comment on the presumably new conception of democracy she would try to bring about. Skirting the question, she replied that "each country's democracy is different, within each country things are changing. . . . For instance when democracy began . . . it meant only a very few people. . . . But . . . the concept grew that more people have to come in."[11]

Although this comment may appear self-serving in 1975, the idea of evolving democracy was one she had articulated many times before. Five years earlier she said: "It is sometimes forgotten that the very meaning of words like democracy . . . keeps changing. . . . As the world changes all concepts and definitions change." A few months earlier she voiced a similar view about socialism, which "is not a given, labelled doctrine; it is a changing concept. As we grow, as we develop, as the needs of the nation develop, socialism also will change." What would not change was the fact that socialism should "function for the public good and not for private profit."[12]

In August 1975, the changeability of concepts remained a consistent and favorite theme. Democracy, she said, "is not just, you know, what are known as the outer trappings. . . . You cannot consider it confined to, say, freedom of the press or voting or anything else. . . . But if the people were involved from the beginning, then they are the best guardians of their rights as well as the programmes which are for their benefit." But how, I asked, is the people's will ascertained? "By their speaking out primarily, because if they feel in any given small place things are not being done, they create trouble there and then, and . . . their *representatives* will say, well this is what has to be made."[13] In other words, she reaffirmed the system of representative democracy but defined it not simply in terms of ritual activities like voting, but rather as some sort of "participatory" democracy. The manner of participation, however, was left vague.

This theme of popular participation as a criterion of democracy (rather than the "outer trappings") was stressed in speeches from 1966 on. In 1970 she said that the "democracy to which we are pledged is not a matter of parliamentary institutions. . . . [The] feeling of democracy, the involvement or participation of the people, is not confined to voting once in five years for Parliament," but is a "genuine participation in the programmes of our country." Clearly this notion had not been newly fashioned for the emergency period. Nor was the idea of discipline, which she stressed after the emergency, a new theme. In 1967 she had said: "In a democratic society, self-discipline is by far the most effective method." A parallel theme was social good as a guarantee of the individual good: "Our motivations should stem from love of our country, from patriotism and national purpose." Speaking to a group of students in 1969, she decried the fact that: "In India we have too long sought individual salvation. Perhaps that is why as a country we came to grief. We now realise that there cannot be salvation for the individual without social salvation." As early as August 15, 1966, she stressed the fact that individual rights in a democracy have corresponding duties. Nearly a month after the emergency declaration, she stated in Parliament that, "Every right that the State concedes to the individual imposes an obligation on him."[14]

But for all her consistency over time, her thought on all these matters adds up to nothing more than an eclectic collection of themes—not a coherent political ideology about the nature of the state within a well-defined socioeconomic structure. Moreover, there seems to be reluctance to carry some of her ideas to their logical conclusion. Though recognizing that popular awareness and expectations had grown and that violence was inevitable unless government responded quickly to growing demands for justice and equality, she excused the lack of quick action on her part by stressing the importance of going slow with reforms, relying on persuasion, and carrying with her as many groups of people and parties as possible. Would all these groups then be transformed and radicalized? She did not think so, but felt that "social circumstances can compel them to be reasonable."[15]

It was once pointed out to her that her father "thought reformism was an impossible solution when the basic structure had to be changed." She agreed that "radical changes are necessary"—but "without casting out old values indiscriminately."[16] The grim fact, however, is that over the past three decades, neither the slowness of reforms nor "social circumstances" have persuaded the "haves" in India to accede to any very radical changes.

Even so, the one idea emerging clearly and pervasively from her statements about her ideological posture was the need for change. Change, which is necessary for survival, should be welcomed as a friend and acknowledged, as it was by ancient Indian philosophers, as the only constant in life. Yet she persisted in articulating the end result of change in the vaguest and most general terms. Expressing her views about socialism, for example, she said that socialism means the "welfare of the entire Indian people" and that its shape will emerge out of "the product of our experience."[17] There was little specific exposition of socialism as an ideology or the means to bring it about. What was expressed tended to be confusing. Her clearest statement about socialism was that it "implies distributive justice," which she conceded, could only be accomplished "by taking away from people who have more than enough."[18] In another context, she accepted her father's views that socialism might have to be brought about through coercion; yet she insisted that she would enforce only such coercive measures as were sanctioned by the constitution and legislative measures.[19] Nor would she be prepared to bring about "distributive justice" by taking over rural and agricultural property. In the 1971 election manifesto, in fact, she assured capitalists that the Congress "has no intention of abolishing the institution of private property."[20]

Both these outlooks found shelter in the concept of "mixed enterprise." In economics the important thing is "to steer clear of the extremes of ideologies, whether capitalist or any other." Under the mixed economic system, she conceded, monopolistic tendencies have developed among some families; but it was "not possible, in the circumstances in which we are, to put a sudden brake" on such tendencies. At the same time, however, changes do have to be effcted and "in a way which lessens the delay." She firmly believed that Congressmen "should remain centrists but left of centre."[21]

Such temporizing and contradictions abound! Asked her views on whether socialism is compatible with sizable private ownership of industrial capital, she could throw no light on the implications of this obvious contradiction: "In a way this is an easy question to answer and in a way a very difficult one because we get into the whole question of what socialism is."[22] Here was the crux of her ideological problem, as well as of the difficulties and inconsistencies that beset her policies: she had no clear conception of socialism. She dimly recognized that social and economic relations have to be restructured in favor of greater "distributive justice" but had no clear idea of exactly how to go about it. She accepted her father's definition of a socialist order as a "classless society with equal economic justice and opportunity for all, a society organised on a planned basis."[23] So defined, socialism would appear to be valued for itself; but, she said, socialism was not a goal but a means to an end, "the most effective way of taking us towards this type of equality."[24] And equality itself was at times perceived as a means to an end. "Once equality has come in, then opportunities should open out for everybody to be enriched . . . in the mind and in the sense of appreciating certain values." Compounding the confusion, she concluded: "How this will be done, I don't know."[25]

By stressing the need to enrich the mind and appreciate "certain values," she seemed to acknowledge the need to bring about some sort of cultural revolution. Socialism and equality, she said, must be thought of not only in terms of economic programs but also in terms of social attitudes and behavior. Barriers of caste and community clearly negated social equality and political democracy. An educational system combining "practical experience with theoretical study" would change the attitude of superiority characteristic of the educated classes, and another barrier between man and his fellow would fall.[26] She often referred approvingly to the part of Gandhi's scheme of basic education that tried to teach Indians the dignity of labor and emphasized work-experience as a "bridge between manual and intellectual work, between hand and head, between town and country, between rich and poor." She also believed that the emphasis on material incentives (such as pay raises and bonuses) for improving work needed to change. The goal was to create "a new type of society" where material motivations are a "secondary consideration."

Similarly, she decried the fact that young people remained self-oriented and motivated almost exclusively by material and status rewards rather than by larger national aspirations. She acknowledged that educational policy had evolved no "scheme of social service for students as part of the educational system" and disclosed that though since independence there had been much talk about "some kind of selective national service for young people," nothing of substance was ever done about it.[27] Bemoaning the fact that government had failed altogether to mold the educational establishment as an instrument of social change, she admitted that Indian education narrowly channeled ambitions toward office jobs, "instead of encouraging self-reliance, resourcefulness and a spirit of adventure." The universities' role, she thought, was to promote the "scientific temper in our people" and loosen the "stranglehold of obscurantism" that pervaded the Indian mentality. They should "make the people more deeply conscious of the powerful forces of social change which have begun to operate in the Indian society." She urged the intelligentsia to become "conscious of its social responsibilities and identify itself with the well-being and aspirations of the masses."[28]

Having expressed all these opinions, however, she was found wanting when it came to doing something concrete about it. She explained that education (like agriculture) is a state subject over which the center has no legislative authority. Nor is it "easy to change (the system of education) now because it means such tremendous dislocation that we shall have all the parents, students and teachers up in arms. . . . The question is are we willing to sacrifice something for the next generation?" The answer, by implication, was no: "because for this generation it will be a big hardship. It is by persuasion, by trying to win over the people, that this has to be done."[29]

Vacillations such as these frustrate any effort to understand her political philosophy. For as she was agonizing over the hardships that educational reform might cause the present generation of medical students, 75 percent of the doctors in India—as she herself confessed—were treating only 10 to 15 percent of the people and were concentrated in urban areas. Although she acknowledged the possible benefits accruing to the poor as a result of the Chinese experiment with the "barefoot doctor," she was not enthusiastic about adopting such a model for India. On the other hand, she perceived that "there is need for people to go into the villages and into the hills."[30]

Again and again, though significant problems and needs were clearly recognized and freely acknowledged, her statements conveyed unwillingness—at worst—or helplessness—at best—to do something about them if actions seemed likely to evoke serious opposition from the privileged classes. Her strategy appeared to be to alienate as few of the influential classes as possible at any given moment. Her style was thus clearly reformist, though her rhetoric sometimes sounded revolutionary. Time and again, she revealed that her principal concern was to maintain stability, which she judged a necessary precondition to economic progress.

A Defective Engine of Change

A similar lack of will was noted in her efforts to transform the Congress party into an effective agent of social change, thus complementing its electoral function. She recognized that it had to be something more than a vote-getting machine and criticized fellow members for devoting "too much attention to elections at the cost of the solid field-work which alone builds the party's base." Above all, she said, the party must "reflect the popular will and at the same time, *mould it.*" The only way to "take our message to (the people) . . . is by way of mass contact."[31] She saw the party, then, as an instrument of mass education.

Efforts to revitalize the Congress to make it a potent socializing agent were initiated as early as December 1969, shortly after the split. At an AICC session in Bombay, the decision was taken "to build an army of dedicated cadres." The objective was "to involve the young and educated people in our party activities, to transform the Party which was reduced to a huge election machinery into a dynamically effective instrument of social, economic and political change." Nearly three years later, however, the head of the AICC's cadre-building department disclosed that the state Congress units had resisted the program and withheld their cooperation, perhaps because it would set up alternative bases of power to their own. Having done away with "the stalwarts of the Syndicate," he said, the party had "opened the door [to] (the protegés of the Syndicate) to be found in States, districts and blocks to stealthily enter into the Congress." It was envisaged that at least one trained cadre (and more in larger places) would be stationed in each of India's three-hundred-some odd districts and that eventually, a million trained cadres would make the Congress "a mighty weapon of social, economic and political change."[32] But by July 1972, only four cadre-building camps had been organized.

The very conception of the cadre-training program as a means of building the attitudinal base for a socialist society was flawed from the beginning—first by giving primacy to urban rather than rural problems, and second by recruiting youth from the upper strata rather than making an effort to search out youth with firsthand knowledge of the problems to be dealt with. The emphasis on the urban areas suggests that the program was first and foremost an effort to counter the opposition's propaganda, which was also concentrated in urban areas. The incongruity inherent in the shortsighted conception of the scheme is evidenced in one of the activities undertaken during a six-day camp in New Delhi. On the last day, "the cadres were taken around the city's slum areas to acquaint them with the real problems of slum dwellers."[33] How could such youth possibly be expected to identify with the problems of the poor? Could they, after a few hours' exposure—even on a periodic basis—be expected to draw sufficient insights so as to make meaningful contributions to the program's goal of spreading "mass consciousness about the socialist programme of the Congress and also the problems and their solution for the metropolitan city"? If they had led such sheltered and comfortable lives that they were not even acquainted with the "real problems of slum dwellers," how well suited were they to "look after the problems of jhuggis and jhonpris (slum settlements), drinking water, elementary schooling . . . unemployment" and other similar problems? The fact that these cadres were so innocent of the plight of the poor amongst whom they lived and the fact that such types were recruited at all suggests not so much poor faith as a lack of sensitivity on the part of the organizers. And how could it be otherwise, given their own high social and economic standing?

Nothing much was heard about these camps until the end of 1974, when the political movement organized by Jayaprakash Narayan had reached its peak. At a meeting on October 19, 1974, the Congress Working Committee "decided that a massive counteroffensive should be organized to defeat attempts to subvert Parliamentary Democracy and constitutional processes in our country." At stake, according to the Congress, was "the very survival of the values of democracy, secularism, social justice and self-reliant economy."[34] Almost the same terms were later used in the rationale for the emergency declaration.

Toward the end of November 1974, an AICC central training camp was organized in Narora, Uttar Pradesh. Its immediate aim was to deal with the political challenge mounted by the forces of the political opposition. The Congress Working Committee "decided to launch a programme of mass education and mass organization in order to defeat this threat of subversion of democracy."[35] According to Congress President D. K. Borooah, the antidemocratic forces were the same as those who in 1971 had forged a grand alliance to defeat the Congress party. Now, they threatened democracy, unity, and the independence of the country. The more long-range purpose of the training program, however, remained the same as that articulated in 1972: "to make the Congress a more effective instrument of social change, to make our active workers—cadres—to participate more actively in day-to-day organization and to project the Congress ideals and ideology among the masses."[36] The opposition movement had jolted the Congress out of a prolonged period of lethargy; over the three-day secret talks, there was a lot of soul-searching by Congressmen and many frank confessions of failure to fulfill their promises.

The minister of agriculture, Jagjivan Ram (later minister of defense in the Janata party government) expressed some anxiety about the fact that many rural and agricultural workers were beginning to think "that the work for their betterment can only be done by the political parties other than the Congress. And it will be suicidal for the Congress if this impression is reflected throughout the country." He spelled out a number of urgent steps to be taken to prevent this feeling from growing "to the detriment of the interest of the Congress." This same minister had been found to have evaded his taxes for a number of years and was himself a big landlord. Another minister, I was told, had boasted that if efforts were made to take any of his land, which was above the pre-scribed ceiling, he would fight it in the courts. Although this story was confirmed by others with whom I spoke, it is still hearsay. Whether true or not, many people believed such stories and were distressed by the apparent gap between Congressmen's professions and their actions. Such gaps eventually eroded the credibility of the Congress and made possible the 1975 crisis.

Other grave shortcomings in performance were acknowledged at the Narora meetings. One background paper on the rural poor noted that the number of agricultural laborers, as a proportion of the total popula-tion, had increased from 16.71 percent in 1961 to 25.76 percent in 1971.[37] This increase, paradoxically enough, was attributed in part to the passage of land-reform legislation; following enactment, some landlords apparently took back land from sharecroppers, either taking advantage of legal loopholes or just blatantly breaking the law. The tenants were too ignorant of the law and too poor and too afraid to press their claims or even to be aware that they had any. According to one report cited, nearly two-thirds of the agricultural households were indebted to their employer-cum-landowners. Citing another report on a

West Bengal district, it was disclosed that per capita earnings of the agricultural worker were about 26 paise or 3 cents per day.[38] The writer wryly noted "the fact that he (the agricultural worker) exists is a miracle."[39]

Quoting from the "Approach Paper to the Fifth Five-Year Plan," the background paper further reported the Planning Commission's estimate that "the absolute number of people below the poverty line today is just as large as it was two decades ago. And these people living in abject poverty constitute between two fifth [sic] and one half of all India citizens." After enumerating the various legislative measures taken to improve the conditions of the tenant farmer in the rural areas, it was conceded that the "basic principle that land should go to the actual tillers has not been realised" despite land legislation in nearly all of the states.[40]

Finally, it was conceded that "the benefits of agricultural development in the last two decades have gone primarily to the upper income groups rather than to the lowest income groups who need them most." Not only cooperative credit but also fertilizers and improved seeds had been monopolized by the rich farmers. Thus the background paper acknowledged what many other observers, Indian and foreign, had long recognized—that the "gap between the rural rich and the rural poor has widened."[41] A few years ago, an Indian critic of the government's land-reform policy made an acerbic comment on the dilatoriness of its implementation. "In 1949, the Congress adopted and announced its policy that 'land must belong to the tiller.' That was two or three years after General MacArthur had broken up the vast feudal estates in Japan and redistributed them to farmers with a maximum of seven and a half acres per family. What the General from the world's biggest capitalist country did in less than two years after the defeat of Japan, our leaders with all their talk of socialism have not done even in twenty-four years!"[42] The point was well-taken, though in all fairness it must be said that General MacArthur, as head of the American occupation forces, was functioning within the framework of a military dictatorship.

Yet the fact remains that after nearly thirty years of mounting evidence about the widening gap between rich and poor, it took a legitimacy crisis of major proportions for the party to recognize at last that the "only remedy is that the rural poor have to be organised to help themselves." One cannot but decry the belatedness of the Congress's realization that the rural poor had to be organized so that they could "fight against injustices and . . . for their economic uplift-ment."[43] The responsibility for this failure must be laid at the feet of both Indira Gandhi and her father—the two leaders who held the reins of power for the longest periods since independence.

Indira Gandhi's own words reveal some recognition that her govern-ment's performance fell far short of her rhetoric. She had done little more than follow the tradition established by Congress since inde-pendence—whether it was in the area of land reforms, education, po-litical socialization, or the restructuring of the Congress. Nor was she forceful enough in dealing with widespread charges of corruption made by opposition leaders and in the press against some of her colleagues. In early 1975, a debate was raging in New Delhi about the chief minister of Haryana, Bansi Lal, a Congress leader said to be very close to Gandhi. A number of state and central legislators had drawn up charges against him and wished to have him investigated by a formal commission of inquiry. According to Cabinet Secretary B. D. Pande, the government can submit any matter of public importance to a commission of inquiry presided over by a judge.[44] Members of the opposition had asserted that, under the same act, if at least five members of parliament sub-mitted charges for investigation, a commission of inquiry must be ap-pointed. Such charges *had* been submitted by the requisite number of MPs, but no commission was appointed. I asked the cabinet secretary why this had not been done. His explanation was that no *prima facie* evidence of corruption had been presented by those making the charges and that, therefore, the prime minister believed no commission could be established. She did, however, appoint a committee of cabinet ministers (all Congressmen of course); they too concluded there was no *prima facie* case. I asked whether the Commission of Inquiry Act re-quired that MPs submit a *prima facie* case in order for an inquiry to be initiated; surprisingly the cabinet secretary replied in the negative. More-over, he admitted, the Act did not stipulate that cabinet ministers must be appointed to investigate the charges or to establish a *prima facie* case. These admissions considerably weaken the government's reasons for not convening a commission of inquiry to look into the charges against Bansi Lal.

Another indication of the government's lackadaisical attitude toward corruption was the failure to pass a bill setting up a kind of "ombuds-man" organization, known at the national level as Lok Pal and at the state level as Lok Ayukta. The Lok Pal Bill had been pending in the

Parliament since 1968, when it was introduced as a result of suggestions made by the Committee on Prevention of Corruption in 1964 and the Administrative Reforms Commission in 1966.

Many opposition leaders also claimed that the licensing of Indira Gandhi's son, Sanjay, to manufacture a small automobile involved corrupt practices by Sanjay and his associates (including Chief Minister Bansi Lal). Despite considerable investment over several years, no automobile was ever produced. The charges of corruption were denied, and formal charges were not brought against Sanjay Gandhi until the Janata Government came to power in March 1977. The question of corruption aside, however, Gandhi must be faulted, at the very least, for exercising poor political judgment. As the country's leader and public advocate of socialist reconstruction, she and her family ought to have pointed the way towards socialism. Of course, private business *is* sanctioned by the "mixed economy" principle, but only as a necessary evil on which you cannot put a "sudden brake."

Self-Reliance Abandoned

In another critical area—economic self-reliance—the distance between performance and precept proved to be dangerous to Gandhi's political health and that of the Congress.

The pattern of dependence on foreign aid and private foreign investment was well established by the time Indira Gandhi assumed office in 1966 at the end of the third five-year plan. When the United States suspended aid following the Indo-Pakistan war of 1965 a streak of economic nationalism had surfaced. Indian anger was further fueled by U.S. and World Bank pressures to devalue the rupee and liberalize the economy along Western capitalist lines. The degree of their dependence was brought home to Indians by President Johnson's decision to approve "Food for Freedom" shipments on a month-by-month basis during the height of one of India's worst droughts. The goal of self-reliance which had been played down in earlier plans was now vigorously propagated in official circles, especially by the prime minister. The objective of the fourth five-year plan, she said shortly after its inception in 1969, was to enable India "to stand on our feet as soon as possible and not take a very large amount of foreign aid." She conceded, indirectly, that the decision to reduce dependence was in part making a virtue out of necessity: "We are doing with less aid because of our own desire and because less aid is available."[45] External assistance, as a proportion of total plan resources, plummeted from a peak of 28.2 percent during the third plan to 12.9 percent in the fourth plan.[46]

At the same time, there seemed to be some confusion as to exactly what "self-reliance" meant. In 1969, Gandhi defined it as the "gradual" elimination of foreign aid but made no distinction between gross and net foreign aid. The fourth plan, however, defined self-reliance as elimination of net aid by 1980–1981. The distinction is highly significant.

Gross aid includes, along with new grants and loans, amounts allocated for repayment of the principal and interest on past debts. As India has been borrowing substantially from foreign sources since the early 1950s, her debtor position closely resembled that of her own poor farmers and agricultural laborers; after repeated borrowings, they found themselves (and their children and grandchildren) mortgaged to the moneylender. Between the 1950–1951 and 1974–1975 periods, India's total public debt increased ninefold. More shockingly, the proportion of the debt raised outside India increased to nearly 200 percent of the 1950–1951 figure; by the end of the fourth plan in 1974, India's foreign debt constituted nearly 35 percent of the total public debt. What is most telling, from the point of view of distinguishing between gross and net aid, is the fact that total debt servicing had increased more than a hundredfold in twenty-five years—from Rs. 23.8 crores in the first plan period to Rs. 2445 at the end of the fourth plan. By the fourth year of the fourth five-year plan, total debt service payments (including amortization and interest) constituted 59 percent of gross aid disbursed.[47]

Thus, in defining self-reliance as the elimination of net rather than gross aid, a paradoxical situation could be created. As one analyst pointed out, it would be possible (given this definition) for the country to become "technically 'self-reliant' [while] its quest for fresh aid intensifies! This could happen when fresh inflows of aid are falling over time while debt service obligations are increasing. Sometime in future, the two would become equal, and the country would actually have to seek larger fresh aid from that point onwards in order to meet its rising debt service obligations. Otherwise, the country would soon become *over*-self reliant!" Clearly the way to avoid such a Kafkaesque situation is to define self-reliance as zero gross aid within a given period.[48]

Nonetheless, the draft fifth five-year plan (1974–1979) did not dedicate itself explicitly to the goal of eliminating gross aid altogether. Rather, it relied on the third plan's formulation of self-reliance—the elimination of "special forms of external assistance." Zero *net* aid was projected by 1978-1979, the last year of the plan—though it also projected zero *gross* aid by 1985-1986 (i.e., during the sixth plan). It justified foreign aid in the interim as a means of building up "the growth potential of the economy to the level where it can support an adequate level of investment from its own production and savings."[49]

The fifth plan model, however, as one critic pointed out, was suited "strictly to a centrally planned economy with public ownership of the means of production" and did not consider the problems encountered in a mixed economy.[50] Nor did it take into account the interrelated policy consequences of the twin objectives of self-reliance and redistribution of wealth and income for the removal of poverty. Clearly, the elimination of aid would have an impact on the rate of income growth and/or investment. Before setting down self-reliance objectives, therefore, the planners must be assured that during the interim period there will be no need to import food, raw materials, or the capital goods necessary for industrial production and new investment. At the same time, if the objective is to remove poverty, the government must be able to strictly control economic behavior—particularly in those areas of the private sector that affect production, distribution, and consumption of goods and services. Yet, as D. R. Gadgil, deputy chairman of the Planning Commission in charge of drafting the fourth plan, noted in 1972, the Indian economy "operates as almost a laissez-faire economy, in part modified by the operation of particular controls. It also means that where the particular measure is in line with trends set in motion by laissez-faire operation the trend is accentuated; on the other hand, where it seeks to counter such a trend it is usually powerless." Another economist noted that the discretion enjoyed by the private sector to make investment decisions often resulted in underinvestment in the public sector, which prompted the government to seek foreign aid to close the investment gap created by private investment in non-plan projects.[51] The significant point here is that in the past, government had proved itself unable to control the private sector, and there was no reason to believe that the wealthy elements (particularly in agriculture) would be prepared to bear the sacrifices expected of them in the fifth plan. The choice of policy measures was simply not grounded in reality.

One observer placed the planning problem in its proper, and bleakest, perspective: "In view of the various concessions the farm lobby has been able to extract in the last few years and the dismal fate which the proposals of agricultural income and wealth tax have met, it appears well-nigh impossible to think of effective policy measures to curb the consumer expenditure (or income) of the rural elite. When it comes to the urban population that is covered extensively under the taxation net, the problems are no less, though their contribution to total sacrifice comes to no more than 25 percent. Evasion of direct and indirect taxes is known to be rampant."[52] Yet the "Approach" to the fifth-plan document noted that "the attainment of self-reliance to an important extent depends on how soon the middle and the upper income strata exercise the needed restraint on their consumption, *particularly of goods and services that have a significant import content.*"[53]

B. S. Minhas, a member of the Planning Commission resigned in protest against the unrealistic estimates in the draft fifth plan. Experience, he said, had shown that the fourth plan had grossly overestimated the amount of domestic revenue available for plan expenditure; yet similar projections were being made in the fifth plan. Stern fiscal discipline, control of expenditures, and price stability were essential to the creation of a large balance from current revenues. This was all the more true given the rapid rise in prices, which was not considered in calculating the total of planned investment. Moreover, calculations of foreign-exchange requirements for 1974–1975 were far too low; they did not consider the steep rise in the price of imported crude oil and nitrogen. The balance-of-trade gap was thus bound to be much greater than projected and would be reflected in higher foreign-exchange needs, which would be further increased by debt-service payments. In addition, the necessary volume of gross aid was not likely to be available from foreign sources. Even if it were, accepting it would not be consistent with the objectives of zero net aid projected for 1978–1979.

Minhas went on to point out that an increased balance-of-payments deficit, leading to depletion of foreign-exchange reserves would, "in fact, force us into further dependence on aid givers. There is no worse way of perpetuating our dependence on foreign aid and of defeating the objective of self-reliance than to base the Plan on unrealistic assumptions. The Draft Plan, as proposed now, may well lead us into a foreign exchange crisis within a year or two of its commencement."[54]

This dissenting note was written on November 23, 1973. Its prophecy was not sufficiently far-sighted: the crisis had begun earlier that same year. Although the balance of trade, which had been unfavorable since the beginning of the first plan, moved into the black for the first time in 1972–1973, the improvement was largely illusory. It represented a sizable increase in exports to Bangladesh, which were not indicative of the long-term picture. (These exports were financed largely by Indian grants.) Moreover, the increase in value reflected a de facto depreciation of the Indian rupee because of changes in foreign-exchange rates, realignment of the world monetary system, and the linking of the rupee to the floating pound sterling.[55] The export picture was not promising over the longer run, and imports were continuing to rise. The balance of trade was heading for another downturn; by 1973–1974, it reached its lowest point since the inception of the fourth plan.

It was predicted in August 1973 that, owing to an anticipated large trade deficit, decline in net aid, and large debt-servicing payments, the government would not only have to draw on its low foreign-exchange reserves but also seek permission from the International Monetary Fund to use special drawing rights and negotiate additional credits. This prediction proved to be true. The government announced early in 1974 that India had drawn $74.4 million from the International Monetary Fund.[56] By April, Gandhi and her colleagues had to go back to the IMF to negotiate a loan of $301.3 million. This was in addition to the $97.3 million in gold that had been withdrawn in April and another loan of $82.6 million taken in February. Reportedly, the government had resorted to such extensive borrowing as a precautionary measure, so as to be sure it would be able to pay the much higher import bill expected because of price increases for oil and other commodities and additional food imports; it was not certain that its foreign-exchange earnings (through exports) would increase enough to meet this higher bill. At the end of May, a loan of $150 million was agreed to by the International Development Association, which distributes loans on softer terms than the International Bank for Reconstruction and Development. It was the ninth such credit to India IDA had authorized during 1973–1974. In June, the World Bank's Aid India consortium agreed to provide India with $800 million, which was predominantly scheduled for debt relief. In other words, this loan enabled India to pay the principal, interest, and debt-service charges on past loans. Another $600 million was provided for project assistance.[57]

The result of these loans for India was that its goal of self-reliance, even as zero net aid, receded far into the background. The warning voiced by the dissenting member of the Planning Commission proved to be only too true. He had said that "when we run to aid-givers in a crisis, we may not be able to obtain aid on terms and conditions that we would like."[58] This is precisely what happened in 1974.

The Turn to the Right

Some of Gandhi's top economic advisers during the height of the economic crisis of 1973–1974 revealed to a Western journalist in 1976 that the IMF had set conditions to its May 1974 agreement to finance the balance-of-payments deficit. The $1,400 million granted in June by the Aid India consortium also had certain strings attached. Without such a program to stabilize the economy, according to a high official in the ministry of finance, "we would not have been able to achieve either the IMF or aid package."[59] The principal secretary to the prime minister, P. N. Dhar, confirmed the condition and pointed to the main outlines of Indira Gandhi's anti-inflationary program incorporated in a book by a well-known Indian economist, V. K. R. V. Rao and his associates (including P. N. Dhar). The message of the book, which was published in October 1973, conformed closely to the World Bank's well-known predilection for "liberalization" of economic policies in underdeveloped countries.[60]

Distinguishing between the "tactics and strategy" of socialist planning, Rao suggested a short-term, tactical policy to control inflation and "set the economic machinery moving in the direction of greater production." His entire analysis, however, was framed in free-market terms of demand and supply, as were his policy suggestions. Inflation was to be controlled by holding down spending in the public and private sectors and by curbing deficit financing by the government—the "real and most conspicuous single factor" behind the increase in the money supply. The latter had to be reduced in order to stabilize the economy and move it toward "economic growth and social justice." A discriminating policy of price controls designed on free-market principles would remove the incentive for black-market transactions that generally emerged under a system of partial control.

In the area of food distribution he favored a reduction in government's responsibility by increasing production "through ways which reduce excessive dependence on prosperous regions and large hold-

ings." However, he opposed the "draconian" measure of nationalization in the wholesale foodgrain trade, which he believed only subsidized
the consumption of the better-off.

In industry, though he thought it wise over the long run to encourage
production by small and medium-sized firms, he proposed that in the
short run, government policy toward monopolies and oligopolies should
be revised in order to take advantage of their trained and educated
personnel and the managerial and entrepreneurial skills required for
increasing industrial production. To encourage competition among the
oligopolies, the government should promote "new large units rather
than just ban production by the existing large units." Oligopolistic
firms could be licensed to work in backward regions "where there are
natural endowments favourable to production" (one of which was,
presumably, cheap labor). Rao took great pains to stress, however, that
his suggestion to expand the oligopolistic sector was meant only as a
temporary measure to meet a temporary situation.[61]

Indeed, all of his policy suggestions were meant as tactical approaches
to the long-term goal of "real socialist change." However he may have
meant them, what he was saying in effect was that, before you can have
socialism, you must first have a proper capitalist economy. It is highly
questionable, however, whether, having once established such an
economy, it is possible to "plan" a socialist transition; for the capitalist
interests and their political spokesmen would have become even
stronger, as Indian history since independence has borne out. Capitalist
economies in the West started out with something approximating a pure
competitive market but ended up dominated by multinationals and
huge national corporations. Why would Indian capitalists evolve dif-
ferently? Moreover, if only a few Indian monopolies now exert such
important influence on the political process, would many large firms
exert less?

By accepting the Rao approach to "socialist planning," Gandhi had
veered decidedly toward the right, even though her rhetoric—like
Rao's—affirmed a conviction in socialism. Jayaprakash Narayan himself
noted with approval her shift to the right.[62] Among the first signs that
the prime minister was following the Rao recommendations was the
decision, in February 1974, to denationalize the wholesale trade in
foodgrains, which had been undertaken with such fanfare in 1973.

The anti-inflationary package based on Rao's recommendations was first given substance in two presidential ordinances issued on July 6, 1974. They were intended to immobilize moneys accruing to workers and business. All increases in wages and half of additional cost-of-living increases would be deposited in a special account for one and two years, respectively. Workers in both the public and private sectors (about 18 million) were included in the scheme. In the business sector, companies would be permitted to distribute only one-third of their net profits or a 12 percent dividend on shares, whichever was smaller. The ceiling on distributable profits was to remain in force for two years.[63]

A week later, on July 13, 1974, the prime minister detailed the rationale and features of her anti-inflationary policy at the cornerstone-laying ceremony of the Institute for Social and Economic Change founded by Rao.[64] She affirmed government's intention to contain the budget deficit, by reducing government spending both at the center and in the states. Bank credit to the commercial sector would be kept under strict surveillance, and the money supply would be further curbed by impounding wage earner's increments. She pointed out that past wage increases and adjustments in the dearness allowance had been ineffective protection from inflation: "Every rise in wages or dearness allowance becomes a signal for shopkeepers and others to raise prices." The statutory ceiling on dividend distribution was imposed to ensure "equitable distribution of sacrifices." She also planned to "bring self-employed professionals and traders within the tax net."

Within a few days after her speech, described by P. N. Dhar as "the critical moment in our policy,"[65] a new ordinance provided for compulsory deposits by all income-tax payers—agricultural and nonagricultural—who earned an annual income of Rs. 15,000 or more. A few days later, the Reserve Bank of India raised the bank rate from 7 to 9 percent. In September, a new law imposed a tax on loan interest received by Indian banks. Like the increase in the Reserve Bank's rate, the new tax was intended to increase the government's revenues as well as to raise the cost of borrowing and thereby reduce inflationary spending.

Inevitably this harsh stabilization program required coercive measures. The compulsory deposit and restrictive dividend measures were accompanied or followed by other strong-arm tactics. Strict enforcement of price regulation and the distribution of essential commodities provided for under the Essential Commodities Act of 1955 required an

172 / Indira Gandhi

amendment—adopted in August 1974—providing a minimum three months' imprisonment for violators. December 1974 saw a new law to deal with smuggling and other illegal transactions involving foreign exchange.[66] But the harshest action was taken in May 1974, when the railway workers' strike was firmly crushed.

On April 23, 1974, in the midst of the foreign-exchange and general economic crisis, the leaders of railway workers announced a strike for May 8. The notice was issued by the National Coordination Committee for Railwaymen's Struggle (NCCRS), which was formed to organize the workers' action. The Action Committee of the NCCRS was headed by George Fernandes, chairman of the Socialist party (now minister of industries in the Janata government). The demands included a 75 percent increase in wages, to bring railway pay up to that of industrial workers in other nationalized industries, a higher annual bonus, an eight-hour working day, and other fringe benefits. On April 29, the railway ministry agreed to major concessions; these were rejected, and on May 2 Fernandes and three hundred other union leaders were arrested. By May 7, six thousand people were being detained. On the third day of the strike, the government offered to release the arrested leaders and resume negotiations if the strike was ended. This proposal was rejected and the strike, the longest in India's railway history, continued at great cost to the economy. Traffic earnings suffered, and workers lost their wages; banking, insurance, and other business transactions were adversely affected; shipments of coal and other necessary shipments, including food, were stalled; millions of people were unable to get work. The government took very stern measures, arresting thousands of strikers and evicting others from houses located on railway housing estates. A month's back pay owed to the strikers was withheld. Gradually the striking railwaymen began to return to work, and by May 28 the strike had been broken.

While the economic cost of the strike was great, the political cost of breaking it turned out to be even greater. The Indian President, V. V. Giri, himself a former president of the All-India Railwaymen's Federation (one of the main unions involved in the strike), warned Gandhi that lasting bitterness would be created by government's use of harsh methods. The stern measures proved to be the catalyst needed to unite, more firmly than ever before, the disparate political forces of the Left and Right. One day after the strike was called and a week after the arrest of Fernandes and other union leaders, all opposition parties in Parliament united to propose a motion of no-confidence in the prime minister and her government.

In a debate on the night of May 9-10, 1974, Gandhi took note of the opposition's show of unity but vigorously defended her government's stand. In the past, she said, the government had been too lenient in meeting workers' demands; such concessions had always led to an escalation of demands. In spite of the inequities of the wage structure, the critical economic situation and the larger public interest had to be considered above that of any particular section. Everyone was agreed "that the country is passing through an extremely difficult economic situation" and that "the strike is bound to bring about a deterioration in the situation." Nonetheless, the strike notice had been given. A member of the opposition had even indicated in Parliament that he had received many telegrams from railway workers "in different parts of the country informing him of threats, intimidation" and other such pressures to coerce workers to participate. The strike "was hitting at the very foundation of our economy," and the government had to take the actions it considered necessary. She mentioned opposition leaders' proclamations and their intention "to weaken the government." But not only the government or the Congress party had suffered, but also the country as a whole: "The country's interests come first and they are above the interests of any one section. Today we cannot afford the exorbitant demands that have been made, or the others that are being hinted on behalf of other sections." To satisfy them would be to satisfy the few at the expense of the mamy.[67]

The tone of the debate was acrimonious, and it was clear that the opposition leaders were united in their condemnation. It was no less clear that the government was prepared to stand firm to protect the economy from further inflationary pressures and to demonstrate to the IMF and the World Bank that the Indian government was worthy of the international bankers' trust. A similar motivation accounts, in part, for the emergency proclamation and the sterilization program embarked upon during Emergency Rule. As one observer remarked, the IMF and the World Bank "must be forced to realise that their stabilisation policies are often so harsh . . . that the programmes force national leaders, against their own inclinations (as with Mrs. Gandhi), to authoritarian measures."[68]

174 / Indira Gandhi

The railway strike, although critical in bringing opposition forces together, was but one stage of the political challenge mounted against Indira Gandhi's government during 1974. A two-pronged attack was launched from political bases in two states southeast and southwest of New Delhi. Jayaprakash Narayan's "total revolution" movement against Gandhi and her government began in 1974 in Bihar. It was inspired by a student protest movement in Gujarat.

CHAPTER VI

The "J. P." Movement, 1974-1975

Politically as well as economically, 1974 was a year of trials and tribulations for the Indian people. And for Gandhi and her government. The severe economic crisis had demoralized a leadership already badly shaken by two years of economic adversity; scarcities (especially of food), spiraling prices, and unemployment were bound to be reflected, as they always had been in the past, in social and political unrest. This time, however, the growing discontent, particularly in urban areas, was systematically fanned and mobilized by a movement that was born in the western industrial state of Gujarat and took root in the eastern, and poorest, state of Bihar. The movement for "total revolution" led by the widely respected elder statesman, Jayaprakash Narayan, was brought to an abrupt halt by the emergency declaration.

There was little good news to induce feelings of security or pride among Indians that year. Perhaps many felt elated for a while by India's detonation of an atomic device and, thus, her entry into the exclusive nuclear club. Even so the world remained a threatening place. Besides the economic squeeze, it was learned that the United States had decided to end its ten-year arms embargo to Pakistan. At Diego Garcia, a thousand miles from India's southern tip, a naval base was being established by the American government, whose president, Gerald Ford, had claimed the right to destabilize governments it did not approve of. Finally, the situation in the northeastern states of Nagaland and Manipur and in the territory of Mizoram remained highly unstable.

In these precarious circumstances J. P. Narayan's movement for "total revolution?"—by its actions, rhetoric, philosophy, and composition—generated concern not only in governmental circles but also in the minds of people concerned with its impact on the country's shaky economic and beleaguered democratic institutions. Of course, in the eyes of its leaders, the movement was designed to provide a corrective to the government's departures from democratic norms and developmental goals.

It is true that Gandhi's government, like her father's, had fallen far short of meeting India's enormous developmental needs; and Indian democracy was still largely government of, by, and for the privileged classes. Nevertheless, even J. P., as he is widely known, conceded that India enjoyed democracy of a sort. Other opponents of the Prime Minister, such as Chandra Shekhar—a Young Turk Congressman and admirer of J. P. (later president of the Janata party)—rejected the notion that India was ruled dictatorially. Even her archenemy, Morarji Desai, noted in November 1974, at a conference to consider ways of extending the movement to other parts of the country, that they could not have held the conference if democracy had not prevailed.[1] Nor would a tightly controlled state provide police protection to the "dictator's" political enemies; Narayan was accompanied by such an escort during his election campaign in Gujarat in May/June 1975. (On at least one well-publicized occasion, however, Narayan was hurt when a scuffle broke out between his supporters and the police.)

"Total Revolution": A Potential for Violence and a Challenge to Democracy

Even if we acknowledge the weaknesses of democratic performance under the Congress government, we must admit that a strong case can also be made against the movement for failing to nurture democratic norms and practices. There was a serious danger that it might get out of control and lead to anarchy; and it was poorly designed to serve the developmental needs of the poor. The possibility of anarchy was recognized by Acharya Vinoba Bhave, leader of the Sarva Seva Sangh (Association for the Service of All), which propagates the Gandhian philosophy of truth and nonviolence. Bhave feared that the agitation launched by Narayan would trigger off the forces of disintegration in the country. In fact, the Sangh, to which Narayan had devoted many years of work, split over the participation of Narayan and his Sarvodayist followers in the Bihar movement.[2]

Chandra Shekhar conceded to me that the movement's leaders had considered the possibility of anarchy. Narayan too acknowledged its potentiality in April 1975, when he conjectured that the people's anger "might turn into a violent outburst leading to anarchy and dictatorship."[3] In June, he repeated this possibility during an interview, admitting that the movement might lead to anarchy, given the inability of opposition political parties to offer a viable, united alternative to the Congress. "We were doubtful as to what would happen." But he thought, generally, that any power vacuum created by the movement would be filled by the opposition parties. Acknowledging that these parties were badly divided—only a few months earlier they had not even been able to agree on a common symbol to use during the election campaign in Gujarat—he hoped there could be a temporary accommodation among them in Parliament. "Even a federal party would not be a bad thing for a few months as a step towards a merger."[4]

The possibility of general anarchy thus seems a genuine reason to fear the movement at this volatile time. Even so, to understand more clearly why Gandhi's strong response to the threatening situation took the extreme form of an emergency proclamation, we need to know something about the movement itself, its leadership and rhetoric, its outlook, its base of support, and its cadre. In what ways did it threaten democratic and stable functioning?

By the end of 1973, inflation and unemployment (particularly among educated youth) had eroded confidence in the Congress government. The middle-upper classes were particularly badly hit; the students, an inconstant political force, also felt the pinch. In Gujarat, they let loose a storm of protest that at first focused on educational grievances: programs that did not prepare them to earn an adequate livelihood, the high cost and poor quality of the food served in hostels, difficult examinations, increases in fees, and the grading system. Their agitation turned violent, and opposition political parties lent support to student activities that culminated in a demand for the resignation of the Congress chief minister of Gujarat. For the first three months of 1974, Gujarat was in a state of near anarchy. Under pressure, Gandhi gave in and requested the chief minister to resign; he did so on February 9, 1974. The state assembly was suspended, and the president's rule was imposed.

By now the opposition parties (in particular the Jana Sangh) had come to dominate the agitation, and they declared the dissolution of the assembly the ultimate goal of the statewide protest. What had started as a grievance against educational conditions had turned into economic agitation and ended up as a wholly political demand. Businessmen and wealthy farmers, who had not supported the students' earlier activities, supported the demand for dissolution. The former chief minister took his revenge on Gandhi by leaving the Congress, forming a separate party, and joining in the chorus of demands for dissolution. Only the urban workers, the landless laborers, and others of the backward classes stayed out of the action; they saw it as motivated by the parties' political ambitions, rather than a desire to help the poor. It was an anti-Congress movement, and, rightly or wrongly, the Congress was thought to be more in tune with the needs of the poor. Rioting, looting, burning, and stone throwing were, therefore, confined to the towns and cities. Finally, the assembly was dissolved on March 16, 1974, and the militant students' organization quickly disintegrated. The whole episode had hardly been an exercise in democratic functioning.

But it was only the beginning. While the students in Gujarat were engaged in violent protests, their confreres in Bihar had started to organize. Their grievances evolved in much the same way as those of their Gujarati counterparts, but their protest had not reached the same pitch of violence. Soon after the Gujarat Assembly had been dissolved, however, the Bihari students began to make the same demand. This agitation soon came under the direct leadership of Jayaprakash Narayan and evolved into the movement for "total revolution."[5] However much J. P. protested to the contrary, this movement was erosive of democratic institutions, practices, and values as these had evolved or were embodied in the constitution. Judging by the increasingly provocative appeals for "total revolution" made by J. P. to the people at large, at organizational forums, and in public statements directed toward civilian and military personnel, his movement must be assessed as subversive of public order and conducive to anarchy and violence.

The Bihar assembly had been duly elected in 1972 for a five-year period, and a Congress government had been formed by the majority party. In May 1974, Narayan acknowledged that the efforts to remove the Congress ministry and dissolve the assembly were not in consonance with the constitution. "Unconstitutional it certainly is," said he, referring to the movement, "but not anti-democratic." The people had no other recourse, for distortions and abuses had "robbed the elections of much of their value and eroded the people's faith in them." A. B. Vajpayee, former president of the Jana Sangh (now foreign minister under the Janata party government), also acknowledged that the movement was an extraparliamentary action.[6]

Six months later, however, Narayan retracted his concession that the demand for dissolution of the assembly was unconstitutional; it had been made, he said, out of "ignorance." One of his supporters, a lawyer named A. G. Noorani, had apparently persuaded J. P. that the demand was quite constitutional. The revised claim was based on the analysis of a nineteenth-century British scholar, A. V. Dicey, "one of the great authorities on constitutional law"; Dicey, according to Narayan, had affirmed "that the people have a right to call for the dissolution of an elected House if there is misgovernment, if the government is corrupt and anti-people and the elected House continues to support it."[7] The former Swatantra leader, M. R. Masani, a Narayan supporter, also cited Dicey in defense of the action.

Turning to Dicey's argument for dismissal, we see that it refers to a set of undefined "combinations of circumstances under which the Crown has a right to dismiss a Ministry who command a Parliamentary majority, and to dissolve the Parliament by which the Ministry are supported."[8] It is quite clear, therefore, that the matter of dissolution is entirely the prerogative of the Crown (in the Indian context, the state governor or the president of India) and that nothing is said about invoking the prerogative under pressure of street demonstrations. As another scholar has pointed out, the "people" had nothing to do with royal decisions.[9] In any event, there is something rather lacking in creativity and imagination in invoking the dicta of an English scholar writing in 1885 about precedents set in a monarchy one to two centuries earlier, when the Crown was still a powerful force, and trying to apply them to Bihar in 1974–1975.

As for Narayan's claim that elections had lost their value, how can one reconcile this with his acceptance, within a year of this statement, of Indira Gandhi's challenge to resolve the dispute between them by putting the issue of her government's legitimacy before the people?

The first test case would be in Gujarat; there Gandhi, under pressure of Morarji Desai's "fast unto death," in April 1975 agreed to hold elections in June to reconstitute the assembly dissolved in March 1974. Just prior to these elections, opposition leaders were delighted by the loss of several Congress party candidates in by-elections for parliamentary seats and other offices. These losses, they claimed, reflected the disillusionment of the people with the Congress party. One cannot claim, at one and the same time, that elections are unfair and unrepresentative of the voice of the people when they are lost but, when they are won, reflect the electorate's mood. If rigging of elections was as widespread as Narayan and other opposition leaders repeatedly claimed, the 1967 elections would not have resulted, as they did, in the Congress debacle; and the March 1977 elections would certainly have returned Gandhi and the Congress to power, especially with the aid of the authoritarian structure then in existence.

The demand for dissolution of the Bihar assembly and the manner of its presentation—on the heels of the Gujarat assembly's dissolution under pressure from violent street demonstrations—cannot be considered a positive inducement to democratic institutions. By this time Gandhi regretted her decision to sack the Gujarat chief minister under pressure;[10] to give in to similar pressure in Bihar would surely open a Pandora's box and encourage dissidents in other states to resort to similar tactics. No state government—nor the central government— would be immune from mob pressures. For Narayan did not rely merely on peaceful street processions and public rallies. A tactical goal was to paralyze the government until it fell under the pressure of movement activities.

One tactic used was the *bandh* or shutdown of all public activities and transactions. Thus, during the Bihar *bandh* of October 3-5, 1974, Narayan prescribed that: "From this date there would be no trains running through Bihar, buses would be off the road, work in Government offices, including the Secretariat, would be paralysed and shops would remain closed. . . . A week's paralysis would be enough to end the government in Bahar."[11] Narayan ignored warnings that the *bandh* could lead to violence; when it did, he held the government wholly responsible.

Another commonly used device was the *gherao* or encirclement of individuals or groups against whom there was a grievance. The *gherao* first gained prominence around 1970 when used by industrial workers against managers and owners. Students used it against university chancellors and professors. In 1974-1975, it was a tactic frequently used by political dissidents against sitting members of legislative assemblies— both in Gujarat and Bihar. When *gherao* did not work, legislators and their families were threatened with injury if they did not resign. Inevitably, such activities set the dissidents on a collision course with the government.

The Bihar movement started on March 18, 1974, when a statewide student organization launched its protest through a *gherao* of the Bihar assembly and the governor; the intent was to prevent the governor from addressing a joint session of the assembly. The action led to a direct confrontation between students and the police who tried to head them off. The result was violence: government buildings were set afire, government storehouses containing food were looted, and similar incidents occurred. Soon mobs were on the rampage throughout the capital, the administration of the city was paralyzed, and, as in Gujarat, the army had to be called out to restore order. Nearly two dozen people were killed. Incidents of this sort were repeated throughout 1974.

Narayan's rhetoric was certainly not designed to defuse but rather to ignite explosive forces. Though he has been widely hailed as a Gandhian and presumed to believe in nonviolence, his philosophy on this matter, as on so many others, is not very clear. It is worth recalling, however, that unlike Narayan, Mahatma Gandhi had always called off his *satyagraha* campaigns against the British when they threatened to turn violent. Narayan's biographer, however, quotes his subject on the issue of violence as follows: "My sarvodaya friends and my Gandhian friends will be surprised to read what I publicly say now. I say with a due sense of responsibility that if I myself am convinced that there is no deliverance for the people except through violence, then Jayaprakash Narayan will also take to violence. If the problems of the people cannot be solved democratically, I will also take to violence." This statement, oddly enough, was made on the centenary of Gandhi's birth.[12]

Thirty years earlier Gandhi reportedly lamented over "the fact that a future leader of India like J. P. should be so uncertain about fundamentals like the attitude towards violence and non-violence." Masani, to whom Gandhi expressed these reservations, tried to defend Narayan, noting that the latter merely had a short temper. "No, no," said Gandhi, "he does not have a short temper. He harbours anger in his heart."[13] Thirty-six years later, when I met him, Narayan also impressed me as a man who "harbours anger in his heart." When I spoke with Morarji Desai in April of 1975, I asked him about Narayan's tendency to reconcile himself and the movement to violent tactics: "What can J. P. do if he has no non-violence in him. I should like him to be non-violent. But unless he has courage, he can't be non-violent. A coward cannot be non-violent."[14]

In an apparent effort to reconcile his ambivalence on the matter,

Narayan resorted to a rather fine and puzzling distinction between "peaceful" and "nonviolent" means. The Bihar movement, he said, was peaceful rather than nonviolent. Nonviolence required that secrecy be ruled out, while peaceful means did not; thus the Bihar movement was peaceful rather than nonviolent because some of his followers were permitted to go underground.[15]

But while insisting that his movement was peaceful and democratic, the signals for action he transmitted to his audiences seemed designed to provoke popular outbursts of anger and to bypass elected organs of government. Thus in early 1975, for example, he told a rally: "A revolution will not come either through elections or from Parliament or Assembly, but a revolution, peaceful or bloody, will always be of the people and by the people." In May 1975, while touring one of the southern states in his efforts to broadcast his message nationwide, he reportedly urged the people in a fiery speech to remove the central government "even by using force" if it stood in the way of his movement for "total revolution." In the state of Karnataka (formerly Mysore), he advised students to launch a struggle to force government to correct its errors. It was not enough to pass resolutions or hold demonstrations. "You must make the functioning of government impossible if it does not listen to you." A month earlier, addressing an audience in Patna, the capital of Bihar, he called upon his followers to "force" the prime minister to revoke the emergency invoked during the 1971 war with Pakistan.[16]

In the early phase of the movement, he announced that though "he himself would not take part in any armed insurrection or rebellion, he could not restrain revolutionaries from taking to the gun." And while he believed in nonviolent methods, "he would follow the violent method if any Opposition party was capable of toppling the Government violently." Shortly after he took over the leadership of the Bihar movement, he told a vast audience in Patna that: "A stage has now come when a flare-up is a must."[17] A few days later, he was in New Delhi to launch his "Citizens for Democracy," an organization intended to spread his movement throughout the country.

Before the close of 1974, a national conference was held in New Delhi; it brought Narayan and his associates together with the leaders of the main noncommunist opposition parties. The conference was "held against [the] background of the Bihar movement calling for total revolution throughout the country."[18] The first month of the new year marked the beginning of his efforts to so extend the movement. The first target was the neighboring state of Uttar Pradesh, the most populous state of India. Here, a students' struggle committee was formed, modeled after a similar body in Bihar. Its steering committee met in the state capital to map out its program for launching a Bihar-type agitation. At the end of January, Narayan was addressing workers in the capital of Maharashtra, one of the most important industrial states in the nation; he urged them to work with others to forge a statewide Bihar-type movement. During the spring, he toured several other states, conveying the same message. By May 1975, a month-and-a-half before the emergency declaration, Jayaprakash Narayan had covered all the major states. Only the small states and territories on the northeastern border remained to be toured; probably only his preoccupation with the upcoming Gujarat elections in May and early June prevented him from traveling to the rest. The day before his arrest, during a large rally in New Delhi, he announced that within a week a nationwide civil-disobedience movement would be launched.[19]

Inciting the army, police, and civil service As he intensified his efforts to spread the movement in the early months of 1975, Narayan's public pronouncements became ever bolder. The most serious were repeated incitements to the army, police, and civil servants to disobey orders they considered antidemocratic, antipeople, or otherwise improper. Soon the press began to report that Narayan "was being charged by some people with inciting civil servants, the army, and police personnel to mutiny."[20] Narayan denied the charges, adding by way of clarification that he meant they should merely refuse to obey orders that were "unjust and beyond the call of duty." But, he added, the "time could come when a revolt of the type alleged could take place."[21] A month later, on March 31, he declared that at an "appropriate hour" he would call on the army and police throughout the country to revolt against the Congress rulers, "whom they are fast coming to know and analyse." He would give the call "unless he was in prison or out of this world."[22] He spoke in the capital of Orissa—an eastern state that, like neighboring Bihar, is known for its poverty and political instability—at the beginning of his trek southward. He set May 1 as the date for launching a mass movement along the lines of the Bihar agitation.

Repeatedly he was asked to clarify his call to the army and police, and repeatedly he denied that he had asked them to join the movement or rebel against the government. But always his denial was followed by what seemed to be affirmation of the charge; he had merely asked them "not to obey orders that are illegal" or "unjust."[23] In other words, policemen, civil servants, and soldiers were being invited to interpret the legality and morality of their orders.

In one of his clarifications, Narayan clearly assigned the military forces veto power over the actions of the civilian government: "even though it may not be explicitly stated in the basic or parliamentary law of the country, it is the duty of the Army to defend the Constitution from authoritarian threats."[24] This interpretation would, of course, change the whole complexion of the Indian constitutional structure. If the army decided at some point that constitutional amendments dealing, for example, with the right to private property, were beyond the democratic powers of Parliament, and hence unconstitutional, it would have, in Narayan's view, the right to overthrow the government. Such a formulation of the army's role is tantamount to a justification for military dictatorship. Indeed, according to his own admission, as early as 1967 Narayan was reportedly "toying with the idea of military dictatorship in India." He suggested then that, given the conditions of political instability that followed the general elections of 1967, "the nation should summon the services of the army to fill the vacuum and set right the instability."[25]

Eight years later, he was speaking of a violent revolution that, he said, would not succeed "unless the existing state and the ruling class begin to disintegrate, and the bulk of the armed forces, particularly of the army, either remains neutral or goes over to the side of the revolution. In a peaceful revolution, there is no need for any army to do that. But if the rulers do venture to use the army to suppress a peaceful revolution, then the army should not allow itself to be so used. On such occasions, the leaders of the revolution may call upon the army to come over to their side."[26]

"Parallel governments" In addition to the many other activities described, Narayan announced his intention to set up parallel governments and courts in Bihar. In November 1974, he denied using the term "parallel government"; making another dubious distinction, he said: "I have always mentioned a people's government."[27] One of his noted disciples, however, noted that "in Bihar, where an antipeople and usurper government continues in office with the help of guns, and the legislative Assembly too is no longer recognised by the people, Janata Sarkar (people's government) has acquired some characteristics of a parallel government." Narayan himself, as quoted by this disciple, said that: "Paralysing the Government should mean the development of a parallel people's system in place of the official system, and the people should start managing their everyday affairs through their own organisations so as to end official interference in people's lives. Jan and Chhatra Sangharsha Samities [People's and Students' Struggle Committees] can form the base of the people's system."[28] Speaking to the deputy editor of the *Hindustan Times* in August 1974, Narayan used the term "parallel administration" in discussing the Bihar movement. The people, he said, would be told "that instead of taking their disputes to thanas (police stations) or to the courts they should settle them among themselves and in this way develop a 'parallel' administration."[29]

In May 1975, Narayan announced that "Janata Sarkars" would be formed in 300 of the 587 community-development blocks in Bihar by the end of July. He dismissed as inconsequential the Bihar chief minister's determination not to allow a parallel government, saying "it is already there and it is running."[30] Later that month, he circulated in Patna a three-month program for declaring Janata Sarkars in every village and block of Bihar.

Part of his four-point plan for people's governments at the village and block levels, which he had announced in Bihar in October of 1974, was a nontax campaign. Actually, he had asked the citizens of Bihar as early as March not to pay their taxes, and he repeated his directive in July 1974. The people were to decide whether to pay their taxes to the Congress government or to the Janata Sarkar. If the Janata Sarkar collected taxes, said one of his lieutenants, it would "in a way be acting as some sort of a parallel government."[31]

Running throughout his comments on "total revolution" and "people's government" was a populist theme. He had told a national youth conference in June 1974, that he wanted to "give the people's movement a revolutionary direction" so that people could "develop their own power and become the guardians of democracy." Later in 1974, he asserted the fundamental right of the people to self-government. Refusal to recognize a "usurper" government might appear to the prime minister to be open rebellion, he said, but in his view, it was "pure and simple people's democracy." The election and functioning of a people's government and a people's assembly in Bihar was to be "an exercise in political revolution, in political awareness and organisation."[32]

A confused man In spite of his emphasis on participatory and grassroots democracy, Narayan's words have sometimes displayed an outlook that is far from democratic. For example, in accepting the leadership of the movement, he made it clear that he would not tolerate being "a mere puppet." He went on to say that while he would try to take into account all points of view, his followers would have to submit, ultimately, to his decision, which would be his alone: "All of you must abide by my decision." When the acid test of his participatory democracy came during the June 1975 election campaign in Gujarat, he urged the people to vote "blindly for Janata Morcha (opposition United Front) candidates."[33] These candidates had been selected, in the usual fashion, by the political leadership, particularly by Morarji Desai—not the people's committees. (The procedure displeased many of Narayan's staunchest supporters.)

Assessing his public commitment to democracy—his inclination to appeal directly to the people above the heads of their parliamentary representatives, his "toying with the idea of military dictatorship," his ambivalence toward violent versus nonviolent means, his emphasis on a decisionmaking style akin to "democratic centralism," and his appeal to voters to suspend their judgment and accept his in casting their ballots— we can only conclude that his political views betrayed a degree of inconsistency that far surpassed what we noted in Indira Gandhi's thinking.

The utter confusion of his ideas was noted by many who were at times equally critical of the Congress government. One respected newspaper commentator described the "J. P. movement" as a "sad, sad, spectacle." Commenting on Narayan's inclination to go along by trial and error, he observed that "absence of dogmatism is admirable but nothing dynamic or constructive can be expected from a movement so lacking in definition and so dependent on 'experimentation.' . . . J. P. is no nearer a solution than when he started." Having first followed the virtuous path of nonpartisan politics, said the commentator, Narayan had later realized the futility of this for his purposes and accepted Gandhi's challenge to confront her in the electoral arena. Even then, however, he seemed unable to decide which of the two paths was more desirable. "Instead of a steady progression from idealism to unqualified politicking, there is now a hovering between the two, sometimes apparently leaning toward one and sometimes recoiling from it towards the other."[34] Sham Lal, the editor of the respected daily, *The Times of India* (Bombay), noted that Narayan's "total revolution," far from being a revolution, was merely "a ploy to beat the Congress at its own game. What kind of revolution can it be which can dispense with a strategy, a vanguard and even cadres?" The *bhoodan* (land-gift) movement he had embarked on twenty years earlier was also supposed to be a major revolution at the grass-roots level, but it had failed. "What are the new weapons," asked Sham Lal, "with which he intends to fight entrenched communal and caste interests? And what are the new sanctions he plans to forge against all the elite classes which have come to acquire a stake in corruption of one kind or another? Has he ever asked himself why the Mahatma made so little impact even on the men closest to him?" Such questions must be answered: "Talk of a 'total revolution' doesn't even permit a search for an honest answer." In the meantime, continued the editorial, the opposition parties were exploiting his rhetoric for their battle against the Congress. Each side had its own disparate goals. "The two meet at the point where they both want to oust the Congress from power and replace a comparatively well-knit coalition of interests with a loose federation of interests." The danger was that the movement would "only create a political climate propitious not for a revolution but for anarchy."[35]

The Conservative Appeal: What Salvation for the Poor?

If we examine Narayan's Sarvodaya philosophy, his halting efforts at socioeconomic reforms, the class base of his movement and its organizational cadre, and his relations with the opposition parties, the conclusion seems inescapable that the movement for total revolution would not have, either in the short or in the long run, responded effectively to the developmental needs of the poor. Far from being revolutionary—despite the rhetoric—the movement was essentially conservative. His "people's" or "voluntary socialism" (as he had once referred to the Sarvodaya philosophy), his weak socioeconomic program, and his political agitation played into the hands of the conservative political parties and the upper and middle-upper classes. These classes had shied away from the movement until its more radical economic demands were decisively eclipsed by the political demands for dissolution—first of the Gujarat and then of the Bihar assembly. At this point both business and landed interests gave it their full support. The students recruited into the organizational cadre ultimately proved to be as conservative as their upper- and middle-class parents. When it came to promoting even limited social and economic reforms, they were found wanting. What engaged their energies were the "combative" rather than the "constructive" activities—as Narayan categorized, respectively, the political and economic aspects of his "direct action" plan.[36]

The clearest signal of J. P.'s 180-degree turn from a left-wing ideology of his younger days to the rightist views in his declining years was the encomium he sang to the champion of conservatism, Sardar Vallabhbhai Patel, Nehru's political archrival before and, especially, after independence. In 1975, Minoo Masani, a conservative supporter, noted that in the past Narayan had been critical of Patel: "As a socialist leader, he [Narayan] had naturally looked upon Sardar Patel as a conservative and traditionalist. Now he made belated amends by saying: 'I do believe now that, a realist and pragmatist, Sardar Patel would have been a better choice than Nehru who never had his feet on the ground and had his head above the clouds.'"[37]

A more substantive sign of Narayan's conservatism may be seen in the fact that he sought and obtained support for his movement from all the major conservative opposition parties (as recounted in Chapter 4). He even joined hands with the militant Hindu revivalists, saying, "If the Jana Sangh is fascist, then I too am a fascist." On November 26, 1974, an opposition leaders' conference convened by Narayan was held in New Delhi. Represented were the Jana Sangh, the Bharatiya Lok Dal, the Congress Organization, the Socialist party, and other smaller conservative parties. The best organized of these parties, the Jana Sangh—along with its student affiliate, the Akhil Bharatiya Vidyarthi Parishad (the All-India Students' Council), and its paramilitary wing, the Rashtriya Swayam Sevak Sangh—had come to dominate Narayan's movement, which caused considerable concern to his Sarvodaya followers.

The conservatism of Narayan's Sarvodaya philosophy was evident in some of its basic principles, such as trusteeship of property and a radical decentralization—both political and economic—that was to culminate in a "stateless" society. These ideas—along with an emphasis on class collaboration and harmony rather than class competition or conflict, and social change through persuasion and love rather than through laws backed ultimately by the coercive powers of the state—lent themselves very easily to the maintenance of the status quo. Running through all of them is the radically interpreted concept of voluntarism, which Gunnar Myrdal, in his *Asian Drama,* singled out as the pernicious feature of the "soft state" that pervades not only government but the entire sociopolitical structure and culture.[38] It is no accident that the conservative parties had embraced one or another of the Sarvodaya notions in their 1967 and 1971 election manifestoes. The idea of trusteeship in particular appealed to the Swatantra party. One of the ideologues of the 1974 movement had also endorsed it, saying: "The Sarvodaya perspective of economic development is consistent with its socio-political vision, wherein the privilege of property is circumscribed by trusteeship obligations towards society."[39]

The *bhoodan* or land-gift experiment to which Narayan dedicated many years of his life had been predicated on the premise that land reform could be brought about by appealing to sentiments of love for one's fellow man. Attempts were made to persuade landlords to donate some portion of their land for distribution to the landless. After devoting nearly twenty years to the effort, Narayan conceded it had been an ineffective instrument of social change; land donations often remained nothing more than unconsummated legal transactions. Even where land had been distributed, either the land was so poor as to be uncultivable or was later forcibly taken back by the owner, who had, perhaps in the presence of Narayan or Vinoba Bhave—the saintly founder of the *bhoodan* movement—made a show of his generosity and piety. The emphasis on nonviolence and class collaboration had also led Sarvodaya workers, many of whom supported the Bihar movement, to quash as immoral any efforts of the poor to resist exploitation by the rich.

The notion of economic decentralization, in its total rejection of centralized planning, was nothing less than the nineteenth-century doctrine of laissez-faire. In Narayan's eyes, however, it was enveloped in the aura of Gandhian truth and thus seemed beyond controversy.[40] He told Masani, the former Swatantra leader, that he liked "the Sarvodaya idea, Gandhi's idea, that 'that government is best which governs the least.'"[41] The concept led Narayan to cling to unrealistic populist notions that vested a sort of magical power in "the people." Reflecting on the possibility of a people's assembly parallel to the existing legislative assembly of the state of Bihar, he recognized that it would have to work without revenue. Nevertheless, "if the People's Assembly adopted a land reforms measure the people themselves will implement it. There is a lot that the People's Assembly can do *even without funds.*"[42]

The strange alliance Having acknowledged in 1964 that both "Marxism and Sarvodaya aim at a stateless society,"[43] Narayan differed with Marxists only in that they went about their aim in the wrong way— that is, by starting with a totalitarian state. Such a state, he said, would pose a Himalayan obstacle to the withering away of the state; as a Sarvodayist, he considered the democratic-socialist state to be a more advantageous starting point. Even if we concede that Nehru's and Gandhi's governments had made only limited progress toward the ideal of democratic socialism, the parties with which Narayan aligned himself were even less suitable candidates for propagating this ideal. From his own statements, it seems clear that Narayan was in fact dubious that such parties would ever adopt progressive policies of social and economic change. Though he accepted their political support, he acknowledged that the BLD and the Jana Sangh "are conservative (though the Jana Sangh resents the appellation of conservatism) and I do not know about the Congress Organization which claims it is socialist though I do not know how far they would go." Yet he remained optimistic about the outcome. Without any apparent ground for it, he expressed the hope that "these parties themselves will be radicalised" as the movement became radicalized.[44] But the trend of the movement even then did not justify his hopes.

Some of his own loyal followers had expressed concern about the possible politicization of the movement and "the game of politics." He assured them that people and youth power would remain the main moving force of the movement; speaking at a youth conference, he proclaimed that the political parties had not the power to bring about a total revolution. Addressing the national conference of opposition parties one or two days later, however, he assured their leaders they would have a role to play.

The acceptance of support from the opposition parties, along with periodic statements of doubt about their intentions and usefulness vis-à-vis total revolution, demonstrate another of the confusing facets of his outlook. His remarks at the youth conference in November 1974 reportedly "rejected the idea of welding various political parties into a single entity to provide a national alternative to ruling Congress."[45]

In later speeches, however, he said that the multiplicity of parties posed a danger to his total revolution, and he often rebuked the parties for their inability to come together. It was indeed quite clear by the end of 1974—even to supporters of the movement—that the opposition political parties were in complete disarray. It is difficult to understand how Narayan could have placed so much hope in political parties that had been perennially fragmented and internally divided, especially when he had claimed as a rationale for his movement the factionalism of the Congress party.

In spite of all evidence to the contrary, Narayan was still hopeful (though no longer optimistic) in early June 1975 that the opposition parties would merge. As events bore out, it took the electric jolt of Emergency Rule to finally weld them together. Prior to that time, the parties hoped to retain their individual identities in the process of dethroning Indira Gandhi and the Congress. They zealously guarded their separate identities, even though J. P. and a few others tried to bring about a merger.

Narayan's enduring distrust of all political parties is best exemplified by his long-held commitment to "partyless democracy." Even when he conceded that he was prepared to work within the framework of a party system, he held to the notion as an ideal to be realized when a "casteless and classless society" had been achieved. His continued references to such an ideal brought remonstrances by both friends and foes. In April 1975, Desai opposed Narayan's idea of a "partyless democracy," saying it "would be possible only in the communist world or under dictatorial rule." Jagjivan Ram (minister of defense in the present government) said in March 1975 that he was at a loss to understand what Narayan meant by a partyless democracy to uphold parliamentary democracy. As far as he could see, it would only destroy democracy.[46]

It is clear then that party men of all political stripes were hostile to Narayan's criticism of the party system. It is equally clear that he was highly ambivalent about the political value of parties—not only the Congress but the parties supporting his movement as well. Speaking to Gujarati students in early 1974 at the height of their campaign against the legislative assembly, he seemed concerned with the possibility that the Congress Organization, the Jana Sangh, and the Swatantra might be strengthened after the elections. He thought this would be a backward step. Yet, a year later, he was campaigning for these very parties. Speaking in Uttar Pradesh in early 1975, he decried the fact that political parties had begun, since the inception of the movement in Bihar, to carve out leadership claims. He urged students to take the initiative in starting the movement in U.P. Domination by political parties, he said, would transform the movement.

While expressing hostility to the pro-Soviet Communist party of India, a sometime supporter of Gandhi's government, Narayan urged the anti-Gandhi Communist party of India-Marxist to become active in his movement because, according to press reports, "he had had doubts about the sustained participation of the Jana Sangh and the Congress (O)."[47] The fact that the Jana Sangh was also involved, he told the CPI-Marxists and their union followers, ought not to deter them from joining his movement. He then added a thought which, bereft of a coherent theoretical framework, leaves us without a clear notion of his strategy and even suggests a certain opportunism. It sustains the oft-heard charge that his movement was primarily an anti-Congress, anti-Indira Gandhi movement, and as such was eagerly supported by all opposition parties and leaders. "In a revolution," he said, "it is not important who is in it at the moment, but who will last till the end."[48] The CPI-Marxists at first rejected his overtures, saying that their "perspective to build the unity of left and democratic forces is incompatible with the idea of all-in unity, including parties of the right."[49] Although later the CPI–Marxist was more forthcoming in its support, the logic of its earlier observation is irrefutable.

Narayan too, despite his publicly acknowledged tolerance for political extremes in January 1975, had shifted position only a month or so later. In early March 1975, he strongly berated the people's and youth committees that had been formed throughout India; he said they were "hotch-potch" groups made up of incompatible political elements which led to "vicious internal wrangling."[50] Indeed, he was so disappointed in these struggle committees that he had considered withdrawing their right to nominate electoral candidates—because various opposition parties were "trying to capture them." In fact, he said, in Bihar he had already taken steps to liberate them from political snares by forming a new kind of unit (the Pradesh Chhatra Yuva Sangharsh Vahini), which would permit only students and youth (between the ages of fourteen and thirty) who were not members of any political organization. This plan must have been dropped, however, for later references indicate that the original units continued to function.

Finally, only two months after he had decried the efforts of opposition parties to manipulate the selection of candidates, he gave these parties carte blanche to set up their own candidates in the forthcoming Gujarat elections.

The "organs of people's power" At first glance, this strange alliance and the lack of common ground between J. P. and the opposition parties is puzzling; but it can be illuminated as the story unfolds.

Narayan's views of the role of the struggle committees in the electoral process confounded many observers. In August 1974, he was asked about his next step in the event that the Bihar assembly was dissolved. As in Gujarat, he was concerned, he said, to "create some kind of institution" that would ensure that "good people" were sent to the legislature and that could, in the period between elections, weed out poor choices. He had in mind some sort of "watchdog" body at the village level. Recognizing that the resignations of ministries and dissolution of assemblies would not in themselves solve the problems he perceived as most serious, he wanted to "forge permanent organs of people's power from the village to the constituency to the State level." He had no "rigid ideas as to the shape of the permanent organs of people's power," other than that the organization of "people's committees" at each polling place should consist "of nonparty members with noncaste and nonclass attitudes of mind, pledged to act as watchdogs of democracy and people's rights as well as duties."[51]

The mechanics of nomination and election, to the limited extent they were spelled out, would be terribly complex and hardly conducive to meaningful popular participation, which was proclaimed as his ultimate goal. One way of selecting delegates for this watchdog body, for example, would be for struggle committee members to choose one to three delegates from among the thousand or so voters for each polling booth. These delegates would form a "voters council" in each constituency to choose their candidate. This council would also keep watch on the representative after he was elected. This scheme, if implemented at the national level of elections, would mean that there would be at least 500 voters councils, each of them made up of between 500 and 1,500 people. (Each constituency averages roughly 500,000 people, sometimes less, often more. This rough calculation applies only to national parliamentary elections. A similar calculation would have to be made for state elections.)

It was not at all clear how the voters councils could avoid becoming entangled in party politics, nor indeed remain immune to the corrupting influence of "money bags" (as the opposition leaders referred to wealthy buyers of political favors). I asked Narayan's biographer, Ajit Bhattacharjea, how the independently nominated candidates were to be financed: "With a local situation of this type, you do not need too much financing because the candidate would be selected by his constituents by a kind of primary election. Committees would get contributions from local people."[52] The rather naive assumption seemed to be that these 500 to 1,500 people, presumably from the very same villages said to be tainted by corruption, would somehow be incorruptible or that the wealthy villagers, who it is assumed were responsible for the corruption then existing in election politics, would not attempt to influence this particular nominating process.

Bhattacharjea added that J. P.'s organizations were "really service organizations trying to influence the political process, but they are not themselves members of it." Isn't there a very thin line, I asked, between "getting into politics" and "trying to influence politics"? His answer did not shed very much light on the question: "The line is that you do not seek office. These committees are set up by the local groups on the basis of consensus. They are not parties in any sense. This approach is different from the electoral approach. He (Narayan) wants unanimity or consensus. The question of ideology on which such candidates run is not the most prominent." Bhattacharjea did concede that the political parties might not accept the nominee of the struggle committees (presumably because of ideological reasons, among others). But, as the nominee was supposedly selected "because he is representative of that area and he would have the support of all the local people ... the opposition parties would be ill-advised to reject such a candidate." A similar question put to Narayan by another interviewer received a no more illuminating response. Asked whether the setting up of candidates would not make of these committees de facto political parties Narayan replied: "Set up or endorse a candidate set up by others, by parties or non-party candidate independents, etc. It is up to them." This kind of logic is perhaps a variant of what V. S. Naipaul has described as a "defect of vision" among some Indian intellectuals and politicians.[53]

Under these circumstances, the struggle committees would actually be nominating candidates for office, a function central to the role of political parties, and it seems quite probable that the nominees would be leading members of the community or their choices. For the "non-party" nominating body was just as likely as party nominating bodies to come under political pressures from the local potentates to nominate a particular candidate and to be affected by such considerations as caste, class, and religion. Caste in particular, Bhattacharjea conceded, would be a factor for forty or fifty years but "with luck . . . would gradually fade."[54]

As Bihar was touted as the big success area of the J. P. movement, I expected that the opposition parties there would have acted more responsibly than in Gujarat. When I asked for confirmation of this, Bhattacharjea answered: "It is difficult to say." He saw success in terms of the "number of people attending meetings and the funds he (Narayan) has been able to collect."

The picture was further confused by Narayan's endorsement of the political parties' right to nominate candidates too. Some candidates would thus be nominated by the struggle committees and others by the parties. Narayan expected that the names of the party nominees would be submitted for his approval, although it is not clear on what ground he based this expectation. Indeed, when the acid test came in the week preceding the June 1975 elections in Gujarat, this hope was dashed. J. P. was not even consulted when the list of candidates was drawn up by a committee of the United Front. Morarji Desai, the leader of the United Front, rejected the demand for representation from the movement out of hand. Earlier, Narayan had made stinging criticisms of the manner in which Front candidates had been selected; but in spite of such differences, Narayan urged the electorate to vote "blindly" for United Front candidates. He described them as "people's candidates," even though he had earlier asserted that "people's candidates" could only be those nominated by people's and youth struggle committees. He insisted he had no differences with Desai and that he would "always support the supporters of struggle who happened to be candidates in the election."[55] He was saying, in effect, that he would support anyone, regardless of whether or not he was committed to his ideals. This stand confirmed the repeated impression that his primary goal was to remove Gandhi and the Congress from power.

If all this reveals a lack of clear thought and planning for the future, it was a problem that pervaded Narayan's thinking in other matters as well. When asked about "the feeling that the movement lacked a total frame, particularly on economic and social issues," he replied that "it is not wise to spell out everything at this stage."[56] Masani, his Swatantra admirer, also expressed misgivings that "in the absence of a clear-cut economic posture, if a chaotic situation were to develop when he (Narayan) might not be there to control it, the fruits of this agitation might well drop into the lap of the Naxalites and the Marxist Communists . . . rather than into the hands of Liberal Democrats or Social Democrats, as he would presumably prefer." Nevertheless, Masani was "not sure that Jayaprakash would be wise to commit himself to a cut-and-dry socioeconomic programme." As J. P. was on a moral crusade, said Masani, "it would perhaps be a pity if he were to limit his appeal to certain sections of society and repel others by outlining a programme of the nature that various political parties have evolved."[57] We may infer from this that any statements that might alienate the conservative business and landed interests and their party supporters were taboo. Hence, "total revolution" was merely a slogan.

This conclusion may explain why there was hardly any mention of land or other economic reforms during the movement. Yet throughout his life, Narayan had given the question of agrarian reforms the highest priority. According to one of his followers, land was seen by J. P. as "the biggest source of inequality and exploitation," and inequalities were seen as "the central problem of Indian society." If only land-reform laws were implemented, Narayan said in the 1960s, "rural society would be radically transformed—socially, economically and psychologically."[58] Yet in 1974–1975, not only was the question of land reforms shelved by Narayan, but he actually supported the demands of better-off farmers to raise the procurement price of foodgrains (which would inevitably be passed on to the consumer and fall most heavily on the shoulders of the poor).

While his lack of clarity probably stemmed from a characteristic style of thinking—much as it did in the case of Indira Gandhi—it is no doubt true in both instances that it served to hold together a disparate group of political interests and outlooks that might otherwise fall apart—particularly (for J. P.) in the emergent conservative alliance being forged during the "total revolution" movement.

The movement's narrow class base   What was the popular base of J. P.'s movement? In one account of the Gujarat and Bihar movements, it is argued rather convincingly that there was no real mass base supporting the demands for dissolution of the two assemblies.[59] Rather, the upper and middle-upper classes in both areas lent their active support to these demands—particularly after the economic demands for land reforms and the like had receded into the background. This contention about the class base of the movement was confirmed by my own observations during the two days I accompanied Narayan on his tour to some of the Gujarat constituencies in late May and early June 1975. The areas seemed to be, on the whole, far more prosperous than those visited by Gandhi on two of her four election tours I observed in Gujarat. His audiences were made up of clearly well-off people and a predominant upper- and middle-class youth (probably student) component. Further, Narayan's first stop upon deplaning in Ahmedabad, the old capital of Gujarat, was at the home of a wealthy businessman; there Narayan met and was briefed by local leaders. An overnight stay while on tour was made at a hostel (the Jyoti Guest House), which was, according to one of Narayan's lieutenants, owned by a local wealthy industrialist. When I tried to pay for my lodgings and food, I was told that everyone's expenses on the tour would be borne by this same industrialist. Had it been necessary to travel by train (we traveled by automobile), this expense too would have been borne by private individuals. The young lieutenant added, by way of explanation, that "J. P. Narayan coming here was a big event."

It occurred to me at the time that no effort was being made to mobilize the poorer classes among the nonorganized workers, farmers, and landless laborers. This observation was confirmed by a study of the J. P. movement in Bihar; it was found that the movement was most active in the "cities and countryside" of the Ganges belt of north and south Bihar, "particularly where middle peasants have improved their economic condition since the 1960s." According to the same study, "Adivasis (tribals), Harijans (untouchables) and Muslims (about 36 percent of the total population) had, by and large, remained indifferent to the movement, and so had poor peasants, landless labourers, industrial workers and casual labourers." The urban poor, who at first thought that the students might champion their cause, showed some sympathy toward the movement, but withdrew their support when they failed to see how dissolution of the assembly would benefit them. Very minimal efforts were made to mobilize the working class and the poor peasants.[60] This impression of the limited class base of the movement was also widespread among many politicians and nonpoliticians I spoke to in New Delhi.

An additional indication of this weakness may be found in Narayan's admission that "organisationally we are not yet as strong and have not gone down deep enough. . . . The programme was that this [the formation of struggle committes] should have gone down to the block level, and, wherever possible, even to the village level."[61] This admission was made in August 1974, the fifth month of the movement; it is possible, but not likely, that lower levels were tapped later on.

Reliance on a Youth Strategy

The likelihood that little was done to reach the poorer classes is borne out by Narayan's announcement, on February 10, 1975, that he would change the tactics that had kept the student and youth activists "pinned down to Patna all the time." He wanted them to "spend a larger part of the time in the countryside in the work of building up the organs of people's power."[62] In early March, he appealed to the youth to go to the countryside to restructure rural society and expressed regret that many had failed to respond to his call to abandon their studies and plunge into the movement. Thus, as late as March 1975, he was encountering difficulties in mobilizing the students to whom he had referred in August 1974 as the "soldiers" of his movement.

One reason for the emphasis of the youth strategy may be found in his perception of the revolutionary potential of the working class. He saw it as "more or less a petit bourgeois class. Their standard of living is higher than the living standards of the lower-middle class, for instance. If you compare their wages with the wages of agricultural labour, they (the industrial working class) are much better off. So I don't think they are a revolutionry force at all."[63] There is some truth to the contention that the Indian working class had become increasingly conservative, but it is a partial truth, perhaps applicable only to the small organized sector of workers. Narayan's conception, however, leaves out the majority—in both urban and rural areas—who are not organized and whose living standards are among the lowest. His view has been properly criticized as elitist. Even if Narayan's perception of the "embourgeoisement" of the workers had been correct, as a true revolutionary he should have concentrated all his efforts on awakening and rallying this class, and particularly the rural workers, landless laborers, and poor sharecroppers or very small landholders who are the most depressed of all classes in India. Despite his observation about the relative poverty of agricultural laborers, he did not choose to mobilize them and gave no explanation of the fact. If standard of living was the criterion, the students certainly could not qualify as a vanguard class. Yet "I worked it out in my mind that it is the youth who must take the lead in this."[64]

His first experience with such "soldiers" could not have been very edifying. Only a few months before assigning them this leading role, he had seen the student movement in Gujarat collapse as soon as the demand for dissolution of the assembly was conceded. The economic demands of the early phase of the movement were simply shelved once the political demands (which, significantly, coincided with those of the opposition political parties) were met. He noted that he had once urged Gujarati students to forge people's organs at the village level, like the voters councils described earlier; but nothing came of this suggestion. Surprisingly, even though he gave them such a prominent role in the movement, he was dubious about whether they possessed the "stamina to carry on a long-drawn struggle."[65] He did not seem to appreciate the seriousness of this weakness, which had proven to be the downfall of the Gujarat movement. If Narayan was primarily interested in the long-drawn struggle of socioeconomic change, as he often said, his choice of "soldiers" was very poor indeed. But if his intention—which he repeatedly denied—was merely to create sufficient instability to bring about the defeat of Indira Gandhi and the Congress, his choice of the students as the vanguard of the "revolution" was felicitous.

Actually, it is difficult to decipher his strategic priorities from his statements. On the one hand, he often said his movement was not intended merely to replace one set of politicians with another. Rather, it was to bring about a total revolution—in the economic, political, cultural, and social spheres. On the other hand, he was prepared to relegate "constructive" (i.e., economic and social) reforms to the background and give primacy to agitational activities. His actions were more consistent with this latter assertion; yet he often said he would be satisfied with nothing less than a "total revolution." He also said, however, that he did not expect "miracles" from his movement and would be "very happy if reform takes place"[66]

Perhaps his strategy was first to topple the Congress and then to proceed with his "constructive" program. If so, he ought to have considered carefully his choice of instruments. If, as he had thought, the students did not have the stamina to carry out a long-term struggle, did he plan after the agitational phase to start developing a different, more committed cadre to take up the constructive work? Where would he recruit this cadre? Perhaps he believed that the "permanent people's organs" would have been forged by the end of the agitational campaign and could take on the onerous responsibilities of social transformation and political vigilance. But it must have been clear to him that the students on whom he counted to forge these people's organs would fail him. That he was aware of this is clear from a statement of March 1975, to the effect that the political parties had lent "basic dynamism" to his movement, while the people's struggle committees "had proved ineffective under non-political persons."[67]

By neither temperament nor class character were the students suited to carry on a sustained struggle for social and economic change. Their strength lay in agitation, not in construction, which requires sacrifice and dedication over the short-term and long-term. One analyst of the Bihar movement assesses the students' role in the following way: "Processions, demonstrations and bandhs attracted them in large numbers, but not so the picketing of liquor shops, visiting villages, and leaving colleges. In the course of the movement, they lost their credibility in the eyes of the masses. Several respondents, including Sarvodaya workers, reported to me that students were irresponsible and corrupt."[68] Even Narayan once conceded that he had evidence of corrupt practices by students working in his movement. He had, moreover, chided his young followers for being power hungry.

A respected newspaper editor pointed out that the students had for the most part ignored J. P.'s appeal to leave their schools and colleges for a year to lead the "total revolution." They were, he said, more interested in passing their examinations without having to do their homework than in overhauling the system.[69] Examples of the frivolity of student demands common to both Gujarat and Bihar were those for concessions on cinema tickets and easier examinations. Even Narayan acknowledged in February 1975 that 99.9 percent of the students had gone back to their studies. Although earlier on he would have considered this a setback, he now professed not to be distraught by it; he was convinced he could count on at least three thousand students to lead the agitation.[70] Another estimate, made by a highly credible supporter, was far more conservative. Referring to a time period around November/December 1974, Masani said: "Students were given the option either to plunge in for total involvement in the campaign for a whole year or to give the movement one day of each week, thus combining studies with agitation. Of the 13,000 students in Patna University, 300 opted for total participation, while 2500 opted for partial participation." Nearly 80 percent, it appears, opted for complete non-participation. As Masani said, "This was certainly a setback for the movement."[71]

This was to be expected. They were a transient group whose primary interest was in securing a career. Even those who might have been susceptible to Narayan's idealistic appeals were often compelled by their parents to appear at examinations. The problem was the nature of the class on which he depended to bring about revolutionary change; it was itself a part of the establishment, and the changes it was interested in were those that would further increase its benefits.

The logic of this situation seems to have escaped Narayan. He often berated the students for acting in accordance with their class character. The movement undertaken by students against profiteering, black marketing, and hoarding failed because, reportedly, it had been infiltrated by the sons and relatives of the people who were guilty of these practices. According to one respected daily, hoarders and profiteers were financing the students. "Significantly, the godowns (storehouses) owned by profiteering wholesalers or shops belonging to retailers who raise prices without any provocation have not been picketed by students."[72]

The drive against corruption entrusted to students was also a flop. J. P. had made corruption a prime issue of his agitation. Yet here too he was thought to have failed to give his followers the quality of leadership expected of him. He had once blamed the government for corrupting businessmen and had tried to assure the latter that his movement was not directed against them. In a wholly unrealistic effort, he appealed to them no longer to "grease the palms of officers."[73] For all his genuine concern with the disease of corruption, which he acknowledged had touched the entire nation and undermined all developmental efforts, he was not prepared to disown the corrupt elements that were reported to be supporting his efforts. Indeed, when queried "about a drive to end corruption with the financial help of businessmen engaged in corrupt practices," Narayan's retort must have surprised and perplexed even his most ardent followers. He replied that "his 'total revolution' was a mass movement and nobody could keep anybody out."[74] One cannot help but wonder how he would square such an attitude with his commitment to Gandhi's Sarvodaya philosophy, one of whose cardinal principles insists on "the right means for the right ends."

Perhaps the most striking example of such questionable support was that provided by Ramnath Goenka, the owner of the daily, *Indian Express,* for the financial support of the Sarvodayist journal of political commentary, *Everyman's Weekly,* which was founded in July 1973. According to the editor of *Everyman's* (Ajit Bhattacharjea, Narayan's admiring biographer), "The *Indian Express* prints *Everyman's Weekly* under some sort of license arrangement under which the printing and publication of *Everyman's Weekly* is financed by Goenka who owns the *Indian Express.* There are also some common personnel between the two newspapers."[75] Goenka was under indictment for corruption on several charges under Gandhi's government, and even when the new Janata government came into power, the charges were reportedly pursued, although nothing has come of them.

In any case, whether in a drive against corruption or for land reforms, student efforts invariably fell short of expectations. They were not even up to effecting such minor social reforms as discarding the sacred thread (which distinguishes upper- from lower-caste Hindus) or fighting against the dowry system. Narayan had urged the young men participating in his movement not to accept dowry in marriage, for that would be a "betrayal of the cause." He goaded them to fight against casteism and ostentatious expenditure at their weddings. He appealed to them to begin the struggle for total revolution in their own homes and abandon the double standards that guided their actions. But such exhortations fell on deaf ears, and once the young men even laughed at their old leader. Angered by this, he rebuked them: "Fools, your sisters are drowning themselves in wells because your fathers cannot give dowry to the greedy vultures who want to sell their sons and you are laughing."[76] Stung, some students pointed out that obedience to their parents' wishes in such matters as dowry was unavoidable, since they were unemployed and thus dependent on their parents. In an angry but futile exchange, J. P. asked them whether they accepted the inevitable, and, if so, then "what is the meaning of total revolution?" A student asked: "What *is* total revolution?" "You shouted 'total revolution' at the airport," retorted J. P. "What did you mean by it?" The question apparently had not been and could not be answered fully to the satisfaction of the movement's participants. By May 1975, Narayan had finally come to the conclusion that the students' views on social and economic problems were conservative.[77]

This realization, along with the students' increasingly evident ineffectiveness as instruments of "total revolution," revealed the ideological and strategical bankruptcy of the movement. This recognition was decisively reflected in Narayan's complete surrender to the political parties that came to dominate the 1975 elections in Gujarat. Narayan's statements and strategy indicate that he was trying to use them; and there can be little doubt that the opposition parties were using him. Jana Sangh leaders, in particulai, and their student affiliates, opposed J. P. on some economic matters. One of them said that "if after the dissolution of the (Bihar) Assembly JP gave some economic programme they would oppose him." A prominent student leader of the state-level organization of the Jana Sangh's student affiliate was reported to have said: "I do not think that some big changes will take place after the dissolution (of the Bihar Assembly). JP will be busy with his Sarvodaya work and we will be busy with Vidyarthi Parishad (the student organization)."[78]

When J. P. called for a nationwide civil-disobedience campaign on June 25, 1975, Indira Gandhi was desperately trying to nurse an ailing economy back to health. Her political legitimacy had been dealt two serious blows—by the Gujarat election defeat and the High Court's ruling against her in the election petition case. The prospect of a national upheaval along the lines of Bihar and Gujarat could not be lightly discounted. J. P. had shown that he could inspire people—even if he could not lead them. He had shown that he could paralyze governments—but he could not ensure their stable functioning. He sought change but could not pursue or organize political power effectively enough to effect it. His partners, the opposition parties, sought power, but they did not want change. Nor could they submerge their differences long enough to offer a stable alternative to the Congress government. The possibility of chaos and violence, which could threaten both the Indian political institutions and economic stability, loomed large. The stakes were high. The prime minister had to respond quickly and firmly to the challenge.

CHAPTER VII

Emergency Rule

The decision to declare an internal state of emergency, taken by Prime Minister Gandhi on June 25, 1975, seemed destined to alter the course of Indian political history. Since then it has cried out for an explanation. Why, though enjoying formidable constitutional as well as political power, did she feel the need to further strengthen her hand? We have sought the answer only partly in her personality, seeking the primary cases in the constraints on action generated in the larger political environment and in her own leadership style and strategy. The latter, of course, were shaped by subjective as well as objective considerations.

Against the wide time perspective and the broader canvas of events sketched in the preceding chapters, I believe we can fruitfully assess the declaration of emergency. Of course, any analysis made at this time must be tentative; one is best advised to tread with caution in judging momentous historic events. However clear-cut the issues may appear to contemporaries, it invariably turns out that the full array of facts has not been known (postemergency revelations notwithstanding). It also bears repeating that my analysis focuses on the decision to declare a state of emergency and its antecedents—not on the events that followed the declaration. An understandable preoccupation with the excesses of Emergency Rule has obscured the events that preceded it; we have therefore sought to restore perspective to this period.

The prevailing somewhat superficial interpretation is that the Emergency Declaration was an unprincipled power grab motivated solely by Gandhi's selfish desire to bolster a weakened political position. In this view Congress' loss of the Gujarat elections and her conviction by the Allahabad High Court were most important. In fact these events, along with the political turmoil generated by them, forced her hand.

No plausible reasons have been offered as to why she did not choose to ride out these two storms. All other things being equal, she could have survived the loss of Gujarat to the opposition parties; in any case, the election was lost by a narrow margin. In a country where defections from one party to another are the norm, the fall of the United Front government could have been engineered in Gujarat; the prime minister could simply have waited until it fell, as well it might, under the weight of the internal divisions so characteristic of such coalitions. Although the loss of the election-petition case weakened her politically—especially within the party but also to a lesser extent throughout the country—she could have survived even this loss. A year later, the high court's decision was in fact overturned by the Supreme Court.

No matter how one explains Indira Gandhi's reaction to the Gujarat election loss and her High Court defeat, there is still no satisfactory explanation as to why she allowed a free election in 1977—if, indeed, she was determined to retain power "anyhow, anyway" (as Desai put it to me). It has been suggested that she hoped elections would placate world opinion, and there may be some validity to this idea. It seems more likely, however, her decision was motivated by a compelling need to refurbish her self-image as a democrat. Such a motivation does not, of course, square with assertions that she was obsessively motivated by power. Moreover, as a meticulous political strategist, she must have recognized the danger that Jagjivan Ram, having been denied the opportunity to run in the forthcoming elections, would defect to the opposition. Ram's defection being a distinct possibility, she would have calculated that her party's election chances were not good. The risk need not have been taken at this time (even if she was misled about the party's popularity), particularly by one "obsessed" with the desire to retain power.

However, Gandhi's response to the Gujarat and election-petition blows—which admittedly precipitated (but did not motivate) the emergency proclamation—does make sense in the context of the events of the preceding several years and of the period shortly preceding June 25. Her decision is perhaps best understood as the mark of a crisis at the national and individual levels of leadership.

On the national levels, competing forces struggled to gain or retain control of the governmental machinery. The J. P. movement and the activities of the opposition parties amounted to organized efforts to effect a coup d'état by paralyzing government at the state and central levels. The authority and legitimacy of government were critically challenged, and political stability and social order were threatened.

At the individual level, the leadership crisis was a signal of the prime minister's failure to evolve a clear ideology and strategy of action. It underscored her inability to resolve contradictions within the ideology of democratic socialism and, more specifically, to carry her democratic and socialist ideals to their logical conclusion by reshaping the Congress party into an instrument of social and political change. The June decision can also be seen as a confession of the failure of her "go-slow" strategy and her desire to effect voluntary change through persuasion.

The political power struggle had gone on for many years—under Nehru, Shastri, and Indira Gandhi. It was chiefly a struggle among the various "have" classes or, more precisely, among the politicians who spoke for them. The ideological struggle was waged by the conservative forces—the Swatantra, the Bharatiya Lok Dal which merged with the former in 1974, the Congress Organization (which split off from the ruling party in 1969), and the Jana Sangh. They aimed at limited government through decentralization and/or the expansion of free enterprise. Socioeconomic reforms that threatened the social status and economic foundations of privilege were frowned upon. Yet, intent on maintaining their separate identities, they remained too divided to speak effectively for the upper- and middle-upper classes they aspired to represent.

Others of their class sought a voice in the ruling Congress party, under whose umbrella both conservative and moderately progressive forces found shelter. Congressmen generally sought to increase government's role in economic and social matters and to preserve a mixed economy that favored public enterprise.

The left wing, beleaguered by conservatives inside and outside the party, periodically exerted itself to introduce socioeconomic reforms and claimed to be spokesmen for the poor. Such reforms were diligently blocked or delayed by opposition and party conservatives—through constitutional channels or informal means. The resulting emasculation of reform was grudgingly tolerated by Congress leftists as the inevitable outcome of the pluralist, democratic process whose legitimacy had been accepted by all the major contenders. Some attempts to circumvent blockage were undertaken within existing political, parliamentary, and constitutional arrangements, but the power mechanics of the system dictated that the incumbent Congress respond sympathetically to conservative pressures for snail-pace reforms.

Both the ruling Congress and the fragmented right-wing political forces then vied for support of established and nouveau riche classes. Hence, the ideological parameters of the struggle for power could never encompass a complete restructuring of society and the state. The political realities of parliamentary democracy precluded it, and the propagation of gradual social and economic change deflected it.

Within the Congress party the compulsions of the nationalist struggle had brought together strange bedfellows, who could be expected to part company once independence was attained. But the process of disassociation was stunted for a long time (and is not likely to be peacefully completed). The first sorting out of conflicting class interests took place in 1948, when a group of socialists left the party. In 1951, the Congress Left gained ground within the party after the death of archconservative Sardar Patel and Nehru's victory over Patel's man, Tandon. Later small fragments of the right wing broke away; the Swatantra party was founded by former Congressmen in 1959, and a number of new state parties formed in 1967. The latter joined the Congress Organization or other right-wing parties at the time of the big split in 1969.

However, even the departure of the extreme right-wingers, did not produce a clear socialist orientation. The Congress "leftists" remained in a blurred no-man's (and everyman's) land, slightly to the left of center. The Congress never became a clearly ideological party. It continued as a coalition party, akin to those in the United States, except that, unlike the latter, it was saddled with a socialist program it was prepared neither to shed nor to fully implement. As it had under Nehru, the Congress under Gandhi continued to seesaw between progressive and conservative policies.

Prime Minister Gandhi herself must share a major portion of the blame for failing to provide a clear ideological lead. Having recognized the need to build the Congress as an instrument of mass education, she invariably succumbed to the conflicting need to maintain it intact as an instrument for mobilizing votes; ideological issues were thus muted for the sake of the continued support of conservatives. Five years intervened between the initial efforts in 1969, to mold the Congress into a socializing agent, and the second attempt in 1974. In the interim, as national and state elections had brought into prominence many men of

Gandhi's own choosing, more progressive policies might have been expected. Once elected, however, the new members forgot their populist slogans and their inarticulate and poverty-stricken constituents to fight with their rivals over the spoils of victory. Although politically obligated to Prime Minister Gandhi and pledged to promote Congress socialist aims, they were no less obligated to local conservative power structures; Gandhi was either unable or unwilling to hold them to their promises. In 1974 the threat of the J. P. movement spurred Congressmen and the prime minister to think once again about arousing ideological fervor and mobilizing the poor, but no significant steps were taken.

By June 1975, when Gandhi was most in need of a strong party to back her, Congressmen were divided on ideological issues and over whether to stand with their leader to confront the J. P. movement and the opposition parties. After the ruling went against her in the election-petition case, it was widely rumored that some colleagues were advising her to resign. Others pressed her to stay on. Clearly the party was divided. Congress conservatives had been disenchanted by her leftist policies, and the leftists by her retreats from progressive policies. Almost all were disillusioned by her defense of Sanjay Gandhi's small-car project and by her response to widespread charges of corruption in government.

The plain fact is that she did not articulate unequivocally her views on democracy and socialism nor did she take action to implement the views she did espouse. On the one hand, she anticipated that without strong government action to effect "distributive justice," violence might break out. Yet prior to the emergency, her watchword was moderation. Although she conceded that expropriation of wealth was a means to socialism, she assured the affluent that their property rights were safe. Her pronouncements and policies on education were similarly ambivalent; she saw the need for progressive educational reforms but was not prepared to undercut the academic ambitions of middle-upper-class youth.

Her actions reflected these ambiguities. Little was done to implement land or educational reforms. And, although the twenty-fourth, twenty-fifth, and twenty-ninth amendments to the constitution struck a serious blow against private business and landed interests—as did the nationalization policies of 1969 and 1971-1972—when faced with the economic crisis of 1973, she retreated. (For example, she quickly yielded to pressures from the landed interests to denationalize the wholesale wheat trade.) By 1974, she was clearly moving away from progressive policies; that year her anti-inflationary package was based on the primacy of the free-market mechanism as an instrument for stabilizing the economy. The working classes, not the business interests, bore the brunt of the harsh economic measures. By 1974–1975, the socialist model of development, embryonic though it was, had been abandoned in favor of the World Bank model.

By this time, it was clear that the much-touted goal of economic self-reliance had been abandoned in order to stabilize the economy. Faced with a systemic problem of serious proportions—maintaining order while attempting to stabilize the shaky economic conditions—she was forced by the J. P. movement to give priority to stability in order to salvage her economic-stabilization program, which she perhaps saw as a precondition for further change. In the past, the conflict between order and change had been resolved by democratic procedures. Now, not only was there no agreement about the means and ends of government among the political "ins" and "outs," but opponents were threatening to flout the democratic rules of the game. She thus had the limited option of either succumbing to political blackmail or imposing order from above. She had to calculate the costs and benefits of coercive action against the potential gains or losses—to her development strategy—of inaction which might lead to chaos and violence. She chose to impose order from above.

Her choice of the coercive alternative reflected her own emotional and intellectual ambiguities on the merits of democratic solutions, and it was a betrayal of her commitment to gradualism and persuasion. Had her policies during Emergency Rule fulfilled her frequent promises to advance socialist goals, the betrayal may have been at least logically consistent with her socialist pledges. As it turned out, neither democracy nor socialism was advanced during Emergency Rule.

While the emergency decision as a conscious, deliberate action can be explained by the situation created by the J. P. movement and the economic crisis that preceded it, it is to her personality that we must turn for clues to her emotional and intellectual predisposition to resort to such a drastic measure. Throughout her life, she had tended to shift sharply from indecision to resoluteness. In the months preceding the Emergency Declaration, many wondered why no action was being taken against the subversive activities of Narayan and his associates (as people had been puzzled by her inaction in 1971 when the Bangladesh crisis was building up to dangerous proportions). Recalling other significant decisions in her life—whether to form the children's Monkey Army, marry Feroze Gandhi, or split the Congress in 1969—we find she was impelled to take resolute action when her will or dignity or beliefs were somehow assaulted. Viewed from that perspective, the emergency decision was a defensive reaction against threats to her self-esteem, resolve, and her vision of India. The tendency to react sharply to opposition is also indicated in her shifting moods—from aloofness to aggressiveness. When personally challenged, she periodically emerged from her ivory tower in an aggressive, defiant mood; at such times her stubborn streak was most apparent. Following an established pattern, in 1975 she seemed resolved to thwart her enemies' plans to unseat her. Determined to be master of her political life and environment, and perceiving herself as one who would not be deterred by "mountainous" obstacles, she no doubt felt she had to overcome any difficulties thrust in her way. Rightly or wrongly, she saw her authority and her economic goals imperiled by the J. P. movement. She had set in motion a program to stabilize the economy, and she was determined to see it through.

The manner in which the emergency decision was reached and implemented clearly reveals Indira Gandhi's fatal leadership flaws. Self-sufficiency, independence, and autonomy, which, when displayed in good measure can be virtues, became flaws. They grew to be obsessively guarded ends in themselves rather than means to a healthy self-fulfillment. Her inability to communicate effectively with people at an intermediate level, where most political relationships operate, meant that she often failed to inspire trust and confidence in associates who did not know her well. Nor were they reassured by her inclination to make decisions in isolation. While she may have sought her colleagues' views before reaching decisions, she secluded herself to make up her mind. Because of her overwhelming need to preserve autonomy, she discouraged even friendly intrusions into her private political world.

The "return to democracy" in 1977 probably signaled her need to be respected by others. Her ambivalence toward authority and its exercise had been temporarily resolved in 1975, but in time the decision created an inner conflict regarding her self-image. Holding elections may have been her way of restoring damaged self-esteem, which in the past had been linked with the championing of democracy. At the same time, she may have realized that control of the decision-making machinery was slipping out of her hands and that she was no longer master of the political situation—and soon might not be master of herself. Her impulse to mastery, over herself and her environment, was too strong to permit that to happen.

As we saw in Chapter 3, Gandhi's decision to impose authoritarian rule may be traced to a certain ambivalence—inherited from her father—to democratic institutions and values. Throughout her life, she defied labels of any kind and recoiled from rigorous definitions of political concepts. Her commitment to socialism never rested on intellectual grounds; there is no evidence, for example, that she ever systematically studied socialist thought. There was thus a certain superficiality in her socialist outlook. The same may be said of her democratic view. The most charitable interpretation of the 1975 decision is that it was a desperate effort to reconcile the yawning gap between socialist promises and action. Her familiar theme of reconciliation, balance, synthesis, and integration had been echoed and reechoed in public and private expressions. It was perhaps inevitable that she would fail to find such a reconciliation, for she had no clear ideology and lacked the machinery to implement progressive goals.

During her tenure, while she strove to find a balance between her democratic and her socialist inclinations, changes were taking place at the social level. As political groups jockeyed for power, the program of industrialization and agrarian modernization proceeded apace. Some social classes were becoming more clearly differentiated and were entering the political arena; these new classes tended to weight the political scales more and more toward the Right. The "green revolution" swelled the ranks of the richer farmers, while industrialization increased the numbers of big and small businessmen—merchants, traders, industrialists, and bankers. As schools and newspapers proliferated, the government bureaucracy mushroomed; and as the judiciary expanded its role as arbiter of socioeconomic conflict, new classes of professionals and intelligentsia developed. All were well-organized and articulate, in sharp contrast to the still largely undifferentiated masses for whom the Congress also claimed to speak (though it had not bothered to mobilize them). The interests of the organized groups were the perpetuation and strengthening of their traditional or new-found privileges and rewards. As they pressed their claims, Congress responded indulgently, for their political and economic resources benefited the party. The party sought and obtained their political and financial support, and their managerial, economic, scientific, and technological skills were recruited.

From 1969 on, however, the left wing was in ascendance, at least until 1971–1972, and the level of socialist rhetoric rose. Some party policies even seemed to be aimed at curtailing the gains of these privileged classes. But as the Congress veered to the Left, the more articulate classes appeared to veer toward the Right. The economic crisis of 1973–1974 sharpened their consciousness, and the J. P. movement provided them with the opportunity to organize against the Congress party—to forge the alternative that had eluded them over the preceding years. Unable to win control of the government through the electoral process, the conservatives seized on the opportunity offered by Narayan's movement to destabilize the government, hoping, in the ensuing chaos, to realize their ambition to steer the ship of state.

We have seen in Chapter 4 that the non-Congress conservative forces shared certain goals with their sympathizers within the party. Attempts were made in 1967 and 1969 to establish a beachhead of power in the office of the presidency; but these efforts were thwarted by the prime minister. During the first ten years of her term, the edifice of economic reforms built by Nehru was sustained and expanded by his daughter and challenged by the forces of conservatism.* The judiciary had proven a willing partner in opposition endeavors to dismantle it. The constitutional right to private property became their chief haven against encroachments on this bulwark of privilege. The courts became their preferred arena of struggle.

In spite of the strong right wing, the Congress, however, was able to maintain a broad base of popular support. In addition to the struggle among established economic classes, there was an ongoing conflict among subnational groups that retained separate social identities—sometimes transcending, sometimes coinciding with their economic interests. At the level of national politics, they were gradually being sorted out in economic terms. Minority groups like the Muslims and untouchables were among the poorer and more disadvantaged segments of society; they aligned themselves with the Congress because of its secular image and its rhetoric in support of the underprivileged.

---

*Perhaps it is no accident that within a year after the conservatives' accession to power, there were signs that efforts were under way to diminish Nehru's stature and to install in his place another nationalist leader, Subhas Chandra Bose, who is believed to have died in an airplane crash in 1945. Bose had made Nazi Germany his base of political operations for organizing the Indian National Army, which fought the British on the Japanese side during World War II (*The New York Times,* January 30, 1978).

Parliament was the nearly exclusive power preserve of the Congress reformers led by the prime minister. With judicial decisions and legislative acts as their respective weapons, conservatives and progressives crossed swords, sometimes in one arena, sometimes in the other. By 1973 there was a growing realization that such confrontations would ultimately end up in a deadlock or in defeat for the conservatives. In the electoral field—the only other legitimate arena for competing middle- and upper-class interests—the opposition parties were at a clear disadvantage vis-à-vis the better organized and broad-based Congress machine. Throughout the years preceding the J. P. movement, opposition efforts to merge, federate, or even form electoral alliances had invariably ended in miserable failure; party leaders seemed incapable of shedding their party identity and submerging philosophical and personal differences. It is ironic that Gandhi's Emergency Rule succeeded in motivating an alliance that past incentives had failed to inspire.

Frustrated by repeated disappointments, many were losing faith in the entire party system; the J. P. movement to a large extent reflected the eroding legitimacy of the political institutions. This was shown by the movement's reliance on such extraconstitutional tactics as *gheraos, bandhs,* and fasts and its concerted efforts to remove elected legislatures and governments in Gujarat and Bihar. The message of the movement was carried by Narayan to nearly all the other states. Moreover, intimidation and social boycotts of state legislators to compel them to resign their posts or otherwise support the movement hardly strengthened democratic norms. Looting and burning during the riots and demonstrations spawned by the movement could easily have degenerated into full-scale violence and anarchy. Overt instigation to the military, police, and civil services to disobey established political authority—in the volatile economic, social, and political climate of Indian society—could quite conceivably have led to complete anarchy. Efforts to set up "people's governments" or a "parallel administration" constituted a clear defiance of established authority. Moreover, being in an embryonic stage, they could hardly have stepped into any vacuum left if the movement succeeded in overthrowing the government. Nor was the political opposition sufficiently united to ensure strong government—at the center or in the states; the history of these parties' failure to unite behind an alternative to the Congress was hardly reassuring.

Under these circumstances, the call by Narayan and other opposition leaders for nationwide civil disobedience at the end of June could well be interpreted as a dire danger to the nation's democratic development. At the very least, a responsible leader had to consider the possibility, and indeed the probability, of violence and chaos if the movement continued.

It is a matter of political judgment as to how long one in Gandhi's position should wait to see whether instability and violence would result. Our case, however, seems to establish clearly that she acted responsibly in declaring the emergency. In the final analysis the decision required executive judgment. It was a political decision and, therefore, must be assessed by political standards. The Indian people's judgment was clearly against the excesses of Emergency Rule. Whether it was also against the decision to declare a state of emergency is not at all certain.

Recent political developments suggest that the struggle for power among the "have" classes continues unabated under the Janata government. The main contenders still vie with one another, seemingly oblivious to the larger forces for change stirring just beneath the political surface. These are moving slowly but unmistakably toward an outlet. They could be mobilized and guided toward expression by a wise leadership; or they could continue to grope blindly and, gaining force, eventually erupt uncontrollably—smashing the antiquated, corrupt, complacent, and repressive structure on which the present political system rests.

Indira Gandhi, for all her flaws, failures, hesitations, and retreats, recognized the explosive dimensions of the problem and sought to deal with it, plunging fearlessly into the Indian political labyrinth, with its awesome and enticing traps. In the end she may have yielded to them her better judgment and her people's laurels.

CHAPTER VIII

Indira Gandhi "On Trial"

"Mrs. Gandhi on Trial" read a banner headline in a New Delhi newspaper during 1978. Although no formal charges had been brought against her actions relating to the emergency proclamation, the headline reflected the public anticipation, particularly in the cities (and it attested to the press's conviction of her guilt). To many, Indira Gandhi remains a magnetic, enigmatic, and fascinating personality, while to others, she is a sinister specter hovering in the political wings. The possibility that she will emerge publicly and permanently disgraced appears increasingly unlikely. Of late it has seemed more and more possible that she may return to power in time (not necessarily as prime minister). A third possibility discussed in whispers by Delhi elites is that she will be assassinated the moment she comes too close to reassuming political power.

Yet, after her ignominious electoral defeat and the jubilance with which it was greeted in the Indian capital and other cities, one would have thought she would have been quickly and nonviolently dispatched from the political scene. Presumably the Janata party government had sufficient evidence of her wrongdoing and the necessary tools to marshal it against her. A study of the relevant material, however, convinces even a nonlawyer like myself that the government and the Commission of Inquiry appointed to look into emergency excesses have failed dismally to do their legal homework. Or perhaps, the evidence does not lend itself very elegantly to the legal task they have set for themselves? The weak case against the former prime minister may account in part for the fact that—a year and a half after her defeat and the establishment of the commission—she has yet to be brought to trial. Although at the time of writing nearly six months have passed since the commission headed by former Chief Justice J. C. Shah submitted its findings—which detailed the evidence on which she could be charged and tried, the trial is still to be held. The reasons for the delay are both legal and political. I will deal here with the legal problems inherent in the government's case which weaken its chances for victory and thereby place it in political jeopardy.

To understand the shortcomings of the government's case, we must look at (1) their overall prosecution strategy; (2) the charges investigated by the Shah commission and the arguments supporting these charges; and (3) the commission's procedures in conducting its investigation of the actors, witnesses, and complainants.

Prosecution Strategy

Efforts to punish Gandhi for her alleged excesses are doomed to uncertainty because the government is relying on the judicial system to penalize her for crimes that, if substantiated, could best be described as political. Moreover, there is little doubt that many (though not all) Janata leaders want to exact retribution. The present government will not be satisfied with a finding that the Emergency Proclamation was unconstitutional—a judgment the judicial system could probably pass. The purpose of the proceedings appears rather to be both to publicly denounce Gandhi's decisions and actions and to punish and disgrace her—to discourage future politicians from imitating her.

Knowledgeable Indian observers maintain that she could easily have been convicted if the government had set up a special tribunal along Nuremberg lines as soon as it came to power in 1977. Of course, such a tribunal would have shared the principal defect of the Nuremberg court—namely, a trial of the defeated in which the victors' wrongdoings are shielded from scrutiny and judgment. Nevertheless, such a trial could have been held, for at that time, the victors were riding the crest of a unity wave of sorts, and members of Parliament—from the government as well as from the opposition ranks—would have supported such a tribunal; and popular sentiment would have favored it. That opportunity was irretrievably lost, however, as the energies of the leadership had to be devoted to simply holding together the new and uneasy coalition. No such trial is now possible, given the approaching disintegration of the Janata party, the strengthening of opposition forces, and their possible realignment behind Indira Gandhi.

On May 28, 1977, the Ministry of Home Affairs appointed the Shah commission, in response to a "widespread demand from different sections of the public," to inquire into "allegations of abuse of authority, excesses and malpractices" committed during the emergency period "by the political authorities, public servants, their friends and/or relatives and in particular allegations of gross misuse of powers of arrest or detention";[1] actions involving the treatment of prisoners, forcible implementation of the family-planning program, and improper demolition of houses and other structures were also to be investigated. Surprisingly, Indira Gandhi was not named, although no one doubted that the inquiry was intended to establish her culpability.

The specific time frame the commission was charged to look at was the "period when the Proclamation of Emergency made on 25th June, 1975 . . . was in force or in days immediately preceding the said Proclamation." In addition to looking into specific abuses of power and other wrongful actions, it was charged "to consider such other matters which, in the opinion of the commission, have any relevance to the aforesaid allegations."[2] Presumably on the basis of this amply framed guideline, the commission undertook to pronounce on the validity of the proclamation itself. In fact, the entire case constructed against Gandhi rests on the argument that, *prima facie,* the declaration of emergency was fraudulent because there was "no evidence of any breakdown of law and order in any part of the country—nor of any apprehension in that behalf; the economic condition was well under control and had in no way deteriorated." From this Justice Shah concluded that "the one and the only motivating force for tendering the extraordinary advice to the President to declare an 'internal emergency' was the intense political activity generated in the ruling party and the opposition, by the decision of the Allahabad High Court declaring the election of the Prime Minister of the day invalid on the ground of corrupt election practices. Thousands were detained and a series of totally illegal and unwarranted actions followed involving untold human misery and suffering." In short, he concluded, her decision was taken "in a desperate endeavor to save herself from the legitimate compulsion of a judicial verdict against her."[3]

Gandhi's political enemies could hardly have phrased their indictment of her in more thunderous and righteous terms. Much as we may be tempted to read his findings as a judgment of guilt, however, we must take Justice Shah at his word. He cautions time and again that he can make no criminal or civil charges or judgment on the issues; the proceedings of the commission were not "adversary"—there was neither "a plaintiff or defendant or a prosecutor and an accused person." They were neither civil nor criminal proceedings. The commission was "not concerned to determine the infraction of any laws" but rather as an inquisitorial body to ascertain whether any excess "falling within the terms of reference was committed."[4]

Thus, despite frequent headlines that Indira Gandhi is "on trial," has been found "guilty," or has been "indicted," there was no formal charge or judgment of guilt brought against her. Moreover, there is a long road ahead before a judgment can be handed down; for a criminal trial must commence with a "charge-sheet" specifying the charges and the substance of the prosecution's case. Only then may evidence be introduced, and this first stage has not yet been reached. Before the trial the Central Bureau of Investigation must file so-called "first information reports"; these delineate the charges to be investigated. In July 1978, three reports implicating the former prime minister in criminal offenses were filed; an investigation, which is presumably now in progress, follows the filing of such reports.

Thus the commission's year-long investigation will be duplicated by government agencies—the same agencies from which the commission's investigative staff was drawn.

The Charges

From the commission's reports and from the statements made to me by the commission counsel, Karl Khandalawala, and Ram Jethmalani, a Janata MP—who, according to Khandalawala will be trying cases against Sanjay Gandhi—the case against Gandhi will be that the emergency proclamation was fraudulent to begin with, and that, therefore, all the actions following it and justified by it were criminal. Issuing the proclamation, however, will not be considered a criminal offense but, as Shah put it, an "excess." Apparently Gandhi is not to be charged with perpetrating a fraud but with criminal action, such as detention of her political opponents, that *followed* the perpetration of a fraud. Jethmalani told me: "The bogus and phony nature of the Emergency is a part of the proof of the criminal offense of wrongful confinement. Because if the Emergency is phony, then everything she has done in the wake of it would amount to an illegal act."

If the fraudulent nature of the emergency is part of the proof, it, of course, does not have to be proven! Nevertheless, Justice Shah did devote considerable attention to establishing that the emergency declaration was itself fraudulent (on the ground that no law-and-order problem existed); her intent to perpetrate fraud was evidenced by failure to obtain the prior consent of the cabinet, as required by its own rules. Evidence that she conspired with others to keep herself in power was found in her decision to arrest her political opponents—itself deemed an abuse of power—and in the timing of that decision.

It has not yet been established legally whether conditions in June 1975 constituted a threat to the nation's security or indeed whether such a decision lends itself to legal determination at all. Assuming that a threat existed, however, the prime minister (or an appropriate subordinate) had the authority, under the existing preventive detention law, to detain persons deemed a threat to internal security. The right to detention without trial was sanctioned by the constitution and could be exercised even in times of peace. Even the present chief justice, Y. V. Chandrachud, who was a Supreme Court judge during the emergency, had held with the majority that the executive had the right to deprive citizens of their liberty and their right to appeal. More than a year after the lifting of the emergency, Chandrachud stated that the court's judgment during the emergency was a correct interpretation of the law, much as he now wished he had stepped down from the bench to demonstrate his disagreement with the law.[5]

Turning to the conspiracy charge, let us look at the logic of the contention that Gandhi conspired to keep herself in power by arresting her opponents. According to the Indian Penal Code, "criminal conspiracy" refers to an agreement by two or more persons to do "an illegal act" or "an act which is not illegal by illegal means."[6] Obviously, attempts to retain political power are not per se illegal; therefore, the conspiracy consists in arresting her political opponents in order to do so. Because the emergency proclamation was fraudulent the arrests are also viewed as illegal. Thus the entire case rests on whether the emergency was fraudulent; this judgment, in turn, depends on whether the prime minister has the right to decide that an emergency situation exists or whether the courts have that right. A second ground for the impropriety of the arrests is found in the faulty framing of the arrest document and her abetment of the faulty framing. The co-conspirators* would have had to agree, on or prior to June 25, to make illegal arrests—that is, to frame or abet faulty documents. Merely agreeing to arrest opposition leaders was no conspiracy. Proving the existence of such an agreement is unlikely and exceedingly difficult.

Aside from this difficulty, the conspiracy charge bears closer scrutiny, for it appears to me that the commission has neglected to examine the cause-and-effect links between the alleged conspiracy to remain in power and Gandhi's arrest of her opponents. If the opposition had sufficient political strength to form a government, it could justifiably be claimed that by arresting them she prevented them from doing so and thus kept herself in power. The commission did not, however, look for evidence that the opposition was able—or willing—to form a coalition. My analysis shows, on the contrary, that the opposition was nowhere near united enough in the days or weeks or months prior to the emergency proclamation to form a government, although it might have succeeded in toppling the Congress government by creating political chaos and instability. If these disruptive efforts had been established by the commission, the constitutional validity of her action would have been upheld. The commission, however, did not investigate this earlier period but examined only the "days immediately preceding the Proclamation" and concluded there was no law-and-order problem.

I asked Attorney Jethmalani whether—if a law-and-order problem existed for a year or so but had abated for two or three days—the prime minister did not still have the right to decide that the danger of anarchy existed. He thought not; in his view, a condition of anarchy had to exist at the exact time that the emergency was proclaimed.[7] This suggests to me that the head of the government is legally bound to wait until there is bloodshed in the streets before taking any action. The question ultimately depends, of course, on whether the executive has the responsibility and the right to decide when grounds for declaring an emergency exist. The commission counsel disagreed with the contention that the decision is political in nature and repeated that he (and Justice Shah) had concluded there was no emergency.[8] The gist of his

---

*The alleged co-conspirators are R. K. Dhawan, former additional private secretary; Bansi Lal, former Union Defense Minister and Chief Minister of Haryana; Gianni Zail Singh, former Punjab Chief Minister; Harideo Joshi, former Rajasthan Chief Minister; P. C. Sethi, former Cabinet Minister; and Kishan Chand, former Lieutenant Governor of Delhi, who committed suicide.

argument seems to be that any reasonable person in similar circumstances would have decided against a declaration of emergency. In other words, conditions of threat to the security of the country are always subject to a sort of scientific/empirical/legal test, which leaves no room for a difference of opinion and requires no political judgment.

Clearly the Shah commission and the prosecution lawyers view the falsity of the claim that there was a law-and-order problem as proof of the fraudulence of the emergency proclamation. The decision not to consult the cabinet prior to proclaiming the emergency, Shah suggests, was further evidence of her intent to perpetrate fraud, for she falsely stated—in a letter to the president of India asking him to sign the proclamation—that there had been no time to consult the cabinet. She appealed to him to sign the proclamation in view of the gravity of the situation and assured him that she would submit the matter to the cabinet for their ratification early the next morning (which she did). Justice Shah found her assertion of lack of time patently untrue since she (1) had found the time to consult several chief ministers and other confidantes and (2) had probably decided as early as June 22 (or 23 at the latest) to take this drastic step. The chief ministers were contacted so that they might make preparations to receive the political prisoners she planned to arrest.

Even if she had made the final decision on June 25, she could have found the time to consult the Ministers. Gandhi told me, however, that she was fearful of leaks and felt that secrecy had to be maintained at all costs.[9] The relevant question thus is not whether she had time to consult them but whether she wished to do so. Apparently she did not, for she asked a close adviser, an eminent lawyer and chief minister of the state of West Bengal, S. S. Ray, whether she could take such a decision without referring it to the cabinet. Ray testified before the Shah commission that he advised her that cabinet rules allowed her to submit the matter to the cabinet simply for ratification.[10] Prior consent was thus not deemed necessary. Commissioner Shah maintains, however, that the cabinet rules identify an emergency declaration as falling within the category of matters that must be submitted to the cabinet. At the same time, he mentions a rule allowing a departure from the guideline: "The Prime Minister may, in *any case or classes of cases,* permit or condone a departure from these rules to the extent he deems necessary."[11] Shah dismisses this rule by saying he cannot understand how it could be applied to a proclamation of emergency.

The commissioner further decries the fact that the home minister, in whose jurisdiction such matters fall, was not consulted. However, Home Minister Brahmananda Reddy, in his testimony before the commission, indicated that he was called to the prime minister's home on the evening of June 25 and told that "on account of the deteriorating law and order situation it was felt necessary to impose an Internal Emergency." He expressed the view that the situation could be dealt with under the existing emergency but was told this suggestion had been examined and rejected. He reportedly told Gandhi to "do what she thought was best" and thereafter wrote and signed a letter to the president sending him the "appropriate Proclamation for your assent."[12]

Assuming that the emergency proclamation sent to the president was fraudulent, on the grounds noted by the commission, one cannot help but wonder why the cabinet ministers, asked to ratify it the following morning, assented. The obvious legal question is whether these ministers (some of whom are serving in the present cabinet) are not guilty of abuse of power in giving consent to an allegedly fraudulent emergency. When I raised this question with Commission Counsel Khandalawala, he replied that the question was not within the commission's terms of reference. Moreover, "once it has happened, if they say, you are Prime Minister, you can do what you want, you cannot call that abuse of power but rather weakness." Jethmalani too thought that the Cabinet was not culpable: "morally and politically they are, but not legally." Linking the timing of the declaration to her power motive, Shah points out that, according to testimony presented before the commission, the decision to take drastic steps, including the declaration of an emergency, was contemplated as early as June 22. The chief minister of one of the southern states, said to be a confidante of Gandhi, was asked on June 22 to be in New Delhi on June 24, when the Supreme Court was to announce its decision on the election-petition case. Fact-finder Shah asserts that "presumably" the Supreme Court judgment was to be the "deciding factor on whether the drastic action contemplated to be taken, should in effect be instituted. . . . If the judgment had been in the nature of a categorical and an unconditional stay [of the High Court's verdict unseating Gandhi], *probably* no action of the nature which was ultimately taken would have followed."[13]

We are asked to infer, then, that the prime minister decided on June 24, finally and irrevocably, that the danger to her office was clear and present, and that the opposition leaders would have to be removed from her path. In yet another paragraph of the same commission report, however, we find testimony suggesting that the decision to take the opposition leaders into custody was taken on June 23, the day *before* she learned of the unfavorable Supreme Court verdict. Moreover, many of the commission's own witnesses indicated that Gandhi had, even before June 12, referred to her concern with the unstable political conditions in the country and J. P.'s "contemplated country-wide agitation." S. S. Ray—who apparently spent a good part of June 25 with her going over reports of lawlessness or threats in northern India, as well as an account of Narayan's speech to be given later that day calling for a mass movement in all of India—was convinced she was "seriously and sincerely disturbed" about these conditions. It was then he advised her to consider imposing internal emergency under Article 352 of the constitution.[14]

Commission Procedures

Although the inquiry was intended to establish the facts about commission of excesses, malpractices, and abuse and misuse of authority by public servants and others, the case constructed against Indira Gandhi is not only weak on substantive terms, as I have argued, but can also be questioned in terms of the procedures used to obtain information from witnesses and from Gandhi. Ironically, these procedures will probably be among the issues argued in a case initiated by Commissioner Shah when Gandhi refused to testify before him. The case may well provide the central legal arena in which the Commission of Inquiry will be compelled to justify its procedures and demonstrate its judicial impartiality.

One question that has arisen is whether the commissioner followed the sequence of steps set out by him just before he began public hearings on September 30, 1977. Soon after its appointment in May 1977, the commission asked the public to send in complaints; the government also supplied files relevant to the investigation. Out of 48,500 complaints received, more than half were considered too insignificant to warrant the commission's attention; over a third were important enough for inquiry by state governments. This left about two thousand cases involving the central government; and these the Shah Commission was to investigate. During the first two months of the commission's proceedings only twenty-eight cases were looked into. I was unable to get specific information about how many more cases the commission investigated thereafter, but it is believed unlikely that many more were (or will be) examined. (The case against Indira Gandhi, incidentally, rests on fewer than a dozen cases.) On the basis of the government files, *prima facie* cases were established on two dozen or so allegations.

Then followed the fact-finding phase of the proceedings, during which numerous witnesses volunteered information. In addition, notices were sent to persons believed, on the basis of existing evidence, to have information. During the second phase a particular person or persons allegedly involved in the commission of excesses were to be given an opportunity to defend themselves before the commission. Part way through the investigation Justice Shah decided to run both phases simultaneously, in order to save time. (Originally, the Home Ministry had stipulated that the commission wind up its work by December 1977; three extensions have been given and, at present, the term of the commission is scheduled to expire on December 31, 1978). For a case involving the investigation of two thousand complaints and the appearance of large numbers of witnesses, a year is too short a time; besides completing all the phases (including a preliminary inquiry preceding phase one), interim and final reports had to be written. Even with extensions, it seems clear that this telescoping of phases in a "matter of public importance" was bound to lead to injustices.

Justice Shah also departed from the prescribed rules, which stipulate that a Commission of Inquiry "shall, as soon as may be after its appointment" issue a notice to individuals who may have information relevant to the inquiry. A notice outlining areas on which information could be offered was not issued to Indira Gandhi until about six months after its appointment. Simultaneously, she was issued a summons under a provision of the act that states that, if "the reputation of any person is likely to be prejudicially affected by the inquiry," the commission must give "to that person a reasonable opportunity of being heard in the inquiry and to produce evidence in his defence."[15]

Gandhi's counsel has argued that, once accusatory statements alleging impropriety in the conduct of the prime minister were made during the early stages of phase one, the commissioner was obliged to issue a summons to her, as a person "likely to be prejudicially affected" and allow her to produce evidence in her defense. According to her counsel the fact that serious allegations were made means that the proceedings at that point should have assumed the form of a criminal or quasi-criminal trial. Under the circumstances, only a summons, not a notice, should have been issued.

By issuing both a notice and a summons, the commission was in effect requiring Gandhi to reveal in her statement the line of defense she would use as a person "prejudicially affected by the inquiry." No doubt, she would use the same defense later in her criminal trial, so that the prosecution—the government—would enjoy a crucial advantage. Commissioner Shah would also enjoy an advantage in preparing questions for her defense hearing: he could merely refer to the statement submitted in response to the notice. Moreover, in answering questions at her defense hearing, she might be led to make self-incriminatory statements, depriving her of the more stringent legal safeguards provided in a criminal trial.

Although the Commissions of Inquiry Act provides that no statement will be used against a person in a later civil or criminal trial, the relevant provision does not cover incriminating documents, nor does it afford protection against compulsion to give self-incriminating answers. Only Article 20(3) of the constitution does so. According to legal precedent the constitutional protection of this article can be (and has been) invoked before the commission by Gandhi. The privilege against self-incrimination can even be invoked at the first-information-report stage. Gandhi is now in a position to claim that, on those cases where first information reports have been filed (as they were in July 1978), she cannot be compelled to produce documents or make statements before the commission.

All these dilemmas arise because it is not clear whether Indira Gandhi is an accused or merely a witness. Shah insists that she is not an accused. When he summoned her to testify, he did not detail any charges against her; he contended that as no one was named in the government's charge to the commission, he did not know who was involved in the commitment of excesses. Technically, of course, Shah was correct although it is impossible that he did not know about Gandhi's possible involvement in the events being considered by the commission. His guidelines did not specifically instruct him to examine her; but then, he was not specifically instructed to look into the circumstances leading up to the emergency proclamation, nor to go beyond the period "immediately preceding" the emergency (i.e., two to three days before June 25), nor to look at the period between June 12 and 25. Yet, relying on his judgment, he did both of these things. It is difficult to avoid the conclusion that Shah applied rather inconsistent standards of flexibility in interpreting the Home Ministry's notification.

Justice Shah also refused her request to outline the charges against her because, he said, his inquiry was not a criminal proceeding and she was therefore not to consider herself an accused. It is true that she was not and could not be formally accused by the commission; even so, many harsh accusations of criminal conduct were made against her in the course of the proceedings. Moreover, the Commissions of Inquiry Act does seem to recognize a status somewhat akin to that of accused when it refers to persons whose reputations might be adversely or prejudicially affected and when it affords such individuals an opportunity to "produce evidence" in their "defence." Furthermore, according to the Royal Commission on Tribunals of Inquiry, which Justice Shah himself referred to at times to validate his arguments, a person called as a witness in an inquiry must first be furnished with a statement of allegations. In spite of this directive, the wording of the act noted above, and, indeed, the wording of Shah's own public notice—which called on respondents to make oral statements "to meet charges" against them—his summons to Indira Gandhi specified no charges.

The arguments put forth by Gandhi and her counsel amount to a refusal to testify before the commission, either orally or in writing; and that refusal has been interpreted by some as an admission of guilt. It may also be viewed, however, as an eminently reasonable effort not to prejudice her case on the substantive issues now being brought to trial in a criminal court. A former justice of the Supreme Court has argued[16] that a defendant (or potential defendant) is prejudiced when a Commission of Inquiry investigates the same questions as a criminal court, especially when the commission arrives at findings adverse to the "defendant." For a criminal court to depart substantially from the findings of the commission would be to impugn its integrity or methods. It is precisely these methods, and the commission's neutrality, that Gandhi is questioning.

Indira Gandhi's refusal to testify stems from yet another procedural quirk on the part of the commission. According to the act, the person whose reputation is at stake may cross-examine witnesses who have made statements implicating that person in wrongful conduct. Commissioner Shah, however, refused to provide her that opportunity unless she first agreed to make statements as (1) a witness in general, offering information requested by the commission, and (2) as a person whose reputation was at stake and who was making a statement in her defense. Since she could not present an adequate defense without having the charges against her outlined, yet would be required as a witness to give potentially self-incriminating answers (all without benefit of prior cross-examination), she found herself in a Catch-22 situation and refused to answer.

The case brought against her by Shah for refusal to testify before the commission will allow Gandhi to defend herself on these and other issues and will determine whether the Shah commission inquiry is considered criminal or quasi-criminal. If the court rules in her favor in this procedural case and she is relieved of answering questions before the commission, her defense in a criminal court can be prepared with much greater efficiency.

It may be said from a layman's point of view that the procedure used in the Shah inquiry, particularly during the fact-finding phase, amounted to a free-for-all affording an opportunity to anyone who desired, for whatever reasons, to make accusations without substantiation. Although the investigating officers' statements in the case histories prepared by them are by law subject to prosecution for perjury, it does not appear that the commission examined them carefully to establish their accuracy. Yet, the Commissions of Inquiry Act specifies that "the Commission *shall* satisfy itself about the correctness of the facts stated and the conclusions, if any, arrived at in the investigation report submitted to it . . . and *for this purpose* the Commission may make such inquiry (including the examination of the person or persons, who conducted or assisted in the investigation) as it thinks fit."[17] Justice Shah maintained, in defense of his apparent oversight, that as long as no one brought any evidence before him that pointed to inaccurate reporting, he did not need to avail himself of the procedure set forth in the act.

Yet the Commissioner did not have to look far to find the evidence he sought, for in his findings, he virtually indicts the police, the magistrates, and the administrative services as a whole for their conduct during Emergency Rule. "Even the cream of the talent of the country in the administrative field," he observes, "often collapsed at the slightest pressure." He goes on to say: "The politician who uses a public servant for purely political purposes and the public servant who allows himself to be so used are both debasing themselves and doing a signal disservice to the country." Justice Shah's findings clearly assert that public servants allowed themselves to be so used by the political authorities. If he believed so, how could he place any credence in the case histories and generally in the assistance provided to the Commission by members of these services—the police, security, intelligence, income tax, and administrative services—from which the investigative and other staff of the Commission was recruited.

Perhaps the grossest indication of Shah's myopia—if not bias—is to be found in a communication he sent to the chief secretaries of State governments and Union territories when he invited them to testify. Only those who had been guilty of the worst abuses of authority would come within the adverse notice of the Commission, he noted. Those, on the other hand, who might have been "a little overenthusiastic" during the Emergency or who obeyed merely to "get along in the service" ought not to be reluctant or inhibited in testifying before him. Such a letter to public servants can only be interpreted as an open invitation to some to blackball others in order to protect themselves. There is no way such an action can be deemed judicious, coming as it did a couple of months after the Home Minister had proclaimed that all wrongdoers, from the "highest political authority to the lowest functionary of the government would be punished according to the law."[18] (OHT, 9/8/77).

Other procedures of the commission arouse skepticism because the kinds of information sought were not within its terms of reference or did not constitute constitutionally permissible areas of examination for a commission of inquiry. For example, Justice Shah inquired into transactions that occurred during a period beyond that set by the commission's guidelines—about two to three days before emergency was declared on June 25. Commissioner Shah chose instead to begin his inquiry in the period from June 12 to 25, 1975, which provided a convenient time frame for "proving" that Gandhi was moved to act as a result of the election-petition decision, which the Allabahad High Court handed down on June 12, 1975. (It is noteworthy that even within this time frame Shah did not consider the possible adverse effects of Jayaprakash Narayan's inflammatory appeals to the army, police, and administration.)

The terms of reference permit investigation of the period when the proclamation was in force and of the "days immediately preceding" it but not of the act of proclamation itself. When Shah did attempt to probe into the proclamation and Gandhi's counsel demurred, Shah conceded that he could not go into the validity of the imposition of emergency. However, he felt that he was entitled to examine Gandhi's motives, which amounted to doing indirectly what he could not do directly.[19]

Justice Shah also sought to obtain information about the advice tendered to and discussions held with the president of India in connection with the proclamation of emergency. Yet Article 74(2) of the Indian Constitution states very clearly that "The question whether any, and if so what, advice was tendered by the Ministers to the President shall not be inquired into in any court."[20] Gandhi refused to testify about such advice, citing the constitutional bar and claiming a privilege against requests for information on the basis of her oath of secrecy sworn by her as prime minister. This oath binds the prime minister not to "directly or indirectly communicate or reveal to any person or persons any matter" she may have considered or have had knowledge about "except as may be required for the due discharge" of her duties. The Shah commission ruled that, as no penalty for breach of such an oath had been provided and as the central government had directed the commission to obtain information from any minister who had left office, the revelation of such information was not a breach of the oath.[21] No further argument or elucidation was presented by Justice Shah to clarify the logic behind the ruling.

The significance of the many procedural questions lies partly in the distinction between legal and political offenses. Unpopular political judgments, such as the imposition of Emergency Rule, even if they are unwise, should not be confused with offenses in law. Apart from the implications of such a confusion for Gandhi personally, the serious consequence may be a significant transformation of the Indian political system. If a Commission of Inquiry or the courts are to decide whether a given situation constitutes a threat—internal or external—to the national security, a new type of system will be forged; and the decision-making authority in important political matters will not be accountable and responsive to the people or their representatives. The present political leadership should beware of abdicating to the judiciary matters of a clearly political nature—even to settle scores with political enemies.

Much of what went awry during the nineteen months of Emergency Rule has been blamed, by Shah and others, on serious shortcomings in the administrative structure, political conventions and customs, and traditional political relations, attitudes, and expectations. Responsibility for failures in these areas is being laid at the door of one or a few persons. Gandhi can be faulted, along with her predecessors and successors, for these weaknesses; but the fault lies in many, not in a few.

The present political leadership should beware of abdicating to the judiciary matters of a clearly political nature—even to settle scores with political enemies. Punishment can be meted out by the courts for criminal acts and by the electoral or legislative process for political offenses. But it is essential to distinguish between legal and political wrongdoings *before* action is taken in these matters—lest the remedies prove worse than the disease.

The case developed by the Shah commission against Indira Gandhi is basically that she was a power-hungry politician motivated by the desire to keep herself in power. The same allegation was made as soon as Emergency Rule was imposed and was offered in much the same form. The preceding chapters have set forth my analysis of the charges, based on in-depth study of her experience and public career. Observing the political scene three years later, I found nothing to significantly vitiate or invalidate the conclusions reached earlier. If anything, they are substantially confirmed. I have argued that Gandhi was not motivated by a desire for power as an end in itself, but rather as a means to an end—namely, promoting the national interest and the public welfare, as she sees these. Her interpretation of these interests is open to question in many respects and suffers from serious inadequacies. But it is one thing to say that she is at times misguided about what best serves the country and another altogether to say that she cares only about satisfying her hunger for power through any means—even illegal and immoral ones. I totally disagree with the latter perception and have sought to support an interpretation of her that more closely reflects reality.

CHAPTER IX

An Interview with Indira Gandhi

During the summer of 1978 I made another trip to India and was able to talk to former Prime Minister Gandhi for the first time since 1975. At the time she was under investigation by the Shah Commission of Inquiry, and three first information reports—the first step in the criminal indictment process—had been filed against her. As deposed leader and inside observer of the Indian political scene, she had had a year to watch the Janata party efforts to hold together its fragile coalition and to survey the eleven turbulent years of her own regime.

The material reproduced below is from several sessions of talks with Indira Gandhi held in the month of July 1978 and totaling about seven hours. Because of its length, the interview had to be substantially edited. Most of the portions deleted either represented ground covered in other answers or referred to personalities and events that may not be familiar to the general reader. (An entire segment on foreign policy was left out as it was not directly relevant to this study.) The first few questions (omitted here) concerned the Janata government and Indira Gandhi's prophecy that, although it would not fall immediately, it would not last out its full term.

M. C. C. Do you consider the present situation with the Janata a vindication of your emergency decision? How does it vindicate the reported excesses of Emergency Rule, assuming you agree that there were excesses?

I. G. The only vindication is the results achieved during the emergency. Before the emergency, everything was on the downgrade. When I left, India was at its peak in military strength, economic stability, and soundness; and all world economic institutions agreed for the first time that we could have rapid economic growth and that a developing country can solve problems of food and so forth. We built our foreign-exchange reserves, and we were beginning to make a go of the public sector. Production had gone up and corruption had come down, and everything was going much more smoothly. Offices were working smoothly. . . . During the first year of the emergency, everyone (except the smugglers) asked why we hadn't had it earlier. My assessment is that if we had not done something, there would have been widespread violence. My family and I would have been killed (like Mujibur Rahman's family in Bangladesh),* and it would have happened in other parts of the country also. There would have been utter political and economic chaos and nobody to fill the vacuum. I wanted to remain because I did not see who would handle it at the moment. I felt—and some chief ministers also said—that if the opposition sensed a victory over me, they will not allow any other Congress person to remain. I did try to make some friendly gestures, but these were regarded as weakness.

M. C. C. Why didn't you use DIR and MISA† to deal with the problem, instead of declaring an internal emergency?

I. G. The law minister and others advised emergency as the legal and constitutional way. There were certain loopholes in the existing laws, and we could not handle even the smugglers. We thought at the time that it would last only a couple of months. Then when the Bangladesh incident [Rahman's killing] took place, we tightened up things. We got caught up in various things, and when we found it was showing results and the country going ahead in every way, it did not seem the proper moment to stop. As soon as I felt the economy was stable, I held elections.

M. C. C. Your decision to hold elections at that time has puzzled many people, including myself. Why exactly did you decide to hold the elections at that time?

I. G. Prior to that time, the economy was in a state where, had there been agitations—and elections do open out everything—we would not have been able to control the economy. As soon as the

*The Bangladesh prime minister, Mujibur Rahman, was assassinated in August 1975.
†Defense of India Rules and Maintenance of Internal Security Act.

economy was stabilized, there was no logical reason not to have elections.

Earlier, you mentioned excesses. What are the excesses? This has never been clarified. According to the Shah commission, certain appointments I made are excesses. Most of what are regarded as excesses had nothing to do with the emergency.

M. C. C. But I have heard many stories from people who say they have firsthand knowledge of extensive abuses.

I. G. Everybody says it was their personal knowledge, but nothing like this has been proved by all the probes and investigations that are being made. . . . The Shah commission specifically went into the matter. Some people came to me complaining. I asked, have any of you been sterilized? They said no. Have any of your relatives or friends been sterilized? They said no. Then how do you know, I asked? Several people have admitted that they had been given money to say that they had been sterilized.

M. C. C. I have read that you did not consult the cabinet in taking the emergency decision. Is this true and how do you explain this?

I. G. It is a fact. I did not consult the cabinet, but it was ratified by the cabinet immediately thereafter. But that is not the only instance where this is done. The Cabinet is never consulted on the budget. The same is true regarding the devaluation of the rupee in 1966. . . . The prime minister is not bound to put everything before the Cabinet. In this case, we felt that secrecy was essential—if the arrests were to be made. And we were concerned that nothing leak out.

M. C. C. What do you think are the chances of your coming back to power? If you did come back to power, what would you do to prevent a recurrence of such excesses as were reported to have occurred during the Emergency?

I. G. I am not at all interested in coming back to power. I am worried about what is happening to the country. I would like to live a quiet life. For how long, I don't know. I might get bored. But because of the cases against me, I had to remain in Delhi.

You see, basically the fight is between the forces of change and the forces of the status quo. The banks and administrative services are very conservative. In fact, the biggest mistake my father made was not to change the administrative structure. I can't blame him because, due to the partition, the country was weak, and it would have been risky to make such changes. But the whole system is pro status quo.

M. C. C. Then, if there were no excesses, and so many people were satisfied with the Emergency, why did the election result in such a debacle for you and the Congress party?

I. G. The strong measures we took annoyed the administration, which was against us even before. The planning commission, in the name of faster development, undertook certain programs which annoyed the farmers. The bonus was not given to the workers; it was put on deposit for them. But they were annoyed. Then, many people were annoyed because of family planning. Teachers were asked to persuade others, and they were against the family-planning program because it was done so highhandedly.

I think we would have been defeated anyway, because we had been in office so many years. But the main reason was the tremendous propaganda which reached every single house. They had a lot of money to spend. The propaganda was that everyone was to be sterilized, and that if one is sterilized, one cannot be a normal man or woman. Some sections in the Janata party had the support of the Western press, Amnesty International, and other Western organizations. Another section was supported by the Soviets.

M. C. C. Do you think Western involvement contributed to your election defeat?

I. G. I think there was Western involvement which helped to swing the vote; they helped by their propaganda. But by itself, it could not have been decisive.

M. C. C. Returning to my earlier question, if you did come back to power, what would you do to prevent a recurrence of such excesses as were reported to have occurred during the Emergency?

I. G. Of course, I don't want people to be harassed or the press censored. In this respect, I think a reorientation of the police attitude is required. I was trying to do that. . . . Even now, the job is still to change police training.

As for having another emergency if I were to be in power again, I would not allow the situation to deteriorate to the point where such harsh measures are required. My fault was in not taking some measures earlier, which would have made unnecessary the harsh measures later. But having allowed the situation to drift, it was necessary to give a shock treatment. The government was not functioning. Government files were going to the opposition. Ministers had become demoralized.

M. C. C. If you believe that your father made an error in not changing the administrative structure, why did you not take any really substantive steps in this direction during your eleven years in power, particularly during Emergency Rule?

I. G. I did say my father made a mistake in not changing the system; but I qualified it by saying that the conditions at the time of independence were such that it may not have been possible to do so, and later, it was more or less settled. I did try. We had a lot of talk about administrative reform, but somehow, people who looked into it simply couldn't imagine big enough reform, and patchworks made no difference. One has to have somebody who can think in a big enough way to make a complete change. That is not easy to do.

M. C. C. Well, where does this leave India? Are you just going sort of to stumble along with this administrative system?

I. G. On the whole, it is a good administrative system. No country in the world can manage a crisis as well as we can.

M. C. C. As you say, it's extremely conservative. It manages crises, but what it needs to manage, it seems to me, is the implementation of established programs like land reforms.

I. G. In a country of India's size, you have to keep balancing as you go along. A violent revolution would uproot the foundation which will take a long time to build anew. We certainly can't afford that. So, the choices are very limited. As Churchill said of democracy, it is very fragile, yet we have no better system. In India, many changes are needed, and obviously one must work for them. But when one comes to a breaking point, one has to pause awhile.

M. C. C. The question is that, if the administration is not doing its job in certain areas—which you have mentioned to me—whose fault is that?

I. G. In different cases, it may be different people's fault. Basically, it is the system.

M. C. C. All right then. Doesn't the system have to be changed?

I. G. Yes, it has to be changed but it's easier to say than to do in a country of this size, where hundreds of millions are involved immediately. We believe in the educational system being changed. Everybody says so. And yet, it isn't really possible to do it, except in slow, small steps, because it affects so many millions of people whose lives would be disrupted.

M. C. C. But over eleven years, what were some of the small steps taken? Were there any steps?

I. G. Yes, there were many steps. But over the eleven years, we were mostly in periods of crises. We had two major droughts, and then we had the Bangladesh war.The first year, it wasn't possible to do anything much. Then we had the party crisis. In spite of all these faults of machinery and with all the lacunae, nevertheless, the country was working much better than most countries.

M. C. C. So that you don't feel the administration is really basically at fault for not implementing Government policies.

I. G. Things are never completely black or white. It's difficult to make a categorical statement—I can't generalize about the administration. . . . It does not help to have a picture in your mind. One has a general picture but the details have to be worked out according to situations and events.

M. C. C. You say, on the one hand, that the administration is basically good, but it's not a "committed" administration.

I. G. Yes. Whenever there is a crisis, they rise to the occasion, so it shows basic efficiency. But the administration functions with individuals and in different and developing situations. The public as a whole—whether it is the political parties (and I include all the political parties, including Marxist)—are not really for radical changes. They talk about them but they have no conception of the immensity of the country or its future potential.

M. C. C. Are you for radical change?

I. G. Yes, I am very much, but I don't see radical changes in the way that the Communists and so-called socialists see them.

M. C. C. I really don't see how you see radical change. As you describe it, it seems to me you are very much of a reformer, rather than one who is prepared to bring about radical change.

I. G. The question is, how do you bring about radical change. You know about Kemal Ataturk? He wanted to remove purdah, and because he went too fast, they went years behind times. The people weren't prepared for it. And so, that program was completely scuttled for the time being. You can't go faster than your people, unless you want to cut off their heads. Now all you can do is try to educate them and push them along. . . . But you couldn't change education in a hurry, no matter how much you wanted to.

M. C. C. But where is the hurry in what the Congress did? Not very much was done under your father, and not very much was done under you, I believe. Not sufficient was done, particularly insofar as raising literacy rates was concerned. One can say whatever they want to about China, but they had great success in this regard, and so did other countries. It seems to me something could have been done.

I. G. Perhaps we could have done more for literacy, but I don't know how important literacy is. What has it done for the West? Are people happier or more alive to problems? On the contrary, I think they have become far more superficial.

M. C. C. Yes, but I am speaking of education as a tool through which government can communicate its policies to its people.

I. G. I'm not saying there is anything wrong with literacy. But as regards education, I agree very much with Illich. Literacy is something that should come by the way, rather than be the focus of education.

M. C. C. But when do you expect these radical changes to come about?

I. G. They do come imperceptibly. Every step may not be visible. But things are set in motion. Now, take secularism. When I was sent to Assam in the fifties, I found that most of the people wanted to change the chief minister. I was told that the best choice would be Fakhruddin Ali Ahmed, but also that it was not possible to have a Muslim in a Hindu majority state. This came as a shock to me. From then on, I worked toward changing this attitude, and I have got this country to a position where nobody would make such a remark now. Even the Jana Sangh dare not.

Now, the progress of Hindi has been greatly retarded by the

238 / Indira Gandhi

impetuousness of Hindi enthusiasts. So you have to tread very softly. It doesn't mean you are not moving. Sometimes you do have to stop also.

M. C. C. But you're really defining the reformist path.

I. G. The question is whether one merely wants to talk or actually bring about change. . . . The Communist idea of change is based on certain slogans. If you nationalize an industry, you're progressive, regardless of whether that helps the nation, that industry, or those workers. Nationalization of yarn, for example, was undertaken without adequate planning, and it hurt the weavers. So, it's not that you can't do it in the long run, but you have to do a lot of planning.

M. C. C. And you don't feel there's the danger that Gandhi felt—that unless something was done, that unless the wealthy voluntarily gave up their wealth, there would be a violent revolution.

I. G. Nobody is going to voluntarily give up his wealth. During emergency, industrialists and others got together to discuss the Gandhian path. At the end, they said this is just too idealistic. And that was the end of it. So nobody is going to give up his wealth voluntarily.

M. C. C. I don't see much evidence of this gap between the very rich and the very poor closing.

I. G. That is the fault of technology itself. The gap between the rich nations and the poor nations is widening all the time, and for the same reasons.

M. C. C. Exactly; therefore, unless something is done, whether by force or voluntarily, there is going to be some sort of explosion—whether in India or the world.

I. G. No, there won't be an explosion. As we were going, there was no danger of such an explosion, because people felt that we were working for them and that they were improving little by little. And if they feel they're on the move, they are not bothered. . . . If we could proceed at the pace that we were going, there was no danger of explosion.

M. C. C. And might they explode under the Janata if they were to remain in power too long?

I. G. I don't know, because they have become so apathetic and so frightened. Later on, they may do so, but just now, there's a lot of apathy. We had shaken them out of that apathetic stage, but now the dominant classes are harassing any poor person who raises his head, and they just collapse in fear.

M. C. C. I'd like to go back to the question which puzzles many people, namely, why you decided to call for elections in January 1977. First, was there any outside pressure? It has been speculated, for example, that you were disturbed by the national and international publicity against your assumption of dictatorial power. Is there any accuracy at all in this speculation?

I. G. Nothing bothers me less than international publicity, because the West has been against India since long before the emergency. They supported the military dictatorships in Pakistan. They have brought about dictatorships in other countries in Asia, Africa, and Latin America. So, to my mind, what they say about us has no validity at all.

M. C. C. Related to this is the speculation that you felt certain qualms of conscience as Nehru's daughter. That as your father had built up democratic processes in India, you, as his daughter, would not want to undo that work.

I. G. I have no qualms of conscience. I know my first duty is to my country. I have said that strong action had to be taken, and one cannot have qualms of conscience about saving one's country. I do feel that I saved the country. I don't know what would have happened if I had not taken strong action. Bangladesh or a small country like Pakistan can be helped but not India; nobody but ourselves can put this country together.

M. C. C. And at the time you were convinced that you were acting to save the country?

I. G. Certainly I was convinced and most Indians were.

M. C. C. But throughout the period of the emergency, did you not feel that you were going too far?

I. G. No. What went far? You have to choose, are people's lives more important, are the vast majority of the people more important, or a few privileged people? You have to make that choice.

M. C. C. And you think this served the vast majority?

I. G. Of course it did. And that is what people are now admitting and realizing. We brought down prices, reduced the rate of growth of unemployment, we built up our foreign reserves, we built up the food reserve, and we made this country—according to the World Bank and the Monetary Fund, everybody—the strongest and most stable of any period in its long history. This government could not have carried on for a month if we had not left that strong position. Now it is deteriorating very fast under them.

And that is why I had the elections. Because once we reached stability, there seemed no reason not to have elections. Elections had been postponed for a particular reason. When that reason was no longer there, I announced elections. I did not consider whether I was going to win, or whether I was going to be prime minister. Earlier I didn't think elections would be fair because there would have been a great deal of violence. Politically, the emergency served its purpose quite early; and from that point of view it could have been lifted. But economic stability had not come then.

M. C. C. Is it possible that, as time went on and the political process seemed to be stabilizing in an authoritarian mold, you felt you had to abandon this pattern of behavior, lest it crystallize into a more permanent dictatorship?

I. G. Emergency, as I told you the last time, did get a little bit out of hand because people started misusing power at different levels. Some of these things were happening before emergency and are happening very much now. So it wasn't due to emergency, but people focussed attention on these incidents because of emergency.

M. C. C. But you do concede that there were excesses. All you are saying is that there were few.

I. G. What were the excesses, will someone tell me? What has the Shah commission been able to unearth after wasting the time of so many officials, high and low, and spending millions of rupees? What I am saying is that that happens all the time, and it is happening today, except with family planning because they have abandoned family planning. But otherwise, what are now called excesses are happening today even more so. I am using the word "excesses" because other people use it. I don't know what it means. We have expressed regret for any suffering caused. If it wasn't happening today, you could say this was a bad thing that happened. But it was happening before, it happened during the emergency, and it is happening today.

M. C. C. Well, it sounds as though it was a very normal period, as though nothing unusual happened.

I. G. Except for the detention of political persons and press censorship, there was not much that was abnormal. . . . At the Turkman Gate incident, six people died, all from outside the area. Yet that has become a matter of world importance. But now, when hundreds of people are dying in firings, nobody is bothered. The West isn't bothered.

M. C. C. So basically, it was just sort of run-of-the-mill violence?

I. G. There was no violence. That's the point. There were just one or two isolated cases. *Today* there is violence all over. And there was violence pre-emergency. Nobody's life is safe today. How many murders have taken place? And how many political murders are taking place? I just had the Bengal people before you came. Last time I met them, they said ten people had died. Now they said twenty-two. But during emergency, there was no such violence. There were just three cases. Turkman Gate, Muzzafarnagar, and Sultanpur. (The Sultanpur firing was due to a misunderstanding. The Commissioner, who was a Muslim, was surrounded by some people in a mosque. The police thinking he was in danger fired.) Nobody's pointed out a fourth case. Whereas today, it is a commonplace thing in all the Hindi-speaking areas. Industrial workers are being fired upon, agricultural labor is being fired upon. Students are being fired upon.

M. C. C. What about the charge that the government was "turned over" to your son Sanjay? Some people have said that he gave orders to ministers; for example, to Gujral.

I. G. Mr. Gujral came to talk to him as a friend, so he gave his views. It is for Gujral not to take the suggestions. Why should he take orders from him?

M. C. C. But then immediately after that, he was relieved of his duties. People make a connection between this . . .

I. G. No, there is no connection at all. Gujral was no longer an MP so he could not be a minister. We were badly in need of an ambassador to the USSR. I tried to send Sardar Swaran Singh. He wouldn't go. And we consulted with the Russians. Because we wanted to send somebody who was acceptable and friendly to the country. And also because they had always sent very high-up people, members of their Politburo. So this was why we sent him.

M. C. C. What about the press? Some people feel that may have been too strong a step.

I. G. The press *was*. Originally I think, we had to have some kind of control. Then my view was that censorship should be lifted. And I advocated what I had advocated for all the years before—that we should evolve some kind of code of conduct which they themselves could work. Somehow it just didn't work. . . . And, of course, the press had been very much against us. Now it is one thing to be against us and not to support the government and to express views against the government. But deliberately to guide the opposition movement in the way they were doing at that moment was very harmful. . . .

The other problem was that our party didn't function. Even American students who came here commented that nobody in the Congress refuted the persistent propaganda against us. If the party had been alert, they could have stopped it in their areas. Then, too, some of our chief ministers arrested people for no reason at all, I mean just personal enmity.

M. C. C. Another related question with which I have speculated is this. Over the years, you had built up a certain image of yourself. You saw yourself (and still do) as a true democrat. Your actions and those of your government in time threatened to negate this self-image. As your own self-respect depends more on your own perceptions of yourself than those of others, you felt you had to refurbish this tarnished self-image, and this contributed in part to your decision to declare elections. Is there any validity at all to this line of thinking?

I. G. I am not at all concerned about my image. Honestly I'm not. It may be conceit but I think there are very few people whose opinion I am willing to take about myself. And therefore it's more important what I think of myself, whether I am doing the right thing. There are times when some action did damage me politically, but if I felt that it was in the nation's interest, I would do it again. . . . To me, only one thing has meaning. Somebody asked Mahatma Gandhi, how do we know whether we are doing the right thing? He said: "I will give you a talisman. When you are doing anything, you ask yourself, is it of benefit to the poorest in our country? If it is, it is the right thing. If it isn't, it is not the right thing." Now that is my only criterion by which I judge myself or anybody else.

M. C. C. Still, you have some conception of what democracy is and what a democrat is.

I. G. No, I have no conception of a democrat. I have a concept of democracy, and I think that you cannot have democracy which leaves out the majority of the people, which was the situation in this country, and is still the situation. I think that by trying to do things for the poorest, making them alive to their interest, making them raise their voices, we enabled them to take greater part in elections. We were furthering the interests of democracy. And democracy—to say that newspapers which belong to a very narrow group, to a clique you might say, that their voice being allowed is democratic, to me this makes no sense. I don't say they should be suppressed. But I do think that to allow them to function freely at the cost of the others. . . . Justice Holmes said that freedom of expression doesn't mean you can shout fire in a closed and crowded room. Now take family planning. It was said that we were sterilizing children when we were trying to immunize them from diphtheria, tetanus, and whooping cough. Now this is the sort of thing that was happening. The health of all those children was endangered because a few people belonging to the then opposition spread wrong propaganda. And . . . press people . . . at a time of communal riots . . . became highly communal themselves, trying to incite people. Now is that a democratic thing to do?

M. C. C. Nevertheless, you do say you have some conception of what democracy is. That would suggest to me that you would also believe that some people are acting in a democratic way and some people are not, according to this standard.

I. G. I haven't even thought about it, and I certainly don't stop to think, am I doing this democratically or not. I am committed to democracy. I don't think there is anybody who is less authoritarian than I am. I don't know a single person here who has consulted more people over anything—except perhaps emergency. I didn't consult at that time.

M. C. C. It has also been speculated that you came to know eventually that things were getting out of hand, that certain things were happening—arbitrary actions being taken in your name, etc.—which made you unhappy. Assuming this to be wholly or partly true, did it contribute to your election decision?

I. G. It is true that arbitrary actions were being taken in my name—and in Sanjay's. Some people collected money in our name, and that was very worrying.

M. C. C. Did you begin to feel that you were losing control of the whole decisionmaking process? Was this also one of the concerns that contributed to your decision?

I. G. No, I wasn't losing control of the decisionmaking process. I was aware of the conspiracy. Foreign agencies had a big hand in what happened. I have no doubt that some of the incidences which are now being questioned were engineered. Our Delhi workers tell me that some Jana Sangh people infiltrated into our party to do just this. And we can guess from what is happening in other countries.

M. C. C. There was no proof that you could have brought out?

I. G. No, how can you? Now we knew that something was happening in Bangladesh, but Mujib said, what is your proof? I could only say, please be careful. I think something terrible is going to happen. No, no, he said, they're all my children. And if anybody had said about Chile that Allende would be killed as he was, what proof could be produced? Even when I said so, after his death, everybody pooh-poohed me. But later it turned out to be the truth. So these are matters which you have to assess and judge by the overall information and by political sense.

M. C. C. It has been said that you were overconfident regarding election victory, and you thought that early 1977 was an opportune time because, as you said before, the economic situation was good and there were signs that it might soon begin to deteriorate. How accurate is this speculation?

I. G. I certainly wasn't overconfident. I wasn't confident of victory at all. I thought there was a very good chance of losing. . . . I didn't think the economic situation would deteriorate.

M. C. C. I had heard that prices were beginning to go up.

I. G. No, very little. We were able to curb these. Oil had gone up. But nothing like what it costs now.

M. C. C. Others say that you saw certain disturbing developments on the horizon that made you feel that the emergency could not be continued much longer without causing serious political and law-and-order difficulties.

I. G. I don't think there would have been law-and-order problems particularly. As a matter of fact I didn't think of it then, but looking back I feel that most of these political people would have cooperated with us, because they were all trying to negotiate with us. . . . when they were in detention. . . . that they would support emergency.

M. C. C. Do you think in retrospect that it would have been wiser not to call the election at the time?

I. G. This is what everybody says. I felt so strongly that there was no reason not to have elections. Maybe it is a serious lacuna in a politician, but I just didn't think of winning or losing. The single thought was that we have put off elections for one year for a particular reason. That reason no longer exists. How can we put off elections any further?

M. C. C. You must have connected elections with the democratic process.

I. G. Not that way. I had never meant to give up elections. It was only a temporary postponement at a particular time. Just as, in wartime, you don't have election.

M. C. C. And you did not consider that this was an authoritarian period?

I. G. No. Obviously it was authoritarian in some ways because press was censored, and individual freedom was curbed. But the situation was very, very grave and in such a situation, you have to choose whether to consider the interests of the larger mass of people or the fewer.

M. C. C. From my study of you, I have gained the impression that, in political matters, you do not act impulsively but always with careful forethought and with a clear understanding of your options and their consequences. . . . And when you are faced with a challenge, you are going to do whatever you can to overcome it. And therefore, you have to think of options.

I. G. No, such events come about so suddenly that there is hardly time for calculation. . . .

M. C. C. Another question has to do with Jagjivan Ram and your decision not to give a ticket to him. As he is said to have been one of the ministers you least trusted, did you not anticipate the possibility that he might bolt from the party and thereby weaken your chances for an electoral victory? Why did you not consider this? And if you did, why did you decide to take the risk anyway?

I. G. I don't know where this fantastic idea arose.

M. C. C. About Jagjivan Ram? That you were not giving him a ticket?

I. G. Yes.

M. C. C. I thought that that was why he left the party.

I. G. Certainly not. He thought he had a good chance of being prime minister. That's why he left the party. There was no question of not giving him a ticket. He was a member of the Election Committee.

M. C. C. You had fully planned to give him a ticket?

I. G. We just never thought of not giving one. The question didn't arise. . . . If that were the case, I would have removed him from the ministry before. But having him as a minister and not giving him a ticket, that would not have worked at all.

M. C. C. What was the relationship during the period of the emergency? It was all right?

I. G. Quite all right. He never said a word against the emergency. He was the one who proposed the resolution in Parliament. And he spoke up strongly at the Gauhati Session. After announcement of the election, he said we should lift emergency. By that time, the people had almost all been released and censorship lifted But the Home Ministry advised waiting until after the election.

M. C. C. Then he didn't even make an issue of it?

I. G. No.

M. C. C. He didn't appear agitated?

I. G. Not at all. But then he came just before he resigned, and then he said, you should lift it.

M. C C. When was that? Before you called the elections or afterwards?

I. G. No, after. And that time I had said to him that the Home Ministry does not feel we should at this moment. I added that if he felt strongly about it, we could refer the matter to the Home Ministry again. He didn't even repeat himself then, and then he went away. Then, I did feel that something was funny. Just to come and put this question baldly like this and then to go away. But then, you are so busy and all that, I forgot about it.

M. C. C. I would like to go back to the question of you and your party's electoral defeat. It seems to me that even if the intelligentsia, the upper and upper-middle classes, the Jana Sangh, and so forth, had become utterly alienated and actively hostile, you could still have managed to remain prime minister as long as the masses stayed with you. You have touched on this before, but I would like you to elaborate on it further. How did you alienate the people to such a large extent? You have suggested that the main reason was a massive propaganda campaign mounted against you and some of your programs. Further, that the administration, which was conservative and had always been against you, worked actively against you in one way or another, and that this contributed to your defeat. Now this raises several questions.

First, how was it possible for the opposition to mount such a massive, efficient, and effective propaganda campaign when, in relation to you and your government, they must have been working at a considerable disadvantage? To say that they did so in spite of having to work underground for the most part is to admit a colossal failure of your own public-relations program and grossly inadequate control of communications channels when your governmental powers were presumably at their peak.

I. G. Well, many things alienated the people. We had been in power a long time. And the then opposition made wild promises. However, when the new government came in, it was found incapable of tackling problems so people began looking back with nostalgia to the past. But at the time of elections, perhaps they felt that very much more could have been done to remove poverty.

We alienated the workers because of bonus and dearness allowance, and teachers because of family planning, the farmers because irrigation rates were raised in order to mobilize larger resources for the plan, at the request of the Planning Commission, especially in the U. P. Earlier, chief ministers were not much interested in development. The farmers had become alienated because of tremendous propaganda that we were not for them and that our inclination was towards industry, and we were bothered about cities and not the rural areas.

All the peasantry thought we were not doing enough for them. This was the line plugged by the Janata party. The rich landlords, of course, were against us on principle because we wanted land reform.

M. C. C. How was it possible for the opposition to mount that kind of propaganda?

I. G. The Congress has never been effective in propaganda at any time. . . . The others were not organized in the beginning. That's why we seemed more effective.

M. C. C. The point is, obviously they got their message across and you were not able to.

I. G. No. We were not able to because the machinery was not with us. . . . The government employees as a whole were very much against us. . . . Gujral [minister of information and broadcasting], for instance, did absolutely nothing. Even before emergency, he didn't put forth the government's program. And the ministers before him did hardly anything.

M. C. C. That's quite a failure—that the Government is not able to put forth its point of view. Whereas the opposition at the time . . .

I. G. The opposition had a lot of foreign help. Many of the embassies were very busy. Our intelligentsia were against us. And then there was the scare that, if we came in, everybody would be sterilized.

M. C. C. If you say that the administration had turned against you, is this not a confession of failure on your part as a leader? How can one possibly rule a country, especially one as vast as this, without effective command over the administrative machinery?

I. G. Well, it was, except that they [administrators] seem to be very much under the influence of the country where they had studied, whether it is the U.S. or U.K. This is what is wrong with our sociology. It's not looked at from the point of view of India but of the United States; and some of our people are highly vulnerable to opinion abroad. This is the class that would be influenced. This is the top. Now the lower section, the clerks and so on, has an inclination towards the Jana Sangh. It's like it was in Germany. There also it was the clerks, the petty shopkeepers, who were mostly with the Nazis. That whole section here is very strongly Jana Sangh.

M. C. C. Turning to another subject, . . . Don't you think that if the Maruti car project had not been established, many of the complications which have arisen in the Indian situation and in your political situation would not have arisen?

I. G. I don't think the complications would not have arisen, because they had arisen in my father's time, and there was no such question. I feel very strongly that the movement against us was engineered by outside forces. Maruti or anything else was just something they could use, but even if there had been no such issue, these forces would still have opposed us and tried to destroy us.

M. C. C. Certain people I talked to in 1975 told me, with great foresight, it now appears, that unfortunately for India, this will be the undoing of Indira Gandhi. And they were strong supporters of yours. Do you agree that some of the anti-Sanjay feeling started perhaps four years earlier or more, when the car project started, and that it was only accentuated during the Emergency? So that, a small event in your family history has become a major tragedy for India.

I. G. Anti-Sanjay also has nothing to do with the car project. It was because, I think, he showed leadership qualities.

M. C. C. You feel he did show leadership qualities?

I. G. Definitely he has, in organizing the Youth Congress. There's no doubt about it. He has character and discipline. And a mind with regard to problems. He's not literary. He enthused our young people, got their thinking on constructive lines, working with dedication. He built up the Youth Congress in a short time, and it was very well organized.

M. C. C. But he has alienated a lot of people in the process.

I. G. No. It was only the propaganda. This was a clean business. He could have made money, say, like Kanti Desai [son of Prime Minister Desai], doing nothing. But people who have met him—take the lawyers on his case—have the highest opinion of him. And certainly nobody who didn't have character could have faced this situation with the dignity he has shown. . . . What was very wrong was the publicity he got. And it was wrong to lionize him. He and I were acutely embarrassed. I didn't know for some time. I never listen to radio or see TV. He drew my attention to it and asked if it was necessary. And then I spoke to I & B people. They said they couldn't stop it immediately because people would say the opposition had done it.

M. C. C. Do you see a political role for him in the future?

I. G. He's not basically interested in politics. . . . In fact, he wouldn't have been in politics at all but for the criticism and tremendous attack on him. He wanted to stand for Parliament because he felt that only he could reply to the false allegations.

M. C. C. But you do think he has leadership qualities. Therefore you must see some sort of role for him.

I. G. Not necessarily in politics. What I mean by leadership is, he's a good organizer.

M. C. C. As far as the Maruti project was concerned, there was quite a bit of a problem.

I. G. There was a problem because the Government was dead against it. If I had wanted to help him, I could have prevented that. But I didn't interfere because I thought that, whatever the opposition, he just has to face it.

M. C. C. Wasn't property supposedly given to him by Bansi Lal?*

I. G. Certainly not. . . . Two commissions have been going into it for the past year and a half. They have not found any such thing. And that grievance is there wherever there's an industrial estate. The difference is that, in most places, they're poor people; here, people like Haksar had land.† And I'm not sure of the figure because I have never talked about this to Sanjay or anybody, but somebody told me that he [Haksar] bought the land for only Rs. 6,000, and he got over Rs. 26,000 for it. You see, if things had been so wrong, surely

---

*Former chief minister of Haryana state, where the Maruti car project was based. During the emergency, he was appointed defense minister.
†P. N. Haksar, principal secretary to the prime minister from 1967 to 1972.

over the years, with all the administration and all the people working against us, they would have unearthed something.

Now they're desperately trying to pressurize people into giving false statements. And then those same people say afterwards, well, what could we do, we're pressurized. One man from Maruti came, and I haven't told Sanjay this even. [The man] fell at my feet and he said, "I have done something that is unforgivable, but I just couldn't help it." He had given a statement against Sanjay. He said: "I know it's not true, but I'm just so poor that if they—they say they'll break up my family and cost me my job. So I didn't know what to do, so I have done it, and I haven't the courage to tell Sanjay, but I am telling you."

M. C. C. Would you comment on how a leader who is publicly committed to socialism and has referred to private enterprise as a necessary (though temporary) evil could sanction the undertaking of a private-enterprise project in her own immediate family?

I. G. I am not against all private enterprise. As you know, our system is based on a mixed economy; but I do believe that private enterprise should be under control. . . . Where it goes wrong is where there are monopolies, and the profit motive becomes so dominant that it overrides social interests. But I don't think the two are incompatible.

M. C. C. Nevertheless you have said that you are committed to socialism.

I. G. Yes, but our socialism is not what other countries call socialism. In no two countries is socialism interpreted in the same way. Our major aim is not socialism but how to remove the poverty of the people. Socialism is a tool or a path because it seems necessary for what we have to do; and in any case, the development of any system has to be by trial and error. We have to see what actually solves problems. We nationalized yarn and still have not been able to solve the problem of our weavers; we complicated it. On the other hand, nationalization of coal was an essential step because the owners of the mines were not looking after the workers and were exploiting mines in such a way that workers suffered and mines themselves were deteriorating.

M. C. C. How do you respond to the charge that Sanjay, either in your presence or otherwise, acted as though he had official power when in fact he did not?

I. G. Sanjay did not act as if he had official power. If people went and spoke to him, he could not help it. He never ordered anybody about. A lot of things were done in his name and my name, about which we knew nothing, and this I am now discovering. . . . Quite often, somebody would say, we are doing this. He would listen. Then they would give it out that they had his approval. He didn't think it was his business to approve or disapprove and therefore he didn't say anything.

M. C. C. From what you have said to me and in public forums, I gather you do not feel you made any serious errors—either in policy decisions or in actions—during the emergency; and that if any errors were made, they were made by people taking arbitrary action in your name or in Sanjay's name. As a leader, however, you must be prepared to concede that your people will judge you by the people who acted in your name. Therefore, don't you think you should be prepared to accept more responsibility than you have been willing to do so far?

I. G. Nobody has specifically pointed to an error so that I could say something about it. I cannot respond to a general statement. We have said publicly that if there was harassment in demolitions, we are sorry, because we did not mean to harass anybody. Perhaps it was due to general police attitudes—but certainly people would not give the order that the people must be harassed. And the resettlement program was an old program. The main thing is, you cannot change or progress without suffering; people think nobody must suffer, and yet things must be done. All you can do is try to mitigate the suffering.

M. C. C. In August 1975, Parliament passed the thirty-ninth amendment placing election petition cases above the courts of law. This amendment in effect nullified the election-petition case pending against you. Many of your critics maintain that the loss of the Allahabad petition case and of the Gujarat elections immediately before that weakened your political position and prompted you to call the emergency in order to hold on to power. The passage of the amendment has been widely interpreted as a confirmation of your critics' thesis.

I. G. I think I have replied to this earlier. The proof that the emergency was justified is what was done during the emergency. As for the arrests, the top political leaders were given due consideration. They were not imprisoned; they were quartered in houses. And apart from press censorship—which was one thing which we could have lifted much earlier—apart from that, the condition of the country was strengthened in every way. So it is a question of priorities. Is the welfare of the many more important, or the license of small privileged groups? The combination against us was not just foreign agencies. They can function only if there is a base here, and the base was provided by top capitalists, big industrialists, smugglers, and people who had always been against our policies, which all these groups thought were far too radical.

M. C. C. But wasn't this amendment a case of overkill?

I. G. I think it was. But it was not in my hands; the MPs were very agitated. The opposition was threatening everybody; earlier there was an attack on the chief justice. So the MPs thought that thousands of cases might be started. The whole purpose was to get everything back on the rails.

M. C. C. Are there any general comments you would like to address to your sympathetic critics, here and abroad, by way of explanation of what happened and what was reported to have happened in India during the emergency period?

I. G. Most of the specific stories which have been mentioned are without foundation. There was firing at Turkman Gate because people turned violent; six people died. Since then, it has been carried every week that many more people died. Now there are all sorts of atrocities in Bihar, but nobody is speaking about them. An entire Muslim family was mutilated—their limbs cut off one by one in the presence of the other members of the family.

I don't know what else I can say. But there was a conspiracy by foreign agencies, not just during the emergency but from way back. In 1967 several heads of state, in Africa and Asia, asked me why these people are against me. It's people in big business, in Germany, the BBC. There is continuous propaganda against us. I believe it was a continuation of their anti-Nehru policies; and the more effectively I implemented his policies, the stronger became the opposition. Mrs. Bandaranaike did not have emergency, but there the situation followed the same pattern. Mujib also did not have emergency. Why was he killed? Afterwards, ministers were murdered in prison. Nobody thinks that is undemocratic. There was no official visit canceled to Bangladesh after Mujib's death and the establishment of a military dictatorship.

NOTES

CHAPTER I: *The Leader and the Setting for Action*

1. Mrs. Gandhi is not related to the Mahatma; nor was her husband, Feroze Gandhi. For an autobiographical account of the Mahatma's life up to 1921, see Mohandas K. Gandhi, *An Autobiography: The Story of My Experiments with Truth* (Boston: Beacon Press, 1957); the most extensive biographical account is D. G. Tendulkar, *Mahatma: Life of Mohandas Karamchand Gandhi,* 8 vols., 2d ed. (Delhi: Ministry of Information and Broadcasting, 1960).

2. For autobiographical accounts of his life, see *Toward Freedom: The Autobiography of Jawaharlal Nehru* (New York: John Day, 1941); and *The Discovery of India* (New York: Doubleday Anchor, 1960).

3. Amendments were passed covering, *inter alia,* governmental authority to amend the constitution (24th amendment), the right to property (25th and 30th amendments), the "privy purse" system (26th amendment), and land reform (29th amendment).

4. Under British colonial rule, a large number of princes who had ruled former Hindu or Moghul states retained some nominal autonomy. The agreement of independence negotiated between the Indian nationalist leaders and the British permitted these princes the option of entering the Indian union (or Pakistan) or becoming fully independent states. All eventually chose the former option. In India, they were compensated by "privy purses," i.e., an annual pension, along with certain special privileges, granted to them and their descendants in perpetuity. These allowances and privileges imposed no formal obligation upon them of any kind, and they were abolished by constitutional amendment in 1971.

5. The petition was filed in 1971 by Raj Narain, then a member of the Socialist party. He subsequently joined the conservative Bharatiya Lok Dal, which mostly represented landlord and business interests. The BLD merged with several other parties in early 1977 to form the Janata party; and following the Janata party's resounding electoral victory in March 1977, Raj Narain was appointed minister of health and family welfare.

6. Although the outgoing government lifted the 1975 emergency, there was some grumbling about the fact that the new regime did not revoke the 1971 proclamation until 1978.

7. Press communique on the president's proclamation, Press Information Bureau, Government of India, New Delhi, June 25, 1975.

8. The successions of Lal Bahadur Shastri in 1964 (after Nehru's death) and of Indira Gandhi in 1966 (following the death of Shastri) were maneuvered by Kamaraj Nadar, then the top power-broker in the Congress party. In the second succession round, Morarji Desai (the present prime minister) refused to abide by Kamaraj's wishes (as he had in 1964, when he hoped to succeed Nehru); he challenged Gandhi for the post and lost. Kamaraj also engineered Gandhi's renomination in 1967, this time avoiding an open contest with Desai by placing him in the second spot as deputy prime minister.

9. National Integration Sub-Committee of the National Committee for Gandhi Centenary, ed., *Gandhi's India: Unity in Diversity* (New Delhi: National Book Trust, 1968), p. 71.

10. As one Western theorist notes, "democracy presupposes consensus. . . . Where the consensus is lacking, can it be brought about by democratic means?" (Ernest Gellner, "Democracy and Industrialisation," *Archives Européennes de sociologie* 8, no. 1 [1967]). This question is most pertinent in the case of underdeveloped countries like India in which social and ideological conflict is exacerbated by the tendency to interpret social phenomena according to ancient social identities and narrow normative standards.

11. Among smaller parties in India, the most successful were those with tightly organized, well-disciplined, and well-trained political cadres (e.g., the Communist parties and the Jana Sangh). The latter's strength in particular can be traced to strong party discipline and good organization.

12. Many in the Desai government would take issue with the characterization of Gandhi's government, and of Indira Gandhi herself

as democratic. The latter point will be discussed in Chapter 3 and the former in Chapters 5–6.

CHAPTER II: *The Motivation to Power* versus *the Motivation to Achievement*

1. Michael Brecher, *Nehru's Mantle: The Politics of Succession* (New York: Praeger, 1966), pp. 53–54.

2. Ibid., pp. 51, 71. Jagjivan Ram had been a member of the Indian cabinet since Nehru's time and served in various capacities. In Indira Gandhi's government, he held (among others) the post of Defense Minister (1970–1974), to which he was reappointed in 1977 under the Desai government.

3. Welles Hangen, *After Nehru, Who?* (New York: Harcourt, Brace, 1963).

4. Indira Gandhi interviewed by Lord Chalfont for the BBC, October 26, 1971 (hereinafter "Chalfont BBC").

5. According to Abraham H. Maslow (*Motivation and Personality* [New York: Harper & Brothers, 1954]), the foremost exponent of humanistic psychology, human behavior is motivated by a set of basic needs or drives that are hierarchically structured in a pattern reflecting their relative strength. Five types of needs make up the hierarchy: physiological, safety or security, affection and belongingness, esteem (of self and others), and self-actualization. The latter, which constitutes psychic fulfillment or mental health, is the culmination of psychological growth; its attainment is possible, generally speaking, only after the other four basic needs have been fulfilled. Thus, the potency of needs is ranged on a scale which places at one end certain physiological needs common to all biological organisms (food, water, sex, and shelter) and at the other needs that are increasingly idiosyncratic and which are deemed to be "higher" basic needs. They are distinguished from "lower" ones in various ways; e.g., though the satisfaction of higher needs is less essential for sheer physical survival, it is more satisfying subjectively—to the extent one's inner life is rendered serene or otherwise enriched. Such enrichment is often defined in selfless terms, for the consciousness of self in its highest forms implies an ever broader range of empathies. The humanistic ap-

proach shares with other theories the belief that personality factors neither evolve nor manifest themselves in a vacuum but are shaped by the immediate context of action as well as the larger cultural environment. My analysis of Indira Gandhi's personality has been based principally on the tenets of humanistic psychology.

6. Among the most recent and more informative biographical studies are Krishan Bhatia, *Indira* (New York: Praeger, 1974); Zareer Masani, *Indira Gandhi: A Biography* (New York: Thomas Y. Crowell, 1975); and Uma Vasudev, *Indira Gandhi: Revolution in Restraint* (Delhi: Vikas, 1974).

7. Bhatia, *Indira*, p. 73.

8. Quoted in Anand Mohan, *Indira Gandhi: A Personal and Political Biography* (New York: Hawthorn Books, 1967), p. 61.

9. Oriana Fallaci, "A Talk with Indira Gandhi," *McCall's*, June 1973.

10. The Salt March was part of a campaign undertaken by Gandhi in 1930–1931 to dramatize the injustice of British rule and to challenge the legitimacy of colonial rule. Arriving at the Arabian Sea coast after almost a month-long march, Gandhi and his followers walked to the beach and prepared salt from sea water, in defiance of the Salt Acts which made the manufacture of salt a monopoly of the British government in India.

11. According to the evidence I have been able to uncover, this was the first and only prison sentence served by Kamala Nehru. It lasted less than a month. However "happy" an event it may have been for her parents, for their daughter it must have been distressing: Gandhi's memory is that her mother was in prison for extended periods; and whenever discussing this period, she repeatedly refers to *both* her mother and her father being away in jail and being left alone in a big house.

12. *The Years of Endeavor: Selected Speeches of Indira Gandhi, January 1966–August 1969*, rev. ed., (New Delhi: Ministry of Information and Broadcasting, 1973), p. 473.

13. Nehru, *Discovery of India*, pp. 31–32.

14. Sarvepalli Gopal, *Jawaharlal Nehru: A Biography*, vol. 1, 1889–1947 (Cambridge: Harvard University Press, 1976), p. 195 (emphasis added).

15. Interview by Gulshan Ewing, *Eve's Weekly*, May 10, 1975. Nehru wished he could give his daughter a practical education, including even a year's work in a factory, and he regretted that it was not

possible to do so in the political climate prevailing in India. He expressed this idea in a letter written while he was still in jail in April 1934. The letter is quoted in Anil K. Chanda, "The 'Red Lady of Santiniketan," *Amrita Bazar Patrika,* January 19, 1972.

16. *The Years of Challenge: Selected Speeches of Indira Gandhi, August 1969–August 1972* (New Delhi: Ministry of Information and Broadcasting, 1975), p. 266.

17. Fallaci, "A Talk with Indira Gandhi."

18. Betty Friedan, "How Mrs. Gandhi Shattered 'The Feminine Mystique,'" *Ladies Home Journal,* May 1966; Fallaci, "A Talk with Indira Gandhi."

19. Woodrow Wilson did not learn his letters until the age of nine and could not read until his eleventh year (Alexander L. George, "Power As a Compensatory Value for Political Leaders," *Journal of Social Issues,* 14, no. 3[1968]:34). Winston Churchill failed his admission examinations to Sandhurst twice (E. Victor Wolfenstein, *Personality and Politics* [Belmont, Calif.: Dickenson, 1961], pp. 24–26).

20. Chalfont, BBC.

21. Ewing, *Eve's Weekly.*

22. Emile Durkheim, *Socialism and St. Simon* (Yellow Springs, Ohio: Antioch Press, 1958), p. 5.

23. Interview by author.

24. Interview by author.

25. An informal conversation with the author.

26. Interview by author.

27. Interview by author.

28. *Years of Challenge,* p. 170, and *Years of Endeavor,* p. 150.

29. In a speech given at a political rally attended by the author.

30. Chalfont, BBC (emphasis added).

31. Interview by author.

32. Promilla Kalhan, *Kamala Nehru: An Intimate Biography* (Delhi: Vikas Publishing, 1973), p. 137.

33. Stanley Allen Renshon, *Psychological Needs and Political Behavior* (New York: Free Press, 1974), p. 1; Angus Campbell, Gerald Gurin, and Warren E. Miller, *The Voter Decides* (quoted in Renshon, p. 31).

34. *Years of Endeavor*, p. 459; 174 (emphasis added); and Marie Seton, *Panditji, A Portrait of Jawaharlal Nehru* (London: Dennis Dobson, 1967), p. 333.

35. *Years of Endeavor*, p. 205; Seton, *Panditji*, p. 351.

36. Chalfont, BBC; Fallaci, "A Talk with Indira Gandhi."

37. Fallaci, "A Talk with Indira Gandhi."

38. *Years of Endeavor*, p. 258.

39. Jawaharlal Nehru, *Glimpses of World History*, 2nd ed. (Bombay: Asia Publishing, 1962), p. 77.

40. Ewing, *Eve's Weekly*.

41. Bhatia, *Indira*, p. 129.

42. Krishna Nehru Hutheesing, *Dear To Behold: An Intimate Portrait of Indira Gandhi* (New York: Macmillan, 1969), p. 45.

43. Fallaci, "A Talk with Indira Gandhi."

44. Ibid.

45. Friedan, "How Mrs. Gandhi Shattered 'The Feminine Mystique'"; Indira Gandhi interviewed by Mrs. Dies Helb, for *Margriet*, (Amsterdam, Holland) March 28, 1970.

46. Mohan, *Indira Gandhi*, p. 69.

47. Masani, *Indira Gandhi*, p. 15.

48. Arnold Michaelis, "An Interview with Indira Gandhi," *McCall's*, April 1966; Friedan, "How Mrs. Gandhi Shattered 'The Feminine Mystique.'"

49. Interview by author.

50. Nehru, *Discovery of India*, p. 26; Fallaci, "A Talk with Indira Gandhi."

51. Although it is not the purpose of this book to analyze personality changes which took place during the nineteen months of emergency rule, one observation seems in order. It appears that up to the first half of 1975, Mrs. Gandhi had managed to maintain to a large degree a balance between the opposing needs for privacy and sociability and to integrate these creatively with her aggressive impulses. Indeed, there is evidence that she consciously strove to maintain some symmetry among these. But this delicate balance seems to have broken down completely during the months following June 1975, when, it appears, she became increasingly isolated from people and lost her grasp of political realities. What had been

a normal impulse to guard her independence of action and self-sufficiency, as a means to an end, now became an end in itself.

52. Karen Horney, *Our Inner Conflicts: A Constructive Theory of Neurosis* (New York: W. W. Norton, 1945), pp. 86–95.

53. Chalfont, BBC.

54. Quoted in Seton, *Panditji*, p. 265.

55. Friedan, "How Mrs. Gandhi Shattered 'The Feminine Mystique.'"

56. Fallaci, "A Talk with Indira Gandhi."

57. Friedan, "How Mrs. Gandhi Shattered 'The Feminine Mystique.'"

58. Fallaci, "A Talk with Indira Gandhi."

59. Chalfont, BBC.

60. James C. Davies, *Human Nature in Politics: The Dynamics of Political Behavior* (New York: John Wiley, 1963), p. 46.

61. Interview by Uma Vasudev.

62. In a letter to a friend, quoted in Masani, *Indira Gandhi*, p. 55.

63. Quotes in this paragraph from Friedan, "How Mrs. Gandhi Shattered 'The Feminine Mystique.'"

64. Chalfont, BBC.

65. Fallaci, "A Talk with Indira Gandhi."

66. Michaelis, "An Interview with Indira Gandhi."

67. Ibid.; Ewing, *Eve's Weekly.*

68. Quoted in Seton, *Panditji*, p. 137.

69. Ibid., p. 421. A characteristic of detached personalities is "a numbness to emotional experience, an uncertainty as to what one is, what one loves, hates, desires, hopes, fears, resents, believes" (Karen Horney, *Our Inner Conflicts*, p. 74).

70. Maslow, *Motivation and Personality*, pp. 90–91.

CHAPTER III: *Authoritarian* versus *Democratic Aspects of Indira Gandhi's Political Personality*

1. Paul Henry Mussen, John Janeway Conger, and Jerome Kagan, *Child Development and Personality*, 3rd ed. (New York: Harper & Row, 1969), pp. 483 ff.

2. T. Adorno, E. Frenkel-Brunswik, D. Levinson, and N. Sanford, *The Authoritarian Personality* (New York: Harper & Bros., 1950); Jeanne N. Knutson, ed., *Handbook of Political Psychology* (San Francisco: Jossey-Bass, 1973), pp. 52–54; and A. H. Maslow, "The Authoritarian Character Structure," *The Journal of Social Psychology, S.P.S.S.I. Bulletin* 18 (1943): 401–411.

3. K. D. Malaviya, minister of petroleum and chemicals, interviewed by author, April 25, 1975.

4. Indira Gandhi interviewed by Betty Friedan, *Ladies Home Journal,* May 1966, p. 100 (emphasis added).

5. Quoted in Kalhan, *Kamala Nehru,* pp. 53, 57.

6. *Amrita Bazar Patrika,* January 19, 1972.

7. Jawaharlal Nehru, *Letters From a Father to his Daughter* (hereinafter *Nehru Letters*) (London: Oxford University Press, 1929); and *Glimpses of World History,* 2nd ed. (hereinafter Nehru, *Glimpses*) (Bombay: Asia Publishing, 1962).

8. Miguel de Unamuno, *The Tragic Sense of Life,* J. E. Crawford Flitch, trans. (New York: Dover Publications, 1954), p. 1.

9. *Nehru Letters,* p. 178.

10. Nehru, *Glimpses,* p. 983.

11. Ibid., p. 385.

12. Ibid., pp. 390, 393, 846–847, 854.

13. Ibid., pp. 847, 854.

14. Ibid., pp. 549, 239–241; *Nehru Letters,* p. 73.

15. Nehru, *Glimpses,* Letters 131, 176, and 193.

16. Ibid., p. 852.

17. Ibid., pp. 965–970, 854.

18. Ibid., pp. 322–323.

19. Ibid., pp. 390–392.

20. *Toward Freedom: The Autobiography of Jawaharlal Nehru* (New York: John Day, 1941), pp. 433–434.

21. Horney, *Our Inner Conflicts,* p. 38.

22. Masani, *Indira Gandhi,* p. 19.

23. Literally "truth force"—a concept developed by Mahatma Gandhi as the foundation of his philosophy and strategy of nonviolent resistance to colonial rule.

24. Hutheesing, *Dear to Behold,* p. 31.

25. Gopal, *Jawaharlal Nehru,* p. 198; quoted in Brecher, *Nehru,* p. 3.
26. Interview by Tibor Mende, quoted in Seton, *Panditji,* p. 187.
27. Nehru, *Toward Freedom,* p. 333; and Gopal, *Jawaharlal Nehru,* pp. 97–98.
28. Nehru, *Discovery of India,* p. 32.
29. Nehru, *Toward Freedom,* p. 334; quoted in Gopal, *Jawaharlal Nehru,* pp. 189, 191 (emphasis added).
30. Krishna Nehru Hutheesing quoted in Kalhan, *Kamala Nehru,* p. 16.
31. Hutheesing, *Dear to Behold,* p. 25.
32. Irawati Karve, *Kinship Organization In India* (Bombay: Asia Publishing, 1965), pp. 129–130. This conflict between Kamala and her sister-in-law was passed on to the second generation and there is no love lost today between their respective daughters, Indira Gandhi and Nayantara Sahgal. As noted earlier, Gandhi and her aunt, Mrs. Pandit, have long been estranged.
33. Gopal, *Jawaharlal Nehru,* p. 194 (emphasis added).
34. Kalhan, *Kamala Nehru,* pp. 107–110.
35. Nehru, *Discovery of India,* p. 27.
36. Kalhan, *Kamala Nehru,* p. 141.
37. Kalhan, *Kamala Nehru,* p. 137.
38. Seton, *Panditji,* p. 129; Seton in a letter to the author; and Kalhan, *Kamala Nehru,* p. 135.
39. Seton in a letter to the author.
40. Indira Gandhi interviewed on film by Anthony Mayer, 1976.
41. Chalfont, BBC (emphasis added).
42. C. L. Sulzberger, *An Age of Mediocrity: Memoirs and Diaries, 1963-1972* (New York: Macmillan, 1973), p. 523; Seton in a letter to the author.
43. Nehru, *Glimpses,* pp. 177, 491.
44. *Years of Endeavor,* p. 264.
45. Ewing, *Eve's Weekly,* pp. 8–11.
46. Seton, *Panditji,* p. 103.
47. Gopal, *Jawaharlal Nehru,* p. 150; Bhatia, *Indira,* p. 97.
48. Luvraj Kumar, a junior member of the civil service who had been a secretary in the Ministry of Petroleum and Chemicals and was

264 / Indira Gandhi

serving on the Planning Commission when interviewed by the author in April 1975.

49. Chalfont, BBC.

50. Kalhan, *Kamala Nehru,* p. 138.

51. Friedan, "How Mrs. Gandhi Shattered 'The Feminine Mystique,'" p. 167.

52. Nehru, *Discovery of India,* p. 32.

CHAPTER IV: *Overture to Dissent: A Coalescence of Conservative Opposition, 1966–1970*

1. I am indebted to J. C. Kapur for the heading of this section, which he used to denote a minority class comprised of one out of approximately every six Indians (or roughly 100 million in a population of over 600 million people). These are the people "dedicated to the symbols, values and privileges of a consumer society in the midst of an ocean that is the Republic of India. . . . The impulses that guide the citizens of the Island Republic also guide the world's affluent societies." (*India in the Year 2000* [New Delhi: India International Centre, 1975], pp. 4–8.)

2. Indian National Congress, All India Congress Committee, *Resolutions on Economic Policy, Programme and Allied Matters* (1924–1969), New Delhi, 1969; Seton, *Panditji,* pp. 392–393.

3. Rasheeduddin Khan, "Reforming the System," *Seminar* 1, no. 185 (1975): 59.

4. All creeds in India, whether political or religious, seem to partake of the polymorphous nature of Hinduism. One can be a Hindu and yet be an atheist—as Nehru was—or be a deeply religious man—as Gandhi was. One can believe in one or many gods and still remain a Hindu. It is the same with the many and varied disciples, self-proclaimed, of democratic socialism or, indeed, of communism.

5. Except for the Himalayan rivers, which are snow fed and perennial, most of the rivers of India are rain fed and thus seasonal. When the monsoon fails, all that remains are dry riverbeds; as the water level drops, the wells—an alternative source of water—also run dry. The land becomes hardened, making it impossible to plough. Excessively heavy rains, on the other hand, swell the great

rivers of the north as they flow down the snow-capped Himalayas, causing devastating floods.

6. Two monsoon periods permit the sowing and harvesting of most crops. The southwest monsoon, the main rainy season, lasts from approximately June to September. The northeast monsoon, from about October to November, falls on most of the southern peninsula. Duing the *kharif* (or summer) season, lasting from June or July to October or November, the farmers plough, sow, and harvest. A second set of crops is planted and harvested from November to March or April.

7. They are the largest minority in India, numbering approximately 60 million in a population of about 600 million.

8. The servant who worked in the house where I rented quarters in 1975 attended three households in a two-story house for about $4 a week. He did the shopping, housecleaning, some cooking, laundry, and other odd jobs. He lived in a hut in a ghetto area, and the roof leaked whenever it rained. He was one of the "fortunate" ones.

9. The Janata party was created in early May 1977 from the merger of the four leading noncommunist parties: the Bharatiya Lok Dal (BLD), the Bharatiya Jana Sangh, the Indian National Congress Organization, and the Socialist party.

    The Bharatiya Lok Dal (The Peoples Party of India) was a new party, the product of a 1974 merger of several parties, the most important of which were the Swatantra party, the Samyukta Socialist party (SSP), and the Bharatiya Kranti Dal. The SSP, formed in 1964, merged with the Praja Socialist party in 1971 to form the Socialist party, and broke away again in 1972. The Bharatiya Kranti Dal (the Revolutionary party of India) was formed in 1967 by former Congressman Charan Singh. This conservative party was based in the northernmost and most populous state, Uttar Pradesh, where it represented the landed and business interests.

    The Bharatiya Jana Sangh was the largest constituent and the only party to the merger that was not originally a part of the Indian National Congress. This economically conservative party was founded in 1951, and had a fairly clear philosophy and program inspired by the ideal of Bharatiya Sanskriti—defined in practice as Hindu culture. It was committed to a revival of ancient values and traditions.

    The Congress Organization was formed as a result of the split in the Congress in 1969. It too was essentially conservative, though perhaps a bit less so than the BLD and the Jana Sangh.

The least conservative constituent unit is the Socialist party, which was earlier part of an unsuccessful merger of the SSP and PSP.

Shortly after the Janata merger, a fifth component, the Congress for Democracy, broke away from the Congress party under the leadership of Jagjivan Ram, a former minister in Gandhi's government and an untouchable leader. It joined with the Janata party almost immediately and thus did not exist long enough to articulate an independent philosophy or program, although Ram was known as a conservative minister.

10. On June 5, 1966, the government announced its decision to devalue the rupee by 36.5 percent in terms of gold and 57.5 percent against the U.S. dollar, pound sterling, and ruble.

11. *Keesing's Contemporary Archives*, 1967, p. 21910.

12. A party is deemed recognized if it "has been engaged in political activity for a continuous period of five years" and has returned a certain minimum number of members to either the parliament or legislature representing a constituency in one or more states, and if the total number of valid votes polled by the candidates of such a party at state or national elections is at least 4 percent of the total number of valid votes polled by all the candidates. If a party is recognized in accordance with these criteria in four or more states, it is accorded the status of a "national party." A second type of recognized party is a "state party," which has fulfilled the criteria in fewer than four states. The number of unrecognized parties far exceeds that of both types of recognized parties (Government of India, Ministry of Law and Justice [Legislative Department], *Manual of Election Law*, 7th ed. [New Delhi: 1972], pp. 431–432).

13. Interviewed by author on April 25, 1975 (emphasis added).

14. Even after the merger, however, Defense Minister Jagjivan Ram reportedly conceded "that the Janata party continued to function more as a conglomeration of various ideological groups rather than as a unified political party" (*India Today*, August 16–31, 1977, p. 16).

15. S. L. Poplai, *1962 General Elections in India* (New Delhi: Allied Publishers, 1962), p. 62.

16. Bharatiya Jana Sangh, *Party Documents*, vol. 1, Principles and Policies, Manifestoes, Constitution (New Delhi: 1973), pp. 11, 30–33.

17. Jana Sangh, *Party Documents,* vol. 1, p. 6.
18. Ibid., p. 21.
19. Jana Sangh's 1967 manifesto in R. Chandidas et al., *India Votes: A Source Book on Indian Elections* (New York: Humanities Press, 1968), p. 22.
20. Poplai, *1962 General Elections,* p. 56.
21. Like the Swatantra, the Jana Sangh is sympathetic to Israel; in its 1967 manifesto (and earlier), it favored establishment of diplomatic relations with that country. Its stand in this respect is in no small measure a reflection of animosity toward Muslims in general.
22. C. Rajagopalachari, *Swarajya,* July 19, 1968, quoted in Norman D. Palmer, *The Indian Political System,* 2nd ed. (Boston: Houghton Mifflin, 1971), p. 207.
23. Jayaprakash Narayan, *Towards Revolution* (New Delhi: Arnold-Heinemann, 1975), pp. 113–116.
24. Dozens of land-reform laws had been enacted by the states, and a number of these were challenged on the ground that they violated the petitioners' property rights. The amendment brought forty-four of these state enactments under the protection of the ninth schedule to the constitution, thus placing them beyond the reach of the courts.
25. The 1967 Swatantra manifesto in Chandidas et al., *India Votes.*
26. In B. N. Ganguli, *Gandhi's Social Philosophy* (New York: John Wiley, 1973), chap. 13.
27. Ibid. Gandhi's prediction about a possible revolution was not unfounded. One observer of Indian political affairs has remarked on the high revolutionary potential of Indian peasants (although it does not compare with that of the Chinese). This potential has not been sufficiently recognized, at least by South Asia scholars, although one historian makes a very convincing case for this point of view. See Barrington Moore, Jr., *Social Origins of Dictatorship and Democracy* (Boston: Beacon Press, 1966), pp. 378–393.
28. Pyarelal, *Mahatma Gandhi: The Last Phase,* vol. 2 (Delhi: Navajivan Publishing, 1958), p. 133.
29. Quoted in K. P. Krishna Shetty, *Fundamental Rights and Socioeconomic Justice in the Indian Constitution* (Allahabad: Chaitanya Publishing, 1969), pp. 127–128. *Yagna* or *yajna* means sacrifice, one of four kinds of spiritual discipline described in the Hindu scriptures.
30. These include the Swatantra, the Bharatiya Kranti Dal (and the

Bharatiya Lok Dal in which these two later merged), and the Congress Organization. The new Janata party has also said that it subscribes to Gandhian principles. The Jana Sangh's conservatism did not stem from Gandhi's teachings, many of which the party's leaders found abhorrent, but it did derive from the larger Hindu tradition of which Gandhi himself was a part and which is essentially conservative. The philosophical derivations of the Indian National Congress include the teachings of Gandhi, the thought of Nehru, and general Western political thought, especially Fabian socialism.

31. Attorney-General M. C. Setalvad's opinion confirmed that the president of India was merely a constitutional head.

32. George H. Gadbois, Jr., "The Emergency: Ms. Gandhi, the Judiciary and the Legal Culture," mimeographed paper presented at Southeast Conference of the Association for Asian Studies, January 20–22, 1977. *See also* H. C. L. Merillat, *Land and the Constitution in India* (New York: Columbia University Press, 1970), pp. 256–271.

33. Gadbois, "The Emergency," pp. 22–23.

34. Ibid., pp. 25–26, 29, n. 54.

35. Actually it would be more accurate to say that these principles describe social-welfare state goals rather than socialist ones.

36. Quoted in Shetty, *Fundamental Rights,* p. 14.

37. Quoted in ibid. Dr. B. R. Ambedkar, a Columbia University graduate and eminent legal theorist, was an untouchable and chief leader of the Depressed Classes; he served as the first law minister in Nehru's government.

38. K. Subba Rao, *Fundamental Rights under the Constitution of India,* quoted in ibid., p. 19.

39. Interestingly enough, some of those who opposed it—such as K. M. Munshi and M. R. Masani—later became influential members of the conservative Swatantra.

40. Quoted in H. M. Jain, *Right to Property Under the Indian Constitution* (Allahabad: Chaitanya Publishing, 1968), pp. 320–321.

41. H. N. Pandit, *The PM's President—A New Concept on Trial* (New Delhi: S. Chand, 1974), p. 29.

42. This account was drawn from C. L. Datta, *With Two Presidents—An Inside Story* (New Delhi: Vikas, 1970) and Pandit, *The PM's President,* pp. 26–30.

43. Quoted in H. M. Jain, ed., *The Union Executive* (Allahabad: Chaitanya Publishing House, 1969), chap. 6.

44. Speech of Congress President S. Nijalingappa, *Congress Bulletin,* April–May 1969, pp. 72–82, quoted in A. Moin Zaidi, *The Great Upheaval: 1969–1972* (New Delhi: Orientalia, 1972), p. 70 (emphasis added). The President's logic (regarding abolition of licensing and controls) echoed that of a tax-enquiry committee that found, among other things, that evasion of taxes became more pronounced in the higher tax brackets; hence, it was concluded, corruption of this type could be avoided by reducing taxes! (Direct Taxes Enquiry Committee, *Final Report,* Government of India, Ministry of Finance, December 1971, p. 169.)

45. Patil also vigorously opposed bank nationalization and the abolition of the princes' privileges and privy purses.

    The "Syndicate" group of the Congress, according to one analyst, was born in October 1963 as a non-Hindi conservative coalition of party bosses with strong regional power bases (Brecher, *Nehru's Mantle,* p. 18). It emerged as a collective power-broker after Nehru's death and acquired a reputation for strong-arm political tactics (hence its name, derived from American gangland associations). It had managed the succession of the prime minister after Nehru died, and again after Shastri's death. Among the top leaders considered part of the Syndicate were K. Kamaraj of Madras (now Tamil Nadu), S. K. Patil of Bombay, Atulya Ghosh of West Bengal, S. Nijalingappa of Mysore, and Sanjiva Reddy of Andhra Pradesh. Only Sanjiva Reddy, who was unanimously elected President of India in 1977, is still politically active.

46. Indian National Congress, *Resolutions on Economic Policy,* p. 185.

47. Although this body had in the past reached its decisions unanimously, a vote was forced this time. Gandhi apparently proposed Jagjivan Ram as president of India, but the Syndicate insisted that the Congress nominee be Reddy. Ram lost by a 4 to 2 vote.

48. All India Congress Committee, *Rules of the Indian National Congress* (New Delhi, 1974), pp. 17–18.

49. C. D. Deshmukh, *The Course of My Life* (New Delhi: Orient Longman, 1974), p. 119.

50. The petitioners in the case were represented by N. A. Palkhivala, a prominent jurist closely associated with the Swatantra party, who also prosecuted the election case against Gandhi in 1975 (a short time before he had represented her in that petition). In addi-

tion to being a member of the Swatantra, he was director of
Statesman Ltd., a newspaper chain which owns five "Statesman"
(English-language) publications, which had been particularly
critical of Gandhi. Among the larger shareholders of Statesman
Ltd. are firms associated with at least 4 of the 75 monopoly
houses identified in the *Monopolies Enquiry Commission Report
of 1965* (the Tatas, Martin Burn, Binny, and Tube Investments).

51. *Lok Sabha Debates,* vol. 11, no. 23, December 14, 1967, cols.
    6973–6974.

52. *India—A Reference Annual, 1975,* Ministry of Information and
    Broadcasting, Publications Division, p. 149.

53. The Banking Companies (Acquisition and Transfer of Under-
    takings) Act, 1969, brought approximately 80 percent of all bank-
    ing business under state management.

54. Indian National Congress, *Resolutions on Economic Policy,* p.
    179.

55. The petitioners in the case were represented by N. A. Palkhivala,
    who also argued against bank nationalization and is now the
    Indian envoy to the United States.
        Because of a loss of voting power in Parliament following the
    split (particularly in the Rajya Sabha—Upper House—which
    ratifies Lok Sabha legislation), the law derecognizing princes was
    passed by the Lok Sabha but blocked in the Rajya Sabha. Even in
    the Lok Sabha, Congress had had to depend on the support of
    opposition parties sympathetic to the government's policy—in-
    cluding the Communist party of India.

56. *Constituent Assembly Debates, vol. 9,* p. 1272, cited in Shetty,
    Fundamental Rights, p. 127.

CHAPTER V: *A Failure of Leadership: Ideological
Vacillation and Incoherence*

1. At the time there were 280 princes receiving, tax-free, annual
   purses totaling $6.5 million.

2. A. Moin Zaidi, ed., *The Annual Register of Indian Political Parties,
   1973–1974* (New Delhi: Michiko & Panjathan, 1974), pp. 412,
   462.

3. Ibid., p. 513.

4. Dr. Karan Singh, Minister of Family Planning in Gandhi's cabinet, interviewed by the author.

5. Interview by author.

6. One of her colleagues interviewed by author.

7. Interview by author.

8. *Years of Endeavour,* p. 344.

9. E.g., Ram Joshi, "Dominance with a Difference, Strains and Challenge," *Economic & Political Weekly* 8 (Annual Number, 1973), and Rajni Kothari, *Democratic Polity and Social Change in India* (New Delhi: Allied Publishers, 1976).

10. Interview by author (nearly two months after the emergency proclamation).

11. Interview by author.

12. *Years of Endeavour,* pp. 206, 341–342.

13. Interview by author (emphasis added).

14. Quotations in this paragraph in *Years of Endeavour,* pp. 53, 417; *Years of Challenge,* pp. 11, 152, 16; and Lok Sabha Debate, July 23, 1975, "Selected Sayings of Smt. Indira Gandhi," Ministry of Information and Broadcasting.

15. R. K. Karanjia and K. A. Abbas, *Face to Face with Indira Gandhi* (New Delhi: Chetana Publications, 1974), p. 107.

16. Interview to the *Patriot,* November 1973, reprinted in *Prime Minister Indira Gandhi on Questions Facing India and the World* (New Delhi: AICC Publication); Danish television interview with Prime Minister Gandhi, June 28, 1974.

17. *Years of Challenge,* p. 18; *Years of Endeavour,* p. 98.

18. Her concluding speech at Congress Leaders Conference, May 14, 1972, reprinted by AICC, p. 13.

19. Karanjia and Abbas, *Face to Face,* pp. 54–55.

20. Indian National Congress, *Election Manifesto,* 1971.

21. *Years of Endeavour,* pp. 279, 346, 359.

22. Ibid., p. 279.

23. Karanjia and Abbas, *Face to Face,* p. 54.

24. *Years of Endeavour,* p. 342.

25. Concluding speech at Congress Leaders' Conference, May 14, 1972, p. 13.

26. Address at Punjab University Convocation, January 3, 1973. Press Information Bureau, Government of India.

27. *Years of Challenge,* pp. 224–225, 234; *Years of Endeavour,* p. 341.

28. *Years of Endeavour,* pp. 462, 464.

29. Karanjia and Abbas, *Face to Face,* p. 42.

30. Address at Punjab University Convocation, January 3, 1973.

31. Uma Vasudev, *Indira Gandhi, Revolution in Restraint* (New Delhi: Vikas, 1974), p. 533; *Socialist India* 5 (August 12, 1972) emphasis added); and Karanjia and Abbas, *Face to Face,* p. 37.

32. K. D. Malaviya, "The Congress Must Be A Cadre-Based Party," *Socialist India* 5 (June 3, 1972):16.

33. Ibid., 5(July 15, 1972):31.

34. AICC, *Present Political Situation* (New Delhi: 1974), pp. 3, 4, 24.

35. Ibid., p. 5 (emphasis added).

36. AICC, *Organization of Rural Poor* (New Delhi: 1974), p. 34.

37. Ibid., p. 6. According to Labour Bureau, Ministry of Labour, *Indian Labour Statistics, 1974* (Simla: 1974), pp. 6–7, the number was 26.33 percent in 1971, and the increase was due more to women laborers joining the work force.

38. This is much lower than the average daily earnings of agricultural households. According to government statistics, male laborers earn Rs. 1.43 or about 32 cents a day, while female laborers earn Rs. .95 or about 12 cents a day. *Indian Labour Statistics,* 1974, p. 55.

39. AICC, *Organization of Rural Poor,* p. 8.

40. Ibid., pp. 8–9.

41. Ibid., pp. 9–12.

42. Ranajit Roy, "'Socialist Pattern'–A Damned Good Slogan for the Rich," *Young Indian* 3 (January 1973): 10.

43. AICC, *Organization of Rural Poor,* p. 13.

44. Interview by author.

45. Karanjia and Abbas, *Face to Face,* p. 59.

46. *India–A Reference Annual, 1975* (Ministry of Information and Broadcasting, Publications Division: 1975), p. 159.

47. *India–A Reference Annual, 1975,* p. 143; Government of India, *Economic Survey, 1974-1975,* p. 112; Planning Commission, Gov-

ernment of India, *Draft Fifth Five-Year Plan, 1974–1979,* vol. 1, p. 71.

48. Bimal Jalan, "A Policy Frame for Self-Reliance," *Economic and Political Weekly* 7 (April 8, 1972): 757.

49. *Draft Five-Year Plan,* pp. 3–4.

50. Suresh D. Tendulkar, "Planning for Growth, Redistribution and Self-Reliance in the Fifth Five-Year Plan–II," *Economic and Political Weekly* 9 (January 19, 1974): 74.

51. Both quoted in ibid.

52. Ibid., p. 76.

53. K. N. Raj, "Approach to the Fifth Plan: First Impression," *Economic and Political Weekly* 8 (Annual Number, 1973): 309.

54. B. S. Minhas, *Planning and the Poor* (New Delhi: S. Chand, 1974), pp. 131–132.

55. "Lurking Foreign Exchange Crisis," *Economic and Political Weekly* Special Number (August 1973): 1375.

56. "Lurking Foreign Exchange Crisis," ibid. p. 1379; ibid. (Annual Number, 1974), p. 171.

57. *Times of India,* May 30, 1974, and June 15, 1974.

58. Minhas, *Planning for the Poor,* p. 132.

59. Quoted in Jeremiah Novak, "The Role of IMF, World Bank," *Times of India,* July 1, 1977.

60. V.K.R.V. Rao, et al., *Inflation and India's Economic Crisis* (Delhi: Vikas, 1973).

61. Ibid., pp. 3, 34–39, and *passim.*

62. Interview by author.

63. *Asian Recorder* 20 (August 6–12, 1974): 12133–12135.

64. Address in Bangalore, July 13, 1974, Press Information Bureau, Government of India.

65. Novak, "The Role of IMF, World Bank," *Times of India,* July 4, 1977.

66. An official study team chaired by M. G. Kaul found in 1971 that illegal international transactions in one year added up to as much as 15 percent of India's recorded exports. Cited in Lawrence A. Veit, *India's Second Revolution: The Dimensions of Development* (New York: McGraw-Hill, 1976), pp. 351–352.

67. "Debate on No-Confidence Motion, Prime Minister's Reply," news

release, Press Information Bureau, Government of India, May 14, 1974.

68. Novak, "The Role of IMF, World Bank," *Times of India*, July 5, 1977.

CHAPTER VI: *The "J. P." Movement, 1974–1975*

1. *Hindustan Times*, March 22, 1974, May 5, 1975.

2. *People's Action* (March/April 1975): 10, 8–13.

3. *Statesman*, April 21, 1975.

4. Interview by author.

5. Minoo Masani, *Is J. P. the Answer?* (Delhi: Macmillan of India, 1975), pp. 57–58. On March 6, 1975, Jayaprakash Narayan had led a "People's March" to Parliament, where he presented a "People's Charter" of demands to both houses; he called for a regime of national austerity, supported the Bihar movement, and demanded the appointment of judicial tribunals to inquire into allegations against the prime minister and other persons in high positions (*Hindustan Times*, March 7, 1975).

6. Jayaprakash Narayan, *Towards Revolution* (New Delhi: Arnold-Heinmann, 1975), p. 130; *People's Action* 9 (January 1975): 17.

7. Narayan, *Towards Revolution*, p. 139.

8. A. V. Dicey, *Introduction to the Study of the Law of the Constitution*, 10th ed. (London: Macmillan 1959), p. 433 (emphasis added).

9. Cecil S. Emden, *The People and the Constitution*, 2nd ed. (London: Oxford University Press 1956).

10. Stated in interview by author.

11. *Statesman* (New Delhi), September 9, 1974.

12. Ajit Bhattacharjea, *Jayaprakash Narayan: A Political Biography* (New Delhi: Vikas, 1975) p. 137.

13. Masani, *Is J. P. the Answer?*, p. 13.

14. Interview by author.

15. Ghanshyam Shah, *Protest Movements in Two Indian States* (Delhi: Ajanta Publ., 1977), pp. 154–155.

16. *Statesman,* January 13, 1975; *Hindustan Times,* May 5, 1975; *Statesman,* May 17, 1975; and *Hindustan Times,* April 7, 1975.

17. *Times of India,* June 23, 1974; *Pioneer* (Lucknow), June 25, 1974; and Masani, *Is J. P. the Answer?,* p. 62.

18. *People's Action* 9 (January 1975): 16.

19. *Motherland,* June 26, 1975 (one of the few newspaper issues distributed on June 26, 1975 that is available).

20. *Times of India,* February 27, 1975.

21. Ibid., February 28, 1975.

22. *Hindustan Times,* April 1, 1975.

23. *Times of India,* February 27, 28, 1975; April 18, 1975.

24. Ibid., April 18, 1975.

25. *Indian Express,* May 8, 1967.

26. *Times of India,* April 18, 1975.

27. Masani, *Is J. P. the Answer?,* p. 99.

28. *People's Action* (February 1975): 23–24.

29. Interviewed by N. S. Jagannathan, Deputy Editor of the *Hindustan Times,* in *Revolution in the Making* (New Delhi: People's Action, n.d.), p. 21.

30. *Times of India,* May 4, 1975.

31. *People's Action* (February 1975): 23.

32. Masani, *Is J. P. the Answer?,* pp. 50, 81; and Narayan, *Towards Revolution,* p. 144.

33. Masani, *Is J. P. the Answer?,* pp. 69–70; and *Hindustan Times,* June 4, 1975.

34. *Statesman,* May 20, 1975.

35. Ibid.

36. *People's Action* (January 1975): 18.

37. Masani, *Is. J. P. the Answer?,* p. 105.

38. Gunnar A. Myrdal, *Asian Drama,* vol. 1, pp. 66–67; vol 3, p. 1909.

39. Jagannathan, *Revolution in the Making,* p. 13.

40. V. S. Naipaul, in his best-selling book, *India, A Wounded Civilization* (New York: Knopf, 1977), refers to the speech made by Narayan on the evening before his arrest, in which the latter says that "Gandhiji always said that Swaraj (Independence) means

Ramraj (the rule of God on earth)." According to Naipaul, it is a notion of "Paradise Lost," by which Hindu rationalism is invariably engulfed: "We have gone beyond the 'working class' and the antifascist struggle to which Narayan had referred in his speech; beyond political systems and the contemplation of the past, we have gone back to the beginning of the Hindu world, to 'nostalgic memories.' We have gone back to the solace of incantation, and back to Gandhi as to the only Indian truth, as though Britain still ruled in India; as though Gandhi hadn't been created by specific circumstances; as though the Indian political situation remains unchanging, as eternal as India itself, requiring always the same ideal solution" (pp. 155–158).

41. Masani, *Is. J. P. the Answer?*, p. 127.

42. Narayan, *Towards Revolution*, p. 144 (emphasis added).

43. Narayan, "Sarvodaya and Democratic Socialism," *Sarvodaya* 14 (August 1964), p. 57.

44. Jagannathan, *Revolution in the Making*, p. 34.

45. *People's Action 9* (January 1975): p. 24.

46. *Times of India*, May 1, 1975; and *Statesman*, March 8, 1975.

47. *Sunday Standard*, January 26, 1975.

48. Ibid.

49. *Times of India*, March 4, 1975.

50. *Sunday Standard*, March 2, 1975.

51. Narayan, *Towards Revolution*, p. 132.

52. Interview by author.

53. Naipaul, *India, A Wounded Civilization*, ch. 5.

54. Interview by author (emphasis added).

55. *Statesman*, May 25, 1975.

56. Jagannathan, *Revolution in the Making*, pp. 33–34.

57. Masani, *Is J. P. the Answer?*, p. 128.

58. *People's Action* 9 (February 1975): 10.

59. Shah, *Protest Movements in Two Indian States, passim.*

60. Ibid., pp. 128–129.

61. Jagannathan, *Revolution in the Making*, p. 24.

62. Masani, *Is J. P. the Answer?*, p. 94.

63. Quoted in ibid., p. 116.

64. Ibid.

65. Jagannathan, *Revolution in the Making,* p. 24.

66. Ibid., p. 31.

67. *Times of India,* March 6, 1975.

68. Shah, *Protest Movements in Two Indian States,* p. 129.

69. Editorial by Sham Lal, *Times of India,* May 29, 1975.

70. *Times of India,* February 12, 1975.

71. Masani, *Is J. P. the Answer?,* p. 93.

72. *Times of India,* May 7, 1975, quoted in Shah, *Protest Movements in Two Indian States,* p. 121.

73. *People's Action* 9 (February 1975): 18.

74. *Times of India,* May 13, 1975.

75. Interview by author.

76. Narayan, *Towards Revolution,* p. 145; *Sunday Standard,* March 2, 1975.

77. *Times of India,* May 4, 1975.

78. Shah, *Protest Movements in Two Indian States,* p. 131.

CHAPTER VIII: *Indira Gandhi "On Trial"*

1. Shah Commission of Inquiry, *Interim Report I,* March 11, 1978, p. 1.

2. Ibid.

3. Shah Commission of Inquiry, *Interim Report II,* April 26, 1978, p. 141.

4. *Interim Report I,* pp. 9–11.

5. *Overseas Hindustan Times,* May 4, 1978.

6. Section 120–A of The Penal Code (XLV of 1860) in *The Criminal Court Manual,* 8th ed., vol. 2 (Madras: The Madras Law Journal Office, 1973), p. 663.

7. Interview by author, July 1978.

8. Interview by author, July 1978.

9. Interview by author, July 1978.

10. Ray, who testified against Gandhi before the commission, is not among the chief ministers charged with criminal conspiracy, although political opponents of the prime minister were arrested in his state.

11. *Interim Report I,* p. 29.

12. Ibid., pp. 29, 24.

13. Ibid., p. 21.

14. Ibid., pp. 23–24.

15. Ibid., p, 8.

16. *Overseas Hindustan Times,* January 26, 1978, p. 7.

17. *Interim Report I,* p. 8 (emphasis added).

18. *Overseas Hindustan Times,* September 8, 1977.

19. John Dayal and Ajoy Bose, *The Shah Commission Begins* (New Delhi: Orient Longman, 1978), p. 349.

20. V. N. Shukla, ed., *Constitution of India,* 6th ed. (Lucknow: Eastern Book, 1975), p. 208.

21. *Interim Report I,* p.15.

Index

Achievement: lacking in early years, 36; motivation to, 25, 39, 44, 45–46, 66, 102; outlet for aggressive impulses, 27

Adivasis, 197

Administrative Reforms Commission, 164

Affection, need for: in childhood, 38, 90–91; expended on the nation, 38

Aggression: alternates with aloofness, 37; Emergency Rule and long-suppressed, 61–62; power as expression of, 27–28; stubbornness as expression of, 37–38, 45

Ahmed, Fakhruddin Ali, 237

Ahmedabad (Gujarat), 197; 1969 riots in, 110

Akbar, 73, 80–81

Akhil Bharatiya Vidyarthi Parishad, 188, 203. *See also* Jana Sangh party

Allahabad (Uttar Pradesh), youth in, 28, 33, 85

Allahabad High Court, decision to oust Gandhi from Parliament, 4, 151, 204, 217, 228, 252

Allende, Salvador, 244

All-India Congress Committee (AICC), 1964 session, 104; 1969 split and, 138–144; 1972 session, 149–150

All-India Students' Council. *See* Akhil Bharatiya Vidyarthi Parishad

Aloofness, 37–38; alternates with aggressiveness, 37

Ambivalence, Gandhi's character, 37, 39–40, 210–211

Amnesty International, 234

Anarchy, threatened by "J. P." movement, 176–177

Andhra Pradesh state, 149; disturbances in, 112; Girijans revolt in, 110

Anxiety, 84, 90; authoritarian personality and, 64; for mother's health, 28, 31

Army, incited to mutiny, 183–184

Ashoka the Great, 73

Assam state: Gandhi visits, 45; Mizo rebels in, 112

Ataturk, Kemal, 237

Atheist, Gandhi as, 43

Authoritarian personality, 22, 63–64; ambivalence re, 97; signs of, 64–66, 97–101; Nehru rejects, 76–77; political environment and, 22; quest for personal power and, 76

Autonomy, 53–54, 91

Bandaranaike, Mrs. Sirimavo, 253

Bandh tactic, 180, 213

Bangalore (Mysore), AICC meets in, 138–144

Bangladesh, 236; exports to, 168

Banking Laws (Amendment) Act (1968), 142

279

41–42, 245–246; courage, 40, 43,
66, 95; on democracy, 154–155,
243; democractic training, 67, 69,
77; elusive image, 24–36, 39–40,
50–62, 242–243; and Emergency
Rule, xiii, 2, 5, 22, 60–61, 63, 84,
100–101, 204–214, 229–230, 231–
233, 234–235, 239, 240–242, 253;
as father's companion, 25–26, 36,
91; handling crowds, 56; illness, 33,
35; jailed, 35, 47, 49; inability to
relate to people, 51, 60; marriage, 7,
35, 54–56, 58–59, 66, 69, 94–95,
210; on Maruti, 248–249, 250; militancy, 47–48, 53; Minister of Information, 7, 25; at Oxford, 33, 34, 35,
69; as a parent, 25, 35, 57, 91; political ambition, 21–22, 24–25, 26, 27–
28, 47, 53–54, 230; political errors, 9,
151, 163–164, 171–173, 208–209,
234, 247–250; popularity, xiv–xv,
145; on press, 241–242; relationship
with father, 89–94, 96; on Sanjay,
241, 244, 249–250, 251; self-
confidence, xiv, xv, 6, 36–37, 44, 45,
53–54, 60, 66–67, 91; self-
reliance, 37, 44, 54, 55, 66–67, 69;
sense of uniqueness, 30, 32, 55–56;
shy nature, xi–xiii, 7, 25, 30, 31–32,
50; on socialism, 154, 156, 157, 251;
stubbornness, 37, 41, 45; at U.N.,
92; welcomes challenge, 27, 40,
44, 45
Gandhi, Mahatma, 24, 255n.1; civil
disobedience, 31, 65, 258n.10; and
nationalist movement, 1, 8–9, 65,
187; and Nehru family, 6, 32, 68,
94, 97; nonviolence, 65, 84, 181;
personality, 20, 21, 59, 65, 243;
political philosophy, 10, 65, 103,
104, 127–128, 238
Gandhi, Sanjay (son), xiv, 53, 55,
101, 164, 208, 218, 241, 249,
250–252
Gandhinagar (Gujarat), 149
Gherao tactic, 180–181, 213
Ghosh, Atulya, 269n.45

Giri, V. V., 139–141, 172
Girijans, 1969 revolt of, 110
Gita: family readings, 43; socialism
and, 128
Glimpses (Nehru), 92
Goenka, Ramnath, 202
Golaknath decision, 129, 130, 132,
133–134, 145
Government: attitudes on role of, 10,
127; colonial heritage, 106; and economic crisis of 1973, 150; "J. P."
movement paralyzes, 180–186, 205–
206; legitimacy erodes, 112, 162,
203, 205–206, 213; political parties
and, 10–13, 177–178; upper classes
in bureaucracy, 105–106
Government employees, 150, 211;
activism, 111–112; incited by "J.
P." movement, 183–184, 248; wooed
by Right, 119
Guilt, from burning her doll, 49
Gujarat state, 149, 151, 175, 176, 179,
204–205; disturbances in, 110, 174,
177; elections, 179–180, 204–205,
252; Gandhi campaigns in, xii, 41,
43; "J. P." movement in, 186, 188,
197, 199, 213; President's rule in,
177
Gujral, I. K., 241, 248
Gujral, Satish, 35

Haksar, P. N., 250
Harijans, 197. *See also* Untouchables
Hindi language, 121
Hindu philosophy, 72, 84
Hindus: clashes with Muslims, 110,
124; clashes with Sikhs, 112, 115;
social philosophy, 15, 264n.4
Holmes, Oliver Wendell, Jr., 243
Humanism, of Nehru, 71–80
Husain, Zakir, 135, 136–137
Hutheesing, Krishna (Nehru)(aunt), 30,
85

Identity, merger of personal and
national, 102

Ideology: contradictions in, 150–
159, 207, 208–209; Narayan's, 186–
187; wanting in political life, 105,
123
Illich, Ivan, 237
Imperialism, western criticized, 79
Indecisiveness, 37, 40, 209
Independence, personal valued, 57–
58, 69, 70, 91, 95, 102; influence of
others denied, 59; in politics, 95,
239
India: nationalist period, 6, 49, 67–
68; need for change, 6, 10–11;
quest for stability, 2, 7–8; U.S. aid
to, 109; war with China, 5, 45, 83,
135; war with Pakistan, 5, 41, 109,
115, 149, 151, 164, 182
Indian Express, 202
Indian Iron and Steel Company, 147
Indian National Congress: cadre-
training program, 159–160; defeats
in states, 123–125, 130; elites and,
106, 212; Gandhi and, 3, 5, 11, 24,
26–27, 41, 45, 48, 56–57, 96, 159;
internal conflicts, 13, 107, 115;
"J. P." movement and, 191, 192,
195, 199, 207; and nationalist
struggle, 105; Nehru and, 33, 107,
207; 1969 split, 3, 41, 64, 95, 114,
136–141, 142–143, 153, 209;
Parliamentary Board, 139; philosophy, 10, 104
Indian National Congress Organization, 144, 145, 148, 188, 190,
191, 192, 206, 207, 265n.9,
267n.30
Indian Penal Code, 219
Individual: conservatives' emphasis on,
128; freedom of, 15, 77; rights/
duties, 155
Industrial Revolution, 78
Inflation, 4, 5, 107–108, 151, 169,
177, 240, 245
Institute for Social and Economic
Change, 171
Integration, 10–11, 12, 112, 113

International Bank for Reconstruction and Development, 168
International Development Association, 168
International Monetary Fund (IMF),
168, 169, 173, 240

Jalal-ud-Din Muhammad, 73, 81
Jammu, integration urged, 122
Jana Sangh party, 117–122, 124,
125, 126, 130, 132, 137–138, 142,
145, 148, 177, 188, 190, 191, 192,
203, 206, 244, 247, 249, 267n.21
Janata party, xv, 234, 265n.9; polit-
ical philosophy, 14, 267n.30; as
ruling party, xiv, 164, 214, 215,
216, 231, 238, 256n.5
Janata Sarkars. *See* Parallel governments
Jan Sangharsha Samities, 185
Japan, land reform in postwar, 162
Jethmalani, Ram, 218–219, 220, 222
Joan of Arc, youthful fantasies, 47
Johnson, Lyndon B., 164
Joshi, Harideo, 220n
"J. P." *See* Narayan, Jayaprakash
"J. P." movement, 151, 160, 174,
175, 205–206, 208, 210, 213;
appeal to youth, 198–203; class
base, 187–188, 196–198, 212;
parallel governments, 184–186, 213;
possibility of anarchy, 176–177,
178, 213; students and, 177–178,
180–181, 183, 199–202; "total
revolution" phase, 176–187,
196, 199
Judicial system: ally of upper classes,
107, 130–132; constitution amended
re, 145; Gandhi confronts, 145–
147; inquiry procedures, 223–230;
and presidential supremacy issue,
129–132; and the Right, 129

Kamaraj, K., 95, 115, 135, 137,
269n.45
Kamaraj Plan, 135

286 / Index